Way Down in the Hole

Critical Issues in Crime and Society

Raymond J. Michalowski and Luis A. Fernandez, Series Editors

Critical Issues in Crime and Society is oriented toward critical analysis of contemporary problems in crime and justice. The series is open to a broad range of topics including specific types of crime, wrongful behavior by economically or politically powerful actors, controversies over justice system practices, and issues related to the intersection of identity, crime, and justice. It is committed to offering thoughtful works that will be accessible to scholars and professional criminologists, general readers, and students.

For a list of titles in the series, see the last page of the book.

Way Down in the Hole

RACE, INTIMACY, AND THE REPRODUCTION OF RACIAL IDEOLOGIES IN SOLITARY CONFINEMENT

ANGELA J. HATTERY AND
EARL SMITH

RUTGERS UNIVERSITY PRESS
New Brunswick, Camden, and Newark, New Jersey, and London

LIBRARY OF CONGRESS CATALOGING-IN-PUBLICATION DATA

Names: Hattery, Angela, author. | Smith, Earl, 1946– author.
Title: Way down in the hole: race, intimacy, and the reproduction of racial
  ideologies in solitary confinement / Angela J. Hattery and Earl Smith.
Description: New Brunswick: Rutgers University Press, [2023] | Series: Critical
  issues in crime and society | Includes bibliographical references and index.
Identifiers: LCCN 2021058190 | ISBN 9781978823785 (paperback) |
  ISBN 9781978823792 (cloth) | ISBN 9781978823808 (epub) |
  ISBN 9781978823815 (mobi) | ISBN 9781978823822 (pdf)
Subjects: LCSH: Solitary confinement. | Prisoners—Social conditions. |
  Minorities—Effect of imprisonment on.
Classification: LCC HV8728 .H37 2022 | DDC 365/.644—dc23/eng/20211213
LC record available at https://lccn.loc.gov/2021058190

A British Cataloging-in-Publication record for this book is available
from the British Library.

References to internet websites (URLs) were accurate at the time of writing. Neither
the author nor Rutgers University Press is responsible for URLs that may have expired
or changed since the manuscript was prepared.

⊛ The paper used in this publication meets the requirements of the American National
Standard for Information Sciences—Permanence of Paper for Printed Library Materials,
ANSI Z39.48-1992.

www.rutgersuniversitypress.org

Manufactured in the United States of America

We dedicate this book to Correctional Officers Travis, Porter, and Daniel; and to Dr. Emma, Marina, and to all of the people we met in solitary confinement—those incarcerated and those who work there.

You touched us in ways unimaginable. We hope we have done justice to your stories and your lives. We will never forget you.

To the tens of thousands of people incarcerated and working in solitary confinement units across the United States. We hope our book renders you visible.

To our children: Travis, Emma, Porter and Marina. You are our inspiration.

To Earl: I wouldn't have survived solitary confinement without you.

To Angela: I only survived solitary because of you!

CONTENTS

Foreword

In *Way Down in the Hole: Race, Intimacy, and the Reproduction of Racial Ideologies in Solitary Confinement,* Angela J. Hattery and Earl Smith provide what has been sorely missing in the literature about solitary confinement: an understanding of the deep roots of solitary confinement and the entire carceral state in slavery and in the shameful history of racism in the United States. A Black man being beaten by a white correction officer for no good reason in a segregation cell makes no sense on one level. Are we simply choosing racist bullies as correction officers? Or is there something more fundamental going on? It's the same as police shooting Blacks on the street, except there is no body camera. American policing and prisons grew out of slavery, literally, as the post–Civil War South enacted "black code" laws to justify locking ex-slaves in prison and then leasing them to former slave owners to work harder than they had when they were slaves, and to die younger. According to Hattery and Smith, "How do constructions of citizenship impact how we think about locking people up and the Thirteenth Amendment? The same way that defining Black people as not fully human allowed white people to justify slavery, and the coding of Black people as not fully citizens allowed for the justification of Jim Crow segregation, identifying Black people in the hole as not fully human allows us to keep them in torturous conditions, often for decades, and identifying them as not full citizens allows us to rationalize burning them on showers and yard and meals, and reconstructing these as 'privileges' and not 'rights' as well as resenting them when they seem to get more than we do." Deconstructing terms like "race" and "white," the authors provide a deep lesson in critical race theory." Everyone talks about critical race theory, but few apply it with the eloquence, depth, and breadth that fill this book. Having interviewed prisoners and corrections officers (COs) in multiple state prisons, the authors bring us insights we will need to abolish prisons and other forms of abuse. For example, the Black corrections officer is capable of a kind of empathy with the Black prisoner that is out of the white corrections officer's range. The authors wonder, "What would it look like if the COs and prisoners began to see their shared self-interest? How might the structures and policies of

xii   Foreword

solitary confinement be reimagined if the COs understood that they, too, were victims of a system, a system that invests in prisons as economic development, a system that rationalizes dehumanization as a condition of confinement and as a form of punishment but also as a form of racism? As CO Josh notes, this will never happen because prison administrators understand clearly that in order to keep thousands and thousands of people—both prisoners and staff—locked in solitary confinement for days and weeks and months and years requires that they never see their shared humanity." To break through the appalling lack of empathy American racism breeds, the authors propose an in-depth look at how slavery and racism got us here, and how we must work together to attain social justice.

Terry A. Kupers, M.D., M.S.P., professor,
the Wright Institute, author of Solitary:
The Inside Story of Supermax Isolation
and How We Can Abolish It

Way Down in the Hole

Introduction

WE GET UP at 3:30 A.M., shower, brush our teeth, dress quickly, brew coffee and tea for our travel mugs, and pack a small bag with a change of clothes and a cooler filled with snacks to eat while we drive. We pull out of the driveway a few minutes after 4 (A.M.). We meet the rest of our research team at the local fire station, and passengers climb, bleary-eyed, into the back seats of cars, stuffing their bags in trunks and hatchbacks. We pull out by 4:30 (A.M.). As we drive through the rural backwaters of several Mid-Atlantic, Rust Belt states on a warm summer morning, our caravan is heading to one of the state correctional facilities.

Early morning departures and long drives are the norm for researchers, lawyers, and most importantly families with a loved one in prison. In nearly every state, including New York, Texas, and California, the majority of people who are incarcerated lived in a major city prior to their incarceration. Yet prisons are not built nearby; rather, they are located in rural, isolated areas of the state, far away from the major population hubs. The public-facing rationale is that prisons bring economic development to these rural communities. Siting prisons in rural communities has another impact, intended or unintended: it renders them, and the people who live and work there, invisible. Intended or unintended, removing incarcerated people from their communities, their friends, and their families also creates tremendous hardship for those who travel hundreds of miles just to see a client or hug a partner or parent. Ruth Gilmore describes a California highway littered with prisons: "Other buses make this journey every day from central Los Angeles, leaving not from churches but rather from courts and jails. Nine hundred miles of prisons: an archipelago of concrete and steel cages, thirty-three major prisons, plus fifty-seven smaller prisons and camps, forty-three of the total built since 1984."[1]

We will make a journey just like this one, eight times across three summers. And just like the archipelago Ruth Gilmore describes, we will crisscross a state littered with dozens of state, federal, and private prisons, often more than one in the same county. Alongside of the families going to visit a loved one, we eat and sleep in prison towns, where the hospitality industry is built entirely around visitors to the prison. We sleep in motels where the tub doesn't drain even after a short shower, and we feel compelled to sleep fully clothed. We eat way too much fast food.

About halfway into the early morning drive, we stop for coffee, and to pee. For whatever reason, we always stop at Sheetz. The students on the team purchase convenience store sandwiches and candy or power bars, and coffee or Red Bull. As good as all the convenience store food looks, our bodies are happier that we have packed our own breakfast, which we dive into just like the students, inhaling hard-boiled eggs, fruit, and on some mornings even a small peanut butter sandwich. Like the students, we do take the opportunity to purchase some caffeine at Sheetz. Smith prefers coffee, Hattery a Diet Coke. Large, but not too large, so as to limit the stops between here and the prison gates. It's only after our first trip to solitary confinement that we truly understand the importance of a good, healthy, nutritious breakfast. It will be the last healthy meal we eat until we get home several days later.

We always try to drive at least halfway before our Sheetz stop. After two hours or so on the road, we are well past the traffic of the interstate—the Beltway, as they call it, that rings DC—which makes the driving easier. As we leave the urban setting where we live, we also leave behind signs and symbols of the diversity of the region, Korean churches, Mosques for both Muslims and Sikhs, restaurants advertising halal meat or pho. By the time we get to Sheetz, these symbols have been largely replaced by a different set: Trump billboards and yard signs (even though he's been in office almost a year by the time we take our first journey), Confederate flags, and other markers of white nationalism are everywhere. We feel nervous, a white woman and a Black man, traveling with a multiracial team of students, hoping we won't be pulled over, hoping we will be served without incident at Sheetz and every other restaurant and hotel where we will eat or stay the night. The pits in our stomachs are just the beginning of the journey into the invisible and highly racialized world of solitary confinement.

This book is about solitary confinement, but it is also about race. Specifically, this book seeks to answer a fundamental question that emerged in one of our very first interviews, with a correctional officer (CO) who we call Travis. CO Travis began his interview by saying: "We [the COs] are Trump's left behind."

How can correctional officers, who have all of the power in prisons and especially in solitary confinement, come to believe that the people they lock up in cages 24 hours a day, and who they treat like animals, have a better life than they do? How can correctional officers who get to leave every day and go home, come to resent the meals and the TVs and the mental health treatment that prisoners, locked in solitary confinement receive? How can correctional officers like CO Travis come to see themselves, and not the prisoners, as the "forgotten?"

Based on dozens of hours of observation and interviews with both those who are incarcerated and those who work in solitary confinement, this book tells the story of the ways in which, intentionally or unintentionally, the unique structures of solitary confinement produce and reproduce *white racial resentment*.

[Note: we refer to men's and women's prisons because that is the way they are referred to by state departments of correction and the federal bureau of prisons. We acknowledge that prisons incarcerate people who identify as transgender or in other ways outside of the gender binary.]

PART ONE

The Hole

Although we are led to believe that the inmates in solitary confinement are the baddest of the bad, I found that claim to be highly
exaggerated. In the beginning, I had actually hoped it was true as a
means of helping me to justify this brutal punishment. But in the
short time I'd been working in the Bing, I'd discovered that many of
these cells' occupants suffered from impulse control disorders. It's not
so much that they won't behave, it's that they *can't*. I wondered if
someday we wouldn't look back at this primitive punishment and
shake our heads. . . . And even in cases of the very worst sociopaths
held in solitary, the question remained: How could it be that a
punishment that drives *any human being*—criminal or otherwise—to
attempt suicide to escape it, not be considered cruel and unusual?

—Mary E. Buser, *Lockdown on Rikers:
Shocking Stories of Abuse and Injustice
at New York's Most Notorious Jail*

To be imprisoned in such a machine was to be buried alive, removed
from the world to an enclosure with no vantage points from which to
gain a perspective on one's spatial situation.

—Lisa Guenther, *Solitary Confinement:
Social Death and Its Afterlives*

CHAPTER 1

A Day in the Hole

WE ARRIVE AT the prison gates at 7:45 A.M. We park the car and prepare to enter the prison. First: remove watches, Fitbits, all jewelry including wedding bands, change into closed-toe shoes, and check to see that you are not wearing any unauthorized clothing garment, including underwire bras. There is nothing we can take inside that identifies us or has the capability to connect to the internet. Since our team is mostly women we remind each other that if someone is having their period they should be sure they are "covered" for the entire eight to ten hours we are inside. The specifics of menstrual aids are left to individual choice, one of the few things in or on your body that you are allowed to bring in.

When you go into prison, to live or to work, you leave your identity at the metal detector. There are no cameras or recording devices allowed. Like old-school anthropologists, our ethnographic field and interview notes were handwritten, taken furiously with a pen and paper. All quotes were written verbatim and double-checked with the person quoted to ensure as much accuracy as possible when two people talk through the telephone in a noncontact visiting room, at a cell door, or through the holes of a strip cage. The pen and paper, just like us, had to be cleared through the metal detector. Only single sheets or notepads, no staples or paper clips. We relied on ballpoint and felt-tip pens, with as few pieces as possible so that they couldn't be easily dismantled and used as tools of violence.

Conducting research without the use of technology is tedious and mentally draining. The exhaustion of getting up early, driving for hours, before the day even begins, and the stale air, fluorescent lights, and uncomfortable plastic chairs all add to the exhaustion of the work. After we leave each day, we want a drink, a shower, and some comfort food, preferably something fried or heavy in carbs, in no particular order. Our rule of the road is the "Vegas" rule: what's eaten on the road, stays on the road.

Ethnographic note-taking is designed to produce rich descriptions of everything we saw and heard, from the look of the prison grounds to the taste of the food we ate in the chow hall, from the formal interviews we conducted to the casual conversations we had walking cell to cell or from the gate to the unit, so that the readers can see, for themselves, through our thick descriptions, what we saw with our eyes and heard with our ears. We scribbled notes every waking moment, from the time we sat down in the breakfast room at the local hotel to the time we fell asleep in yet another cheap motel at night. The days and weeks following a prison trip were filled with transcribing hand-scrawled notes into typewritten pages that can be analyzed by hand or software packages like NVivo or Atlas. The students on the project were trained on Atlas. We, on the other hand, used the "old school" method of generating thematic codes manually, by reading and rereading interview transcripts and ethnographic field notes. The goal is to transcribe and analyze as soon as possible after each trip so that the details of one's notes don't lose their precision.

We wonder what we are doing. No one volunteers to go into solitary confinement if they are in their right mind. Yet, as a result of this rare and unprecedented access, the days we spent talking with those who are incarcerated and those who work in solitary confinement revealed much more than the traumatic impact of being confined with minimal human interaction. It exposed the ways in which in a rural, economically depressed community, the structures of solitary confinement contributed to the exacerbation of white supremacist racial ideologies. These racial ideologies not only shape the behaviors of incarcerated people and correctional officers but also spill out into the surrounding communities, contributing to the perfect storm that descended on these communities as Donald Trump ran for and was elected the 45th president of the United States.

Solitary confinement is invisible. Solitary confinement units are hidden, out of sight and out of mind, even from many people who are incarcerated and work in prisons. No one wants to go to the hole. Very rarely do outsiders get access to solitary confinement units. Staff will argue that it's because solitary confinement units and supermax facilities are maximum security facilities, so there is too much risk in allowing outsiders in. We also believe that staff and administrators are not keen on outsiders peeking into the realities of these severe punishment units that are built on the premise of maximum isolation.

After passing through metal detectors and having our driver's licenses checked or held (the policy varied from prison to prison), we were escorted into the bowels of the prison. Because the prisons in this state are all built on the same architectural plan, after a couple of visits, we knew just where to find the solitary confinement unit, or at least we thought we did! There was always more than one route, but regardless, we passed through both indoor and outdoor sections of the prison on our way to the "hole." We passed the visitor rooms, with murals, and playground equipment, and toys and highchairs, where families meet as often as they can with their incarcerated loved ones. Depending on the route, we often passed through the "clinic" waiting room, where incarcerated people line up, alphabetically, in the "pill line" to receive medication each day.

Just as predictable as the toys and highchairs in the visitor rooms were, so was the complexion of the prison. As we walked across the grounds on our way to the solitary confinement unit or to the chow hall for lunch each day, we saw a sea of Black faces all dressed in identical brown uniforms, their status as prisoners of the Department of Corrections emblazoned boldly, so as to leave no room for doubt, on their backs: "DOC." [We acknowledge here the debates around the language used to describe people who are incarcerated and we provide a full discussion in part 4, chapter 17.]

We also saw dozens of correctional officers and other staff, in their own uniforms, emblazoned not with the generic identifier of the prisoners' uniforms but with markers of their identity or station. Members of the leadership, including captains, sergeants, and lieutenants, wear white shirts, and incarcerated people often referred to them simply as "white shirts." Correctional officers, or COs, wear dark gray. Staff who work in facilities or maintenance wear clothing suitable to their work, as do medical staff, who wear scrubs. Civilian staff, including mental health staff, counselors, and office staff, wear street clothes which can best described as casual: khakis or jeans, polo shirts, and sweaters, depending on the weather. All staff members, regardless of the type of uniform or clothing they wore, have an ID card that is always visible and a nametag. Last name only. But a name. A designation of their humanity. Nearly every staff person we saw was white, and most were men. The contrast in both race and uniform was clear to everyone who paid attention.

When we arrive at the solitary confinement unit, one of the first things we notice is that everything except the floor is painted a pale green or gray; some on our research team say it's aqua. The doors of the units are painted. The doors to the offices and bathrooms are painted. The tiles on the walls, which remind us of a middle school or church basement, are painted. Many of us say that the buildings (and the food) remind us of a middle school. Public buildings constructed with taxpayer dollars, using similar architects and building suppliers.

The size of solitary confinement units varies by prisons, but all have some structure to isolate incarcerated people who officers believe cannot be managed in general population. Some prisons, the "supermaxes," as they are often called, are built entirely for isolation. Every prisoner incarcerated there is housed in solitary confinement. Others have a unit designed for solitary isolation, and some may have just a few cells. The size of the solitary confinement unit is dictated in part by the overall size of the prison itself, comprising a proportion of the overall beds and cells. Other prisons, as was the case in the state where we conducted our research, house especially high-risk prisoners—those who have been violent toward an officer, those with known gang affiliations—from across the entire department of corrections in a high-security solitary confinement unit in one location.

The size of the solitary confinement unit doesn't necessarily dictate its location in the prison or its overall structure, but it does dictate the size of the visiting room and the amenities offered.

THE VISITING ROOM

The visiting rooms in the prisons' solitary confinement units held between five and ten noncontact visiting rooms for incarcerated people to meet with family or their lawyers. All incarcerated people are entitled to contact with their lawyers. Incarcerated people on administrative custody (AC) status can have regular visits, and incarcerated people on disciplinary custody (DC) status are allowed one visit per month. Most of the people we interviewed hadn't had a single visitor while they were in solitary confinement and most said they didn't want one.

The days we were in the prisons, there was the occasional visit between an incarcerated person and a lawyer, but we didn't witness more than a few in the weeks we spent there conducting research.

Just in case there is a visitor, the visiting room had several rows of chairs, the plastic kind that are connected to each other, like you might find in a run-down airplane or Amtrak or bus terminal, where people can wait for their loved one or client to be "loaded" into the noncontact visiting room.

The chairs are also aqua or tan. Having spent many hours over the course of our time sitting in these visiting rooms, we can personally attest to the fact that they are not comfortable. The color scheme of the unit continues through the visiting room, walls and doors painted aqua. There are two bathrooms, both unlocked, marked simply "visitor." One of the two announces, via signage "Koala Kare," that it has a baby-changing station. We wonder what it's like to visit your parent or sibling in solitary confinement. What's it like to have to manage baby food and bottles and diapers? How do you entertain a toddler, or for that matter a teenager if you can't bring in a Gameboy?

Just inside the door to the visiting room in the solitary confinement unit is a bookshelf. There are religious books—the Bible, Qur'an, Book of Mormon—which seems to tell us something about who is incarcerated and who visits. There are also kids' books—Dr. Seuss, *The Night the Toys Had a Party*—and books that are for youth, including *New Jersey*, which we peruse. It's a book about New Jersey (go figure) with sections titled "Who Lives in New Jersey," "Black People Who Live in New Jersey" (we are *not* kidding), and "Economic Industries in New Jersey." We wonder what it's like to bring your family here. Do kids run around, hide under the chairs, read on the chairs, perhaps sit on the lap of a parent or grandparent? Do they go into the noncontact room or wait outside while their family member is with their incarcerated loved one?

Visitors, or in this case researchers, entered individual noncontact visiting rooms from one side. Incarcerated people are "loaded" into the other side, with access only to the solitary confinement unit, not the visitor room. Noncontact visiting rooms are about the size of a telephone booth, each side an identical twin to the other. They are not a place in which one would get too comfortable. There is a plastic chair on each side of the plexiglass window that separates the free person from the incarcerated. The chair can be pulled up to a narrow counter, maybe 6 inches wide. Wide enough to hold a notebook. Incarcerated people we interviewed were always shackled and often hand-cuffed while on their side of the noncontact visiting room. The interview was conducted through a phone we each held, which often posed difficulties for the prisoner to hold when they were handcuffed. Maybe that's exactly why the correctional officers [COs] kept them handcuffed, not just for security but also to keep them from getting too comfortable. Sometimes the phones didn't work and we had to sit up on the narrow counter and lean close to the glass, where there is a seam, and talk, or more often holler, through the small crack. Though we were able to develop rapport rather easily, despite these conditions, we wondered, each and every time we were there, about what it's like to visit one's family member this way. So close and yet so far away.

Every visiting room, regardless of size, has an observation room or "bubble" where an officer is stationed to keep watch over the visitors, to ensure they are following the rules, not passing any contraband, and so on. A large research team like ours spent hours in the visiting rooms either waiting for incarcer-ated people whom we would interview in the noncontact visiting rooms or waiting to be escorted back and forth into the solitary confinement pods to recruit incarcerated people for the study or to interview staff. For those of us going back into the unit itself, and we were always accompanied by at least one CO or white shirt, we had to first be buzzed through a secure door. Not only do we pass through the door many times each day, but we are sure to spend some time in the bubble talking with the officers. Inside the bubble are video monitors on which the officers can see all the doors that lead into the space surrounding the bubble. One of the doors is the one we pass through. Another is the door that leads to the solitary confinement unit itself. Every time officers escort incarcerated people to the visiting rooms or researchers into the solitary confinement unit, they must be buzzed through the door connecting the visitor area and the unit itself. The space between the unit and the visiting room is 100 percent secure so that incarcerated people and visitors (or in this case researchers) have no physical contact. On the days we are there, with perhaps fifty incarcerated people being moved through on a single day, and researchers going back and forth between the visitors' space and the unit, the officers in the bubble are busy. We imagine that on many days, the job in the bubble is boring. We get a sense of this when we hang out in the bubble with the officers. They talk trash, they count the number of hours until their shifts are over, they count the number of years until they can retire, and they share information that is unique to their environment. They even talk about each other.

During shift change one afternoon, a Black woman civilian staff exits the unit on her way home. She is wearing skintight pants and a tight-fitting top.

The COs in the bubble have their eyes glued to the window while they make derogatory comments about what they would like to do with her body. In our interview with her, she acknowledges that prisons are a really hard place for women to work and especially for women of color. All of the men, COs and prisoners alike, think they can hit on her, they think she might want to date them, and they think they can take advantage of her because she is a woman.

But the COs don't just stare at and make derogatory comments about the women staff, they also do the same about the young white women students on our research team. One of the women on our team, a blond, blue-eyed, very attractive woman, spent some time in the bubble hanging out with the officers, as we encouraged them to do. This is how to do ethnography, we tell them. Hang out and talk to people. After she came back to the visiting room, one of the white COs she had been talking with came out to where Smith was seated. He leaned over, gesturing, and said, "Hey man you're lucky you get to hang out with *that* all day!" The race and gender implications are clear. A Black man gets to "hang out with" white women ("that") all day, something that many white men both fear and envy. Relationships, really of any kind, between Black men and white women reinforce the stereotypes of Black masculinity and white women's vulnerability. The entire racial history of the United States confirms this claim. Between the end of the Civil War and the 1940s, tens of thousands of Black men were lynched based almost entirely on the *accusation*, almost always false, that they raped a white woman. Hundreds of *innocent* Black men have been wrongfully convicted and served decades in prison for the rape or murder of a white woman. But, it's not just interactions between men and women that threaten the racial hierarchy of the United States. Interracial intimacies of all kinds have always been strictly policed because they challenge the racial hierarchy on which white supremacy is built. And, it is precisely these intimate interactions that are necessitated by the structural conditions of solitary confinement that lead to the production and reproduction of white racial resentment among many of the COs we interviewed.

Interestingly, this interaction between Smith and the COs was one of the few instances in which COs would talk with Smith. For the most part they ignored him or seemed surprised when he was introduced as a professor and one of the lead researchers on the team. We had many conversations about the different ways that we (the researchers) were received. The rest of the team, all white women, were, for the most part, treated with respect. And, though administrators, white shirts, and COs all made it clear that they were in charge and we were guests in their world, they were, for the most part, pleasant and reasonably helpful. We considered these differences many times and concluded that the COs have few, if any, regular interactions with Black men who are *not* behind bars. They have likely never encountered *professional* Black men—doctors or dentists or college professors. And, thus they were surprised to encounter a Black man who had more education than they did, who makes more money than they do, and by all accounts has more status than they do. Heck, he even gets to "hang out" with white "girls" all day. Thus it was that one point of confluence, their identities as men, that opened up the rare occasion in which the COs willingly engaged with Smith.

THE WAR ROOM

Just before the door where staff are buzzed through to the hole, every solitary confinement unit has what we refer to as a "war room." The war room is filled with the equipment officers use when they have to use force or conduct a cell extraction. The equipment can only be described as high-tech riot gear. Full body armor and a helmet with a gas mask, like a cross between SWAT and a moon walk, Iraq meets the International Space Station. In many ways, it's a perfect descriptor of solitary confinement. When the COs don this gear, are they headed into combat? Most officers would say yes, the work they do is dangerous and this equipment is necessary for their protection. Some officers we talked to say they like it when they have to use force or conduct a cell extraction because of the adrenaline rush it brings. Solitary confinement is a combat zone, negotiated through force, cell extractions, strip searches, and the wicket.

One of the things we learn from interviewing staff, both COs and white shirts, is that a high percentage of them transferred from careers in the military to careers in prisons. As we will detail in our chapters that focus on staff experiences, there are preferences for hiring veterans, there are bonuses for veterans who sign on to work in prisons, and the transition for most is fairly seamless. And the war room tells the story. When people enter the military, they are trained to fight and if necessary to kill the enemy. COs and white shirts who are veterans bring that experience to their work in the prison and in solitary confinement in particular. The war room, though a bit shocking to us, is familiar to them. The same gear, the same tactical maneuvers they were trained on and implemented in far-off places like Iraq and Afghanistan are now deployed in the United States. As Radley Balko argues in his book *The Rise of the Warrior Cop: The Militarization of America's Police Forces*, the War on Drugs fueled a steep rise in the use of military-style equipment and techniques by local police departments in places as sparsely populated and remote as rural Maine.[1] We underscore Balko's argument in our book *Policing Black Bodies* where we demonstrate that the so-called War on Drugs is a thinly disguised War on Black people. In an interview with Dan Baum which was published in *Harper's* magazine, John Ehrlichman, who had been Nixon's domestic policy adviser, provided the proof that the War on Drugs was designed to criminalize Black people. He said:

"You want to know what this was really all about?" he asked with the bluntness of a man who, after public disgrace and a stretch in federal prison, had little left to protect. "The Nixon campaign in 1968, and the Nixon White House after that, had two enemies: the antiwar left and black people. You understand what I'm saying? We knew we couldn't make it illegal to be either against the war or blacks, but by getting the public to associate the hippies with marijuana and blacks with heroin, and then criminalizing both heavily, we could disrupt those communities. We could arrest their leaders, raid their homes, break up their meetings, and vilify them night after night on the evening news. Did we know we were lying about the drugs? Of course we did."[2]

COs transition from waging a war on enemies in foreign lands to waging a war on Black people. This time, though, like fish in a barrel, the enemy is locked, twenty-three hours a day, in a cage.

THE HOLE

In the twenty-first century, "solitary confinement" in most prisons no longer consists of simply throwing prisoners into a room with cement walls, a dirt floor, and nothing but a hole in the ground in which to urinate and defecate. Many solitary confinement units are high-tech spaces filled with steel and concrete and doors that open and close not with keys but by the push of a button by a CO in some office that may, or may not be, close to the unit itself. Though newer units are made of the same materials used to construct modern-day skyscrapers, the solitary confinement units where we conducted research feel just like what their name implies, like a hole. There is very little natural light inside solitary confinement, only fluorescent lights in the hallways, lamps in the offices, and safety lights in the pods. There is no other way to put it than to say it is dark. The air is stale. Inside you have no idea what's going on in the outside world. After six or seven trips, we finally said to each other, it's so interesting that prisoners and guards refer to going "down" to the hole. Yet it is not underground. We could have sworn we had walked down some steps or a sloped walkway. But no, it's ground level just like all the other units in the prison. The feeling of being underground, of being invisible, of being in a cave is something we never shake.

Eddie Griffin who was incarcerated in a prison in Colorado describes it this way: "A prisoner in the confinement unit [CU] has had his life spared from execution but a meaningful sense of social life has been drained from his existence. A vague but bleak sensation invades a man's being when he passes through the grill doors into the prison's interior. Each electronically controlled grill seems to alienate him more and more from his freedom—even the hope of freedom. A sense of finality, of being *buried alive*, is raised to the supra-level of his consciousness."[3]

The first thing to greet the prisoner who is being processed into solitary confinement is the strip cage. In many units the strip cage was in a property room, the place where the prisoners' property was stored while the COs prepared it for delivery to cells. Sometimes the room was small, the strip cage taking up most of the room, and in other cases, the cage was just one of many things in the room. The door to the room was never closed when people were being strip-searched, and there was always a camera installed so that a white shirt or unit manager could watch the strip from his office. The camera doubled as video backup in the event that either the prisoner or the officer made a claim about the search, for example, that it was overly intrusive and violated the Prison Rape Elimination Act (PREA) or that an officer found contraband that the prisoner claimed had been planted.

On one visit, we were hanging out in Unit Manager Steve's office which was located directly across the sally port from the strip cage, the last point of entry before the highly secure unit. That day some construction work was being done in the unit. Safety glass was being installed in showers, and ceiling panels in the hallway and offices that contained asbestos were being removed and replaced. John Woodward, who was formerly incarcerated, makes a profound observation: prisons and housing projects are both sites of environmental hazard.[4] Prisoners and COs alike face potential exposure to asbestos just as children living in the high- and low-rise projects in West Baltimore, people like Freddy Gray, are exposed to lead paint. Or children living in the blighted urban ghettos of Flint, Michigan continue to be exposed to poisonous water.

In any case, the maintenance staff included incarcerated workers who were assisting with the maintenance work. The working teams came in and out of the unit several times across the day, and we noticed that incarcerated workers were subjected to strip searches each and every time they went into or out of the solitary confinement unit. No one seemed to pay any attention, not the unit manager or the prisoners. Strip searches were simply business as usual in solitary confinement.

Yet while routine, strip searches are simultaneously an activity that is of the most intimate in nature. During a strip search, prisoners are required to remove all of their clothes, stick out their tongues, cough, lift up their genitals, turn around and spread their cheeks, all while an officer looks carefully at their naked body to ensure that they are not smuggling contraband—a cellphone, a packet of drugs—out of, or more often into, the solitary confinement unit. When we talked with COs about conducting strip searches, their perspectives varied. Some shrugged it off as if to suggest it was no big deal. Others complained about the fact that they had been accused during strip searches of looking too closely and thus, according to the prisoner who accused them, of violating his PREA rights. One officer in particular, who had been accused more than once, told us that these accusations threatened his marriage; his wife wondered what it was he was doing at work, the implication of course is that he likes looking at naked men. He also worried that if any of the PREA allegations "stuck" (none had when we interviewed him), he would have a sex offense on his record which could bar him from coaching his kids' Little League teams. Others told us that as uncomfortable as the strip searches were to conduct, they were essential to maintaining the security of the solitary confinement unit, slowing the movement not only of drugs but also of shanks and other tools that could be used to harm another prisoner or perhaps, more importantly, an officer. For these COs, strip searches were a critical security tool which they took seriously and performed professionally. Incarcerated people also varied in terms of their perceptions of being subjected to strip searches. Some remarked that they simply got used to it, others argued that they felt sexually harassed (a violation of their PREA rights), and others told us that they believed some officers "got off" on looking at their "packages." The strip search was both a site of contested terrain and a site for reinforcing race and gender stereotypes about Black men's bodies and their sexuality. A point to which we will return.

The hole itself is a long hallway with strip cages, offices for psych staff and the white shirts (captains, sergeants, and lieutenants), and two bathrooms (not locked), one marked "inmate" and the other marked "staff." Officers said we could use either bathroom but suggested we not use the one marked "inmate," as it wasn't clean. Honor prisoners who do the janitorial work in the unit told us just the opposite. We used both. It would be a good bet to determine which was the better choice. Both were filthy. Because there are few women who regularly come into the hole, the men run the bathroom, and you can tell. The toilet seat is almost always left up. The toilet paper is rarely on the roller and more often can be found sitting on top of the tank or on a shelf by the door. Hattery learns to look for it before she sits on the toilet. There is often "reading" material, probably from the prison library, the battered paperbacks telling stories of rugged men and romance.

In some units there is a room marked "library," which held a cage but no books.

Like any workplace, off the hallway in solitary confinement units are offices. Unlike most other businesses, or certainly the offices where we have worked, offices in solitary confinement units are a combination of minimalism and clutter. It's a bit like walking onto the set of *Madmen*, minus the bar cart, of course. The furniture and fixtures qualify as minimalist. Each office has a steel desk and chair, the kind that you might find in an old government building or in an office from the 1950s. One thing that abounds in solitary confinement units, and in prisons more generally, are one-piece plastic chairs. Frequently they are dragged from office to office or room to room so that more people can congregate, including researchers. Sitting in these chairs for hours, as we often did, gave us a backache. Computers also fall in the minimalist category. Unlike the typical office in the twenty-first century in the

United States, the only offices with computers are for "civilian" staff, including psychologists and unit managers, and "white shirts," lieutenants and sergeants. The computers are—how else can they be described?—dinosaurs, and they don't connect to the internet. They are connected on a sort of internal "net" that allows staff to put information in that can then be accessed by other staff. For example, psych staff can submit a report that is then reviewed by the supervising psychiatrist, and searches can be performed on internal DOC "websites"—for example, to locate an incarcerated person who has transferred to another institution. The phones provide another throwback moment. Welcome to the world of landlines! Just as we researchers are not allowed to bring in cellphones or Fitbits that connect to the Internet, as these pose a security threat, neither are staff. Each office has a landline phone—brace yourself—with a cord! Some offices also had cordless landline phones, allowing staff to move about the office while talking. Phoning is also an internal-only experience, no calls home to alert your spouse that you have to work an unexpected double shift or to GrubHub for food delivery.

Then there is the clutter. Piles of paper, official DOC inmate handbooks from the early 2000s, blank commissary order and grievance forms. Often while conducting an interview we would learn some new piece of information and ask the staff if they could teach us more about it. For example, many incarcerated people we interviewed who were on DC status indicated that one of the things they resented the most about their time in solitary confinement was the limited commissary they could order. We asked officers about it and they steered us to stacks of paper, sometimes organized, sometimes not, that included blank commissary order forms denoting those items which were approved for prisoners on DC status and which were reserved for those on AC. The more we picked through the paper, the more we realized it was mostly useless. On the one hand, we wonder why all this clutter is there. On the other hand, it is by far the least of anyone's concern, so no one seems to take the time to organize it and discard what is outdated or no longer needed. The blank forms also tell a tale of the process by which people incarcerated in solitary confinement can access their rights. Stacks of blank forms are there so that when a prisoner makes a request, an officer can find the appropriate form and deliver it to their cell, sliding it through the seam in the door window, just as we did when we recruited participants for interviews. The stack of forms also tells the tale of the way time moves in prison and in solitary confinement in particular. The one thing incarcerated people have plenty of is time. Twenty-four hours a day. For years. And we regularly observed the ways in which COs used time as a way to punish those confined in solitary. On many occasions prisoners told us that they had been in solitary confinement for more than a week without getting their property, which they are supposed to be given as quickly as possible. In fairness, we saw property rooms that were bursting at the seams. Officers told us that because they had been short-staffed, no one had time to sort and deliver the property. They had more pressing things to do like strip searches and cell extractions, or the daily mundane, reoccurring, and time-sensitive tasks like bringing meals and escorting prisoners to showers and the yard. We also heard unit leaders respond to requests for property flippantly, telling us, "Hey these guys are in for ninety days; what's the rush? He'll get it when he gets it." All the while, he leans back in his chair and spends an hour telling us about his career trajectory. Was he really that busy, or was he "burning" [the term "burning" means to deny someone their rights, for example to a shower, to a meal, or in this case to their possessions] the prisoner for whom he felt no sense of urgency? Imagine being locked in a cell twenty-three hours a day, waiting on the only possessions you own in the world—a book, some letters, and photographs—in your undelivered property box sitting in the property room or unit manager's office.

★   ★   ★

The year 2020 was a particularly difficult year for most people. As the United States seemed to be coming apart at the seams, at least politically, one common experience for nearly everyone living in the United States was the COVID-19 pandemic. Many of us struggled, as people incarcerated in solitary confinement do, with time. A common experience for those of us working and learning from home was losing track of the days. Without a commute or a reason to put on work clothes, and with many of us working into the evenings or on the weekends to make up time we lost during the regular work week while we supervised children's home-learning or cared for aging parents, like people incarcerated in solitary confinement, it was easy to lose track of time.

We wrote the first version of this chapter during the summer of 2020, and we revised it in April 2021, thirteen months into the COVID-19 pandemic. We heard many people compare their quarantine conditions to solitary confinement. We will just say this: if you felt isolated, if you felt lonely, if you felt stir crazy, and most of us did, you may be able to relate to what it's like to be incarcerated in solitary confinement. But let us be clear: no matter how isolated you felt or how much time you have lost track of, our lives in the COVID-19 pandemic are luxurious compared with life in solitary confinement. Chances are you still had your Netflix, HBO Max, Amazon Prime. You could get groceries delivered from Instacart and prepared food from your favorite restaurant from GrubHub. You could take a shower anytime you wanted to. You could make as many phone calls or send as many emails or text messages as you liked, anytime you liked. No one called you a "dog" or "n———." No SWAT team arrived to forcibly extract you from your home. You were never subjected to the dehumanizing strip and cavity search. And though it might have seemed like it would never end, we all know it will. For thousands of people locked in solitary confinement units in U.S. prisons, there is no end date; sentences are interminable, often lasting decades. Decades.

We believe that the comparison between solitary confinement and the COVID-19 pandemic may be a way for the average person to get a *small* sense of what solitary confinement is like. In fact, in our classes we invite students to participate in a solitary confinement simulation, spending twenty-four hours in a bathroom or closet, an assignment we were first introduced to by our colleague and friend Professor Danielle Rudes. But we suggest that these comparisons be undertaken with caution so as not to minimize the realities of solitary confinement as it is designed and implemented in the United States.

★　★　★

Off of the hallway are four pods, A, B, C, and D. Entrance into each pod is through a steel door, which, once again, requires buzzing from the CO in the bubble. Inside the solitary confinement unit the bubble is much bigger than the bubble in the visitors' space. Although the precise location varies, in the majority of the prisons where we conducted research, the bubble was a rectangular room on the second floor that ran between the pods in such a way as to give the officer a clear view of each pod and nearly every cell in each pod, including those on both the first and second floors. There were a few blinds spots, but very, very few. The bubble, like everything else in a solitary confinement unit, is accessible only through a secure door. Officers and researchers who want to access the bubble push a button next to the door and they are buzzed up.

Visualizing the space of solitary confinement is critical to understanding the impact of the space on the social interactions and intimacy we interrogate in this book. Therefore, we included artists' renderings of the space in order to help the reader "see" solitary through both pictures and words. We commissioned this diagram of the unit from our friend and colleague, Taylor Sprague (Figure 1).

Each pod has a cement floor and a fairly big common area, which is an interesting space design choice given the infrequency and few exceptions in which people incarcerated in solitary confinement, who are locked in their cells twenty-three hours a day, are allowed to be with one another in the common area.

The aqua color scheme continues. Everywhere you look you see the same color, the kind of color that in a weird way reminds you of vomit. Or maybe it's just that these are the same colors that we find in places that we associate with being sick, like bathrooms in middle schools. The colors are not soothing or welcoming. The only exceptions are the strip cages and therapy cages, which are painted brown. Whether by design or not, the monochromatic interior design contributes to sensory deprivation. After a while we forget what the

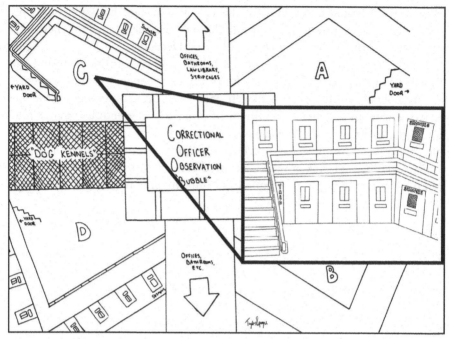

Figure 1. Diagram of the Hole. (Illustration by Taylor Sprague.)

actual color of the paint is because there is nothing to contrast with it. Dirt is the only thing punctuating the sea of aqua. The hole is filthy, the kind of filthy that only a good power washing can clean—we mean like an industrial power washing.

In her review of the literature on sensory deprivation, Lisa Guenther details study after study, mostly performed by psychologists, many conducted in part to understand how to best extract information during times of war, that confirm that sensory deprivation quickly produces declines in mental health. After just a day, even less if the sensory deprivation is multifaceted, including visual, auditory, and physical (temperature), people begin to report anxiety and hallucinations.

Sensory deprivation is a deliberate strategy in solitary confinement.

Baxter and colleagues taught a philosophy seminar at the Maryland Penitentiary and they published the reflections of their incarcerated students, including those of John Woodland, Jr., a Black prisoner, who described the architecture of his cell and the cell block:

> It's just enough room to live in. No more. Nothing for relaxation. . . .
> One thing I noticed when I first came to the penitentiary is that the penitentiary design is similar to the high-rise projects in West Baltimore or East Baltimore or wherever. In prison it's the tiers; in the projects it's the floors. . . . Because wherever you go, east or west, you see African

Americans and low-income people packed in on top of one another, with no real space. When you walk down the streets of most inner cities, you feel indifference to everything; This isn't really part of me. I'm just existing here. This is not something I should care about or protect or build up. This is something I gotta deal with until I get out.' I guess that's the same way we look at prisons.[5]

A place to "get through" rather than inhabit.

Saidiya Hartman extends our conceptualization of space as a place to get through, not to be in, by considering the impact of the transatlantic slave trade. She argues:

The slave and the master understand differently what staying implies. The transience of the slave's existence still leaves its traces in how Black people imagine home as well as how we speak of it. We may have forgotten our country, but we haven't forgotten our dispossession. It's why we never tire of dreaming of a place that we can call home, a place better than here, wherever here might be. It's why one hundred square blocks of Los Angeles can be destroyed in an evening. If we stay there, but we don't live there. . . . Two people meeting on the avenue will ask, "Is this where you stay?" Not "Is this your house?" "I stayed here all my life" is the reply. Staying is living in a country without exercising any claims on its resources. It is the perilous condition of existing in a world in which you have no investments. It is having never resided in a place that you can say is yours. It is being "of the house" but not having a stake in it. Staying implies transient quarters, a make-shift domicile, a temporary shelter, but not attachment or affiliation. This sense of not belonging and of being an extraneous element is at the heart of slavery.[6]

Solitary confinement, and prison more generally, is a transient place, even if one's stay is long, even if the stay is nearly one's entire life, as it is for the nearly 2,500 men who were sentenced as juveniles to life sentences without the possibility of parole. Or for COs who will work an average of sixty hours a week, for twenty-five years, in solitary confinement. No one plans to stay here forever any more than people living in urban and rural ghettos, characterized by substandard housing, underresourced schools, and retail inequality, plans to live there forever. Yet research on social mobility suggests that not only do few people escape the urban or rural ghetto, for most people living there, it's an intergenerational experience.[7] Places to survive, not places to thrive.

★ ★ ★

In many, though not all, of the pods there is trash littering the floor. Sometimes it seems to overflow from a clear plastic trash bag, like you might see at a tailgate party or public park or highway rest stop. Other times, the trash is arranged as if it is a perimeter between the cell doors and the floor of the pod. It's as if those incarcerated in solitary confinement wait for the wicket to open and then they throw out items for which they no longer have any use: empty food containers, pieces of paper. Though there are plenty of people who could clean up the mess, no one does, and no one seems to care or even really notice. John Woodward Jr. seems to be right.

A place to get through isn't a place to clean.

The monochromatism that pervades solitary confinement is broken up only by murals in the visitor room and diversionary treatment unit (DTU). In some prisons, officials are experimenting with a new kind of solitary confinement unit, a DTU, for prisoners with serious and unmanaged mentally illness who commit misconducts or pose a threat to themselves or who are at risk for being targeted with violence. Ok, so one question you should be asking is why there are people with serious mental illness in prison, let alone in solitary confinement. That is another question for another day, and in fact, this is the type of discussion we defer to our colleagues including Terry Kupers and Mary Buser, and we highly recommend that the reader interested in learning more about mental health in prisons and in solitary confinement in particular read Kupers's 2017 book *Solitary: The Inside Story of Supermax Isolation and How We Can Abolish It* and Buser's 2015 book *Lockdown on Rikers: Shocking Stories of Abuse and Injustices at New York's Most Notorious Jail.*

For our purposes, the importance of the murals is that their presence and the way the staff talk about them is indicative of their understanding of the impact that the monochromatic aqua vomit-colored walls and doors have on people. Often when we arrived at a jail we had never visited before, the staff were eager to show us the murals, brightly colored, often with inspirational quotes. A rainbow with the phrase "Hope Helps." They believed that the visual stimulation had a calming effect on the people who were incarcerated in these units. Many of the prisons we visited had incarcerated artists who vied for the chance to paint murals on the walls in the visiting room or the DTUs. We met a woman, a "lifer" who had been incarcerated in solitary confinement for decades until the state passed a moratorium on the death penalty. Because the only thing holding her in solitary confinement was her death sentence, once the moratorium was passed she was released back into general population to serve out her sentence. She was a talented painter, and she spent many, many days painting murals in the DTU. Staff told us that it helped her pass the time and it gave her a sense of purpose: transforming the place she had lived for so long to be a bit more stimulating and encouraging for the women still locked up there.

In each pod there is an upper tier and a lower tier, each holding about twenty cells. At the end of each tier, top and bottom, is a double shower. Essentially, two cells reconfigured, then divided into two steel cage shower stalls.

Off the back of the pod is a steel door out to the yard, where prisoners are placed in cages that resemble dog kennels for "exercise." Near the door, which is, of course, secure, is a mudroom of sorts with hooks for coats and a space for boots. Some days, in some prisons, it is well organized. Other days, in other prisons, it is a mess, as if a bunch of teenage boys has descended on your house. Some jackets are hung up; others are strewn on the floor as if the previous wearer simply took off the jacket or coat and dropped it immediately upon entry. The boots are the same. Some days, in some prisons, they are orderly. Other days, in other prisons, rather than standing up in a row, they are strewn all over the floor, on top of each other, the task of finding two mates seemingly impossible. It's not quite clear if the coats and boots "belong" to individual prisoners or if you grab what you need, depending on the weather, on your way out to the "yard." Because only a few prisoners are allowed out to the yard at the same time, a small number of coats and pairs of boots in a range of sizes will suffice. One man sloughs off, the next puts on. Repeat. Day after rainy or snowy day.

We, as well as most of the staff and prisoners we interviewed, use the term "solitary confinement," though it's important to acknowledge that most prison administrators argue that they have officially eliminated solitary confinement. Note that we used the term "eliminated" and not "ended the use of."

Regardless of what it is officially termed—secure housing unit (SHU), restrictive housing unit (RHU), diversionary treatment unit (DTU)—the basic idea is the same: prisoners are removed from the general prison population and placed in small cells and deprived of human contact for twenty-three hours per day. Prisoners eat, sleep, brush their teeth, and defecate in this confined space. Terry Kupers refers to these units as "isolation units" because their primary purpose is to use isolation and sensory deprivation as tools of punishment. Through a variety of lawsuits, of which we learned a great deal from both prisoners and staff, prisoners have secured certain rights, even in solitary confinement. In reality these rights are constantly being negotiated and renegotiated in individual units and among individual people. "Burning" is the term both prisoners and staff use to describe instances in which rights are denied. For example, though incarcerated people are entitled to an hour out of their cells each day, in practice this doesn't always happen. For a variety of reasons, including staffing shortages, and the preferences of the guards, most incarcerated people in solitary confinement are, realistically, out of their cells no more than a few hours a week. At many of the prisons where we did our research, showers were given on Mondays, Wednesdays, and Fridays. Showers take only about ten to fifteen minutes. Yet, often, officers argued that a shower amounted to adequate "out-of-cell time," and thus prisoners did not get yard time on shower days and vice versa. Most people incarcerated in solitary confinement reported that they did not get showers or yard time on the weekends or holidays when correctional officers operated on skeleton crews.

In order words, prisoners get a shower on Friday, and they don't get another shower until Monday. Even when the air conditioning is unable to keep up with the heat and humidity and the unit feels like a sauna.

The Shower

Our first day in solitary confinement happened to be a Monday, and it was shower day and we had the rare opportunity to watch the showering procedures up close. At one point we asked an officer to show us the shower. He gave us a surprised look, and we clarified that we didn't mean while a prisoner was showering; we wanted to see an empty shower. He laughed and said, sure, "come with me."

The officer in the bubble buzzed us in and the pod erupted immediately. Prisoners began hollering from their cells trying to get our attention. Among the many things that they yelled, a recurrent theme was the filthiness of the shower. "Nobody 'f-ing' cleans the shower!" to which the officer escorting us replied, "That's your job!" Well, the prisoners weren't wrong. The shower was as filthy as it was tiny. About the width of a bathroom in the economy section of an airplane, and perhaps twice as deep, the shower is a metal cube. The door, identical to a cell door, has a wicket through which the prisoner passes their hands for cuffing and uncuffing, and a window that is covered by steel caging. The window allows light to come in while simultaneously maintaining some privacy, as it runs about the length of the top third of the door. The window also ensured that officers were easily able to see well enough into the shower to tell if the occupant was doing anything dangerous, like cutting themselves.

It was the floor of the shower that caught our attention. The floor is a steel grate that allows water to pass through to the drain. Along the steel floor was human excrement, wet and soiled toilet paper, and other garbage. Though it may not have been any worse than a shower in a national park during a government shutdown, it was certainly not any place we would like to have to routinely shower.

On one wall of the shower is a 10 × 10 polished piece of metal which serves as the equivalent of a mirror. This is the only opportunity the incarcerated person has to take care of their hair on their head or their face. If they are not on a special restriction for cutting or other misconduct, they are entitled to a safety razor. Beyond the fact that the polished metal does not make it easy to shave or groom, we wonder what it's like for people incarcerated in long-term solitary confinement to go weeks, months, or even years without really seeing themselves. For men locked up for fifteen or twenty years in solitary confinement, how do they measure their aging? What is the impact on their mental health and sense of identity? We didn't ask these questions in our interviews, but they came up organically among many of the women we interviewed. In the solitary confinement unit in the women's prison where we conducted research, the mirror was contested terrain.

One might wonder, why all this drama over a mirror? The mirror becomes yet another tool in the tool kit of sensory deprivation. Not only is one deprived of visual stimulation in the form of colors or the natural cycles of dawn and dusk, one is not even allowed to see oneself. Though we mark our aging with our birthdays, most of us also mark our aging by observing changes in our bodies . . . a few pounds put on around the middle, gray hairs, or, for many men, thinning hair lines. What does it mean to not be able to mark the time of the day or the seasons, but literally the passing of your life?

Back in the shower . . . The shower head is attached to a metal ceiling, and along with the controls for heat and cold was a button the occupant pushed to get the water to come out. We were told by both prisoners and COs that an officer could also control the button from the bubble if he felt like a prisoner was taking too long in the shower. Even this moment of privacy can be and often is controlled by the officer. Incidentally, the toilet in each cell can also be operated by the officer in the bubble, and people incarcerated in solitary confinement routinely complained that officers refused to flush their toilets for days at a time as a form of punishment.

In solitary confinement COs exert tremendous control over the prisoners' daily hygiene in ways that serve to both dehumanize and remind the prisoner that the CO has all of the power. And this kind of control is not limited to men's prisons. Shaniqua is incarcerated in solitary confinement in the women's prison. She tells us a similar story. Shaniqua complains about the escort process, as COs move her (and the other women incarcerated in solitary confinement) between their cells, the yard, showers, and even to the law library where we interview her. Shaniqua is secured in a strip cage, handcuffed and shackled, we sit on plastic chairs that we have pulled as close to the cage as possible so that we can hear each other without yelling. Before the interview even begins, she starts complaining that the COs are lazy. She's holding papers in her hand, and we ask if it is the survey we distributed to her in the yard. We tell her that we are happy to take it from her if she has completed it. She shows us the paper. It isn't the survey.

"They took me straight from the yard to PRC [the hearing committee to determine her sentence in solitary] to here. They are too lazy. They didn't want to strip me again, so they brought me from one place to another."
["It's like running errands and doing them all at once instead of going home in between."]
"Exactly! They are lazy. Sometimes they take us to shower first and then directly to yard because they don't want to strip us again. It doesn't make any sense. . . . You take shower, you're clean, and wet, and then they take

us to the yard where we get sweaty, and we don't get another shower for two days. Lazy, that's what they are."

COs see it differently. An officer told us that on days when there is an emergency, like a cell extraction, which requires nearly every CO to rush to the "war room" and don combat gear, a prisoner may simply be left in the shower, often for an hour or more, until the crisis is cleared. The officer considered this a bonus, as if to say, "Lucky him, he was in the shower just when we had to use force to extract a prisoner from his cell." It wasn't clear to us that the occupant had any control over the flow of water in this instance. Perhaps he didn't want to be in the shower that long. Perhaps the officer in the bubble turned off the water and so he had to stand there, waiting to be removed from the shower cage, with only his towel to keep him from shivering. Perhaps many people, including some COs, don't care if a prisoner is stuck in a shower cage or if their toilet isn't flushed or if they go to yard *after* they've had a shower and put on a clean jumpsuit. In their view, people are incarcerated because they have committed a crime and they are in solitary confinement because they have misbehaved in prison, therefore, they aren't necessarily entitled to shower rights. But at the end of the day, they are human beings. Their sentence to prison is meant to punish them for their crime; their sentence to solitary is meant to punish them for misconduct, perhaps having a birthday card from a purported gang member. Do we, as a society, really intend to take away their control over their shower or their toilet?

The answer is that each and every "right" is negotiated through both lawsuits and individual, daily interactions between COs and incarcerated people. As we will document, it is this set of daily negotiations, as insignificant or inconsequential as each may seem, that structures the production and reproduction of white racial resentment.

THE YARD

The "yard" is not the kind of yard that Tim Robbins and Morgan Freeman frequented in the famous prison film *Shawshank Redemption*. For those confined in solitary, the "yard" is more like, in fact it is exactly like, a dog kennel, and both those incarcerated and officers often referred to it as such. A cage that is perhaps ten feet long, five feet wide, and ten feet high. Prisoners can jump and pace and sometimes talk to each other if they are caged near one another. Because this is their only opportunity to go outside, to see the sun and feel the wind and breathe the air, many incarcerated people take advantage of yard time even when it's cold or raining or snowing or over 120 degrees. Others refuse the yard unless the weather is ideal, which depending on the climate where the prison is located means people locked in solitary confinement may go weeks, months, or even years without breathing fresh air or feeling the rain on their faces.

THE CELL

Each pod has an upper and a lower tier with a single staircase up to the second tier. The staircase is a set of stairs that are simply steel grates, the kind of stairs you might encounter if you are touring the Hoover Dam or a power plant or a submarine parked in a harbor or port in New York City or San Francisco.

The cell doors are steel, and on each door there are two plastic holders for prisoner identification cards. Incarcerated people on AC status sometimes have a "cellie" (cell mate), so there is room on the door for up to two people to be identified as its occupants. ID cards have the individual's picture, name, inmate number, a notation of their status, AC or DC, and any restrictions they have. For example, the ID card of a prisoner who doesn't eat pork might have a pink pig with a circle and an X on top of it, that is, "No pig." Just a friendly reminder to the CO serving trays that the person housed in this cell should get the "no pork" meal option.

Prisoners who have cut themselves or others may have razor restrictions, which are noted, along with anything else important. Again, a visual cue to the CO passing out safety razors, as he prepares to escort people to the shower, who can and who cannot have razors. In addition to serving as a visual cue, this notification system, if you will, means that any CO working any shift—indeed, any researcher walking by—can learn things about each person incarcerated in solitary confinement. Of course, all the other prisoners can learn this information as well as they are escorted past cells on their way to the shower or the yard. There is also a shelf outside each cell door. In women's prisons these shelves often held razors and pill bottles and shampoo and menstrual supplies. In the men's prisons, they rarely held anything, but one can imagine if there were more trust between the incarcerated and the COs that similar items could be placed there, outside the grasp of the prisoner but close enough to dispense easily.

The cells in solitary confinement are 12 feet × 12 feet. Each cell has either one or two bunks on one wall, with a desk and a stool on the other wall. In the corner is a sink-and-toilet combination. Everything is made of steel and bolted to the floor and the adjacent wall. The floor and the walls are cement. The walls are painted the same color as the entire unit: vomit aqua. There is a small window in the back of the cell, maybe six inches wide and two or three feet long. It's more like a slit, really. Despite its small size, when we walk to and from the solitary confinement unit each day or when we go to the chow hall for a lunch break, incarcerated people' faces are plastered against these slits, watching us. Sometimes they bang the glass with their hands to get our attention. Sometimes they show off their body parts. Anything to get attention, to break up the monotony of the endless days. Any form of connection with another human being.

Our friend and colleague Taylor Sprague produced the following image in Figure 2 to represent the inside of a cell in solitary confinement.

Figure 2. Solitary cell. (Illustration by Taylor Sprague.)

As often as possible we selected pieces of art to illustrate the experiences of solitary confinement by those who were incarcerated there. This image shown in Figure 3 of the cell door was created by an incarcerated person, D. L. Derrell.

The cells are locked with a steel door that has a small, narrow, long window, which, once again, has a small seam for passing papers or talking. During our many visits to cell doors to speak with incarcerated people about participating in the research, we had a window into their whole lives; their possessions were on full display. People incarcerated in solitary confinement are given a set of bedding, which is certainly not like what you would find in even the cheapest Motel 6 in a prison town. Bedding consists of a thin mattress, black and gray striped, like you see in the movies. A thin set of sheets, pillow, and pillowcase and a thin gray blanket. Prisoners who have money on their books and who are in AC status, can, of course, purchase extra bedding, but everyone is entitled to the indigent bedding package. The same goes with clothing. Incarcerated people are entitled to two or three "oranges," or jumpsuits (browns if you are general population, blue if you are confined in the DTU, and red, the color of blood, for those on death row), underwear, undershirt, socks, and shower sandals that are tan. As with the bedding, those on AC status can purchase more clothing, up to the limits allowed, and higher-quality shower shoes, thermal underwear, and even a tablet, which sells for $147. As noted, there are boots and coats available near the door to the yard which prisoners can put on to go out in inclement weather.

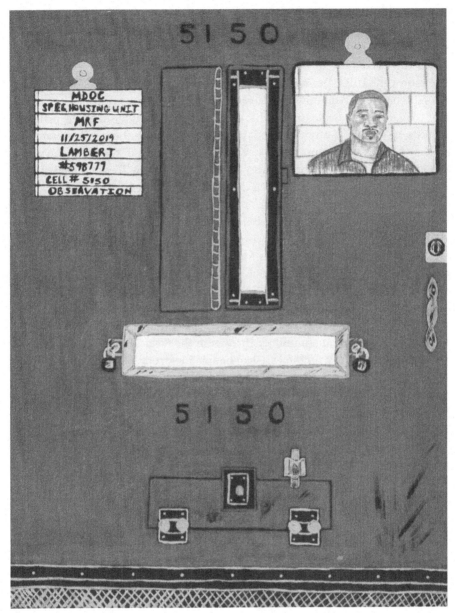

Figure 3. Solitary door with wicket. *OBSERVATION—"Red" Cell.*
(Painting by D. L. Derell.)

We also had the opportunity to observe how incarcerated people organize their meager possessions. Some had books and writing materials on the desk. Some kept fruit served at lunch or dinner to snack on later. Many of the people incarcerated in solitary confinement who we observed strung a line from one end of the desk to the toilet to hang the clothes they have washed in their steel sinks. Some had pictures and posters on the wall, of loved ones or heroes; some hang paper with pictures they have drawn or words they have scribed. Some prisoners are fastidious, their cells as clean as is humanly possible in this incredibly filthy environment. Others, not so much. Even though it's against the rules, some men hang paper to cover the windows on their cell doors. They aren't supposed to cover their windows because the COs argue that they need to be able to see what each person is doing inside their cell. But men do it, and COs often oblige, as a matter of giving those incarcerated in solitary confinement some privacy. We notice that most of the men who cover the window on their cell doors also cover their window to the outside, leaving the cell nearly pitch black even during the day. It resembles a cave.

Each cell door has a "wicket," a basket-like device that allows officers to pass food, medicine, and other materials back and forth to the occupant. This is also the hole through which prisoners put their hands to be cuffed before they are removed from their cells for any reason, including to be escorted to the shower or the yard. The CO has the only key to open the wicket; prisoners cannot open it themselves. Correctional officers treat every instance of opening the wicket with care because it is in this action that prisoners also have the opportunity to pass items through the cell door, including urine and feces, which are not uncommonly thrown in the faces of officers.

Lorna Rhoades, who interviewed people incarcerated in solitary confinement in Washington State, argues: "In a world where your food is thrown at you through a hole, where the head of your bed is next to your toilet, where toilet paper has to be requested, throwing *shit* says something."[8]

It is, as she argues, an act of resistance.

The wicket becomes contested terrain, a war zone in which the prisoner and the correctional officer do battle. They battle for control; they battle for humanity.

The defining feature of solitary confinement, regardless of what it is officially termed, is the absolute deprivation of human interaction.

Mary Buser, who after writing her book *Lockdown on Rikers: Shocking Stories of Abuse and Injustice at New York's Notorious Jail* which pulled the curtain back and unsilenced one of the most notorious jails in the world, became an activist who dedicates her life to abolishing solitary confinement. She shared this story with us about a man she now works with and advocates for, Frank DePalma.

Can you imagine stepping into an elevator car, having the door close behind you and not open again for 22 years? During this time a food tray would be delivered through a slot in the door. You'd have no human contact, no TV, no magazines or books, not even a Bible. For 22 years.

This is exactly what happened to my friend, Frank DePalma, in a Nevada Prison, where he spent 22 years and 36 days in solitary confinement. He entered the cell at 36 years old and did not come out till he was close to

60. He went for 2 years without a mattress, and was forced to extract 4 of his own teeth during his confinement. When he was released from the cell, his vocal chords did not work, he could barely walk, he could not interact with people, did not recognize himself in a mirror, and had no idea how old he was.

After a short period of "rehab," Frank was released to the streets, where he has been trying his best to survive. After a period of homelessness, he now lives in a small room in a boarding house with a shared bathroom & kitchen. His monthly disability check covers his rent, but little else. A bar of soap is a luxury. Despite some poor decisions earlier in his life, Frank DePalma is a good man. Every day is a struggle for him, psychologically, physically, and financially. Frank has known extreme human cruelty in his life and deserves a second chance at life.[9]

We interviewed people like Frank DePalma, people who endured extreme torture and cruelty. People who have made mistakes, some of whom have even done terrible things, but none of whom, we argue, deserve to be treated, as they say, like dogs, like animals in cages. And no one, no matter what they have been convicted of should spend decades lock away in isolation as Frank DePalma was.

Most experts, including those writing the UN Human Rights Articles, agree that the isolation of solitary confinement should be limited in time, ideally to no more than fifteen consecutive days, and should be a strategy of last resort, when all other measures to keep incarcerated people and corrections staff safe have been exhausted.[10] In reality, just like the twenty-three-hour-per-day lockup rule, these limits on the use of solitary confinement are rarely honored. In fact, since the 1980s, stays in solitary confinement can last for months, years, or even decades, as was the case for Albert Woodfox, who was released in 2016 after spending forty-three years in solitary confinement.[11] In many states, including in the state where we conducted research and in the state where Smith worked as a counselor in a maximum security prison, including serving incarcerated people on death row, prisoners serving death sentences are incarcerated in solitary confinement for the entire term of their sentences, released only when the state deems it "time" to take their lives. One member of our research team told us about a prisoner who was released from death row after the state passed a moratorium on the death penalty. On the day he was transferred into general population, after *thirty-six years* in solitary confinement, he asked to linger in the yard a few extra minutes, where he allegedly got down on the ground to smell the grass.

There are now hundreds of super-maximum-security, "supermax," prisons that are carefully designed and constructed entirely of units built for the long-term isolation of human beings. Incarcerated people in the famous supermax in Florence, Colorado, are housed in underground, single cells, where they live, often for decades, with virtually no human interaction other than with the corrections officers who move them to the shower or push their meal trays through the wicket on the cell doors, both activities often done in silence or with the only exchanges being the hurling of derogatory insults. In some supermax facilities, the doors to the cells, showers, and yard, as well as the wicket, are all motorized such that a CO can control them from a remote location. No human contact is necessary even to perform the most basic daily activities.

In her book *Solitary Confinement: Social Death and Its Afterlives*, Lisa Guenther argues that *all* solitary confinement units should be termed "supermax" incarceration.

Solitary confinement is no longer reserved exclusively for incarcerated people who are either in danger or who pose a danger to others. Corrections officers routinely use solitary confinement as punishment for otherwise minimal infractions, including having too many personal items in the one's cell, especially food, or for trading in black market services, such as sewing in exchange for extra food. We interviewed several people who were serving ninety-day sentences in solitary confinement for running "stores." A store is a way to make a living in prison if you don't have a job or you don't have anyone to put money on your books (in your commissary). As explained by one person incarcerated in solitary confinement, a store allows you to get some commissary items and make a profit by selling them at a markup. As he described: "I loan you two honey buns and you owe me three back." One hundred percent interest. In many prisons, there is a limit on how many commissary items you can have in your cell, and thus when officers find a cell with more than the maximum allowed, they can accuse the inmate of running a store—all stores need inventory—and throw you in the hole.

Many incarcerated people who identify in the LGBTQ+ community are routinely housed for their entire sentence in solitary confinement, allegedly to "keep them safe." Other incarcerated people who are confined in solitary confinement for their "safety" include police officers, snitches, high-profile prisoners, sex offenders, and anyone else who either is deemed or self-identifies as "at risk." These incarcerated people have not been sentenced to solitary confinement for misconduct or committing an infraction in the general population, and yet like those who have been, they are forced to endure solitary confinement as the only strategy the staff in the prison can identify to keep them safe. CeCe McDonald, a trans woman who was incarcerated, spent her entire sentence, more than a year and a half, in solitary confinement because her jailers believed this was the only way to keep her safe. She reported being raped by correctional officers no fewer than seven times in these eighteen months. Despite arguing that CeCe needed to be held in solitary to keep her safe, COs were not able to keep her safe, even there, not even from violence perpetrated by other COs.[12]

CHAPTER 2

Solitary Confinement in Context

EACH AND EVERY DAY in the United States there are between 80,000 and 100,000 people locked in solitary confinement units. Though there is no way to track the exact number of people working in solitary confinement units, based on our extensive observations, across all three shifts, in several different prisons, we estimate that there are somewhere in the neighborhood of 30,000 people who spend forty to sixty hours a week *working* in the hole, in a jail, or in a state or federal prison.

Solitary confinement has been a part of incarceration practices since the inception of confinement as a tool of punishment.[1] Beliefs about the utility of solitary confinement have varied across both time and place, including in the United States. At the beginning of the nineteenth century, two theories or schools of incarceration were born. The Auburn system, which was developed in New York, was focused on work camps that were characterized by silence but not restricted interaction.[2] The Pennsylvania system was built on the belief and practice of rigid isolation.

Moving into contemporary times, solitary confinement is a prison management strategy used primarily for two purposes: to house disruptive prisoners away from the general prison population ("general population") and to house incarcerated people who are deemed to be, or self-identify as, at a high risk for becoming victims of violence. Solitary confinement became institutionalized across American penal institutions in response, many suggest, to George Jackson's purported attempted escape on August 21, 1971, from the California prison where he was incarcerated; during that attempted escape, he was killed by a correctional officer.[3]

There are a lot of misconceptions about how people end up in the hole. Some people are sentenced directly to solitary confinement, but that is in fact a rare and exclusive journey. Generally speaking, the only people sentenced directly to solitary confinement are those sentenced to death, including in states that have a moratorium on executions, and those sentenced to supermax prisons like Florence, Colorado, where the notorious Mexican drug lord Joaquín Guzmán, "El Chapo," was sent in the summer of 2019. Other than these individuals, the vast majority of the nearly 100,000 people in the hole are there because of something they did on the inside, not because of something they did on the outside.

In other words, being sentenced to solitary confinement often has little to do with the crime one was sentenced to prison for and everything to do with one's behavior while in prison. People often wrongly assume that axe murderers and serial rapists are in solitary confinement and drug dealers never are. In fact, axe murderers who behave themselves in prison may spend most of their sentences in general population, whereas drug dealers who continue to deal in drugs or other contraband while incarcerated may spend a good part, if not most, of their sentences in solitary confinement units.

Two summers of conducting research in solitary confinement units exposed us to much of the inner workings and daily routines of life in solitary confinement for both incarcerated people and staff. To be honest, much of what we observed contradicted what we expected and debunked many myths we previously held about solitary confinement. Thus, we decided it was important to learn more about the average American's perceptions of solitary confinement. During the first week of July 2019, we conducted a survey using a Qualtrics panel of 2,500 people living in the United States. [Qualtrics is a data management system that researchers use to identify participants and gather data from them.] Based on our interest in understanding more about the ways in which solitary confinement is racialized and the ways in which its structures contribute to the production and reproduction of white racial resentment, we oversampled Blacks, people who live in rural communities, and those with some experience in the criminal legal system. In addition to asking people their demographic information, things like race, gender, religious affiliation, region of the country where they lived, and experience with the criminal legal system, we relied on the Vera Institute for Justice's "myths" about solitary confinement to design the "attitude" questions in the survey. As noted on their website: "Vera is now a national organization that partners with impacted communities and government leaders for change. We develop just, antiracist solutions so that money doesn't determine freedom; fewer people are in jails, prisons, and immigration detention; and everyone in the system is treated with dignity."[4]

For each of the twelve myths identified by the Vera Institute, we included a statement in the survey, such as "Segregated housing is reserved for only the most violent," to which we asked respondents to indicate their level of agreement or disagreement. We chose these myths because we suspected that people with no experience with the criminal legal system, and solitary confinement more specifically, would answer differently from those people who did have experience with the criminal legal system, those who had been incarcerated or worked in a jail or prison.

The mean for nearly every attitude item in the survey, which was scored as 0 = strongly disagree and 100 = strongly agree, was 50. Typically mean scores in the middle of the scale suggest one of two things: either most respondents to the survey are ambivalent and they choose an answer that reflects this ambivalence, indicating, for example, that they "neither agree nor disagree," or the sample is composed of people with extremely polarized attitudes; they either "strongly agree" or they "strongly disagree" with every item and their responses average out to the middle score. In other words, either people were completely ambivalent about the use of solitary confinement, whether it should be continued, whether it kept people safe, or their attitudes were so extremely polarized that they canceled each other out.

Mild though significant differences were found such that older people, those who live in the South, those who identify as conservative, those who practice a "major world religion," and those who are "not poor" were somewhat more likely to have attitudes that were favorable to the use of solitary confinement as well as its continued use. Surprisingly, there were no racial differences in attitudes toward solitary confinement.

We were initially surprised that there were so few significant differences among people's attitudes about solitary confinement, but we conclude that there are at least two explanations for this lack of findings. Knowing that the population of people with criminal legal involvement is relatively small overall, we oversampled for involvement in the criminal legal system, in the hopes of getting a large enough sample to be able to perform meaningful statistical analysis. When we began looking at the data, we were stunned to find that slightly more than half of the sample (51.2 percent of respondents) reported that they had some interaction with the criminal legal system; they themselves had been incarcerated, they had a friend or family member who had been to jail or prison, or they had worked in a jail or prison. A quarter (25.9 percent) of those surveyed had personal experience with solitary confinement; they had friends and family members who had been incarcerated in solitary confinement or had worked in solitary confinement. These extraordinarily high rates of practical experience with prisons and solitary confinement in particular are likely the best explanation as to why there were so few differences in people's attitudes regarding solitary confinement. In short, the responses of those with experience with the criminal legal system and solitary confinement likely canceled out the responses of people with no experience.

One of the most encouraging findings was that there was overwhelming agreement that solitary confinement should *not* be used with children.

Despite what the "average" American thinks or knows about solitary confinement, following the murder of George Jackson, state and federal prisons came to rely on solitary confinement as a *management tool* to isolate away those incarcerated people whom officers deem the worst of the worst, those who are identified as a danger to others and often to themselves. In many cases engaging the rhetoric of "safety" is nothing more than a way to rationalize the use of solitary confinement, as the case of CeCe McDonald, detailed previously, illustrates.

Many people are under the impression that solitary is a punishment practice to address behaviors that contribute to safety concerns inside the prison.

Under this assumption, we could conclude that people are in solitary confinement because they are dangerous or pose a threat to others. Some people are sent to solitary confinement because they are involved in assaults, particularly if their target is an officer. But many, many people we interviewed in solitary confinement and those we observed being "sentenced" to solitary in an internal hearing process were there for breaking minor rules, such as having too many commissary items in their cells or trading sewing services for honey buns. Others were in solitary confinement for more "serious" offenses, such as refusing to take a cell mate, which though it can be interpreted as an act of defiance does not necessarily pose a safety risk. In other words, yes, solitary confinement is punishment, but in a majority of cases, the punishment is for being defiant or for being innovative, not necessarily for being dangerous.

As we found in our interviews with staff but especially with incarcerated people, solitary confinement can be used as punishment for prisoners who are seen as being too critical or too vocal about their treatment in prison, it can be used to isolate incarcerated people who are perceived as organizers or rabble rousers, and it can be used as retribution against political prisoners, as Claude Marks experienced. The definition of "misconduct" that lands one in solitary confinement can be entirely based on an officer's whim, and solitary confinement can be imposed without impunity. Having too many honey buns or being someone who writes too many letters to the grievance board pleading for their rights provides the rationale for sending a prisoner to the hole for weeks, months, or even years. Solitary confinement units are, then, not only utilized to house the most violent, but often those who are perceived as dangerous because of their attitudes and their willingness to fight for their civil and human rights.

As far back as the 1820s, philosophers and reformers described the devastation of solitary confinement. But nobody listened.

The French sociologist and political theorist Alexis de Tocqueville (1805–1859) traveled to the United States in 1831 to study its prison system, and he published his observations in *Democracy in America* (1835). Prior to that book, he and Gustave de Beaumont wrote *On the Penitentiary System in the United States and Its Application in France* (1833). This report demonstrates that the authors were keenly aware of the dangers of using isolation as a form of punishment, especially after their visit to one of the original penitentiaries in New York State: Auburn. They put it thus: "The northern wing, having been nearly finished in 1821, eighty prisoners were placed there, and a separate cell was given to each. This trial, from which so happy a result had been anticipated, was fatal to the greater part of the convicts. In order to reform them, they had been submitted to complete isolation; but this absolute solitude, if nothing interrupts it, is beyond the strength of man; it destroys the criminal without intermission and without pity; it does not reform, it kills."[5]

Despite de Tocqueville's early warnings, today every state in the United States, the federal prison system, and nearly every local city and county jail utilizes some form of solitary confinement. Unlike the system that tracks all incarcerated bodies at the local, state, and federal levels and reports data through the Bureau of Justice Statistics, there is no federal or systematic reporting system that tracks how many people are isolated away at any given time in solitary confinement.

THE NUMBERS

The United Nations report *Seeing into Solitary: A Review of the Laws and Policies of Certain Nations Regarding Solitary Confinement of Detainees* published in 2016 provides the most comprehensive quantitative examination of solitary confinement available. The report includes comparative data on twenty-six countries and thirty-five jurisdictions in the United States. According to the report, on any given day, hundreds of thousands of people around the world are held in some sort of solitary confinement or restricted housing unit. Citing data from the ASCA-Liman Nationwide Survey of Time-in-Cell study, the United Nations report indicates that 80,000 to 100,000 of those held in solitary confinement around the world are incarcerated in the United States. Though we can't know for sure what percentage of all prisoners held in solitary confinement are held in the United States, based on the data we can speculate that the United States utilizes solitary confinement more than most other countries. For starters, the United States incarcerates a disproportionate percentage of our citizenry; the United States has 5 percent of the world's population but 25 percent of the world's incarcerated population. As the United Nations report reveals, the United States allows for longer sentences in solitary confinement than the vast majority of other countries, including indefinite sentences. The report concludes: "In the United States, although there is a diverse legal regime among the states and between the states and federal systems regarding solitary confinement as a disciplinary sanction, overall, many of these laws are written such that *prisoners could be held in solitary confinement indefinitely.*"[6]

Though there are perhaps thousands of incarcerated people serving long-term or indefinite terms in solitary confinement, many more incarcerated people serve shorter sentences. On any given day, 3.5 percent of the incarcerated population is in some form of solitary confinement, but the United Nations report indicates that the total number of people who *are ever* confined in solitary confinement is much higher:

Over the course of a year approximately 20% of all prisoners and 18% of jail detainees spend time in solitary confinement. By any measure the use of solitary confinement in American correctional institutions is a global outlier and human rights crisis. Not only are the numbers of people subject to solitary staggering, the duration they spend in such extreme social and environmental isolation in America is unconscionable. While some prisoners are subject to days or weeks in isolation, too frequently American prisoners are isolated in solitary for months, years, and even decades. In the federal prison system and at least 19 states, corrections officials may hold people in isolation housing indefinitely. A recent study in Texas, for example, demonstrated that the average stay in solitary for prisoners in the state is almost four years; and over one hundred people had spent more than twenty years in solitary confinement.

Twenty percent of all people currently incarcerated in the United States having served time in solitary confinement amounts to 500,000 people. In other words, *annually*, half a million people in the United States spend at least some time in solitary confinement.

Complicating the matter is the fact that "solitary confinement" goes by a number of names, including administrative segregation (ad seg), special housing units (SHU), management control units, diversionary treatment units, behavior management units, and even threat units designed to isolate gang members who are engaged in discernible gang activity. Though there are many different explanations for this change in language, we are not alone in noticing that the renaming of these restrictive housing units corresponds with changes in public opinion, increased pressure by activists, and lawsuits.

States can announce that they have abolished solitary confinement when in fact what they have done is rename it, and perhaps modified it slightly so as to make it seem less tortuous.[7] And, though some of these "reforms" have actually improved conditions in solitary confinement, nevertheless, on any given day, 3.2 percent of the incarcerated population in the United States is in the "hole."

In California, for example, incarcerated people and their families filed a lawsuit, *Ashker v. Brown*, that was partially settled in 2015. According to the lawsuit, California held more incarcerated people in solitary confinement, for longer periods of time, on innocuous charges such as suspected gang affiliation, than any other state. According to reports, suspicion of gang affiliation could be as simple as having "Aztec art or a birthday card from a purported gang member" and could result in an *indefinite* sentence in solitary confinement.[8] Several incarcerated people named in the lawsuit had been held for fifteen years in California's notorious Pelican Bay supermax prison. As a result of the lawsuit, today, prisoners in California are housed not in "solitary confinement" but in a "secure housing unit or SHU." Reports note that the number of incarcerated people sent to the SHU for suspected gang affiliation has dropped, but the unit remains populated through other equally innocuous sentences. "Basically, prison staff are prosecutor, judge, jury, everything," says Jean Casella, codirector of the watchdog organization *Solitary Watch*, noting that the conviction rate in prison hearings is over 90 percent in most states. "If a [correctional officer] wants you to go to solitary, you're probably going to go to solitary."[9]

An early review of the first draft of this chapter raised some concerns that we were misrepresenting the situation at Pelican Bay, which had purportedly eliminated or at least significantly reduced the use of solitary confinement. In response, we reached out to Claude Marks, a former political prisoner, advocate, and cofounder of Freedom Archives (which, according to their website, is "a non-profit educational archive located in Berkeley dedicated to the preservation and dissemination of historical audio, video and print materials documenting progressive movements and culture from the 1960s to the 1990s")[10] who had intimate knowledge of the situation at Pelican Bay. Claude confirmed, and pointed us to several reputable sources that documented this as well, that Pelican Bay did close the "short corridor" where people were incarcerated in long-term solitary confinement. Many, including some of the plaintiffs in the Ashker case and those who participated in the infamous hunger strike, were transferred from the "short corridor" at Pelican Bay to another prison and to a slightly lower level of security–they were phased from level 5 to level 4. In the prison system, custody levels range from 1 to 5; level 5, or maximum security, generally describes supermax prisons or units where prisoners are isolated (solitary confinement) whereas level 1, or minimum security, refers to prisons or units in which people who are incarcerated may live in dormitory style housing and have significantly more freedom of movement, even leaving the secure setting to perform work around the grounds and even in the local community.

As a result of being moved from level 5 to level 4, the prisoners who were removed from the short corridor at Pelican Bay were given slightly more out-of-cell time. *But they remained in long-term solitary confinement.* And because they were suspected of gang activity, they were denied the opportunity to communicate with one another. As reported in the *Bay View News* series "Behind Enemy Lines": "While Plaintiffs admit conditions at Tehachapi SHU are slightly different from the conditions at Pelican Bay, their main contention is the same: Housing inmates in a SHU for prolonged periods of time is cruel and unusual punishment."[11]

We are grateful to Claude for walking us through the intricacies of the Pelican Bay case and pointing us to multiple sources that confirm the fact that although solitary confinement has been renamed and some prisoners have been transferred, California and many other states, including the state where we conducted our research, continue to hold prisoners in long-term solitary confinement.

Contrary to popular belief, and not that it really makes it all that much better, in the prisons where we conducted research, "solitary confinement" did not necessarily mean incarcerated people didn't have cellies, especially those who were housed in administrative custody. In the jails where we conducted research, there were two distinct statuses of people incarcerated in solitary confinement, DC and AC. Prisoners in administrative custody (AC) were there for nondisciplinary reasons. For example, most prisoners who identify in the LGBTQ+ community are housed in solitary confinement for "their own safety" on AC status, as are prisoners who are in "protective custody," including police officers, high-profile people like Paul Manafort, and others who are at risk for but had not necessarily perpetrated or been the victim of violence in general population. During the COVID-19 pandemic, some jails held every prisoner in solitary confinement as a strategy for reducing the spread of the virus. Prisoners on AC status have significantly more privileges than those on disciplinary custody (DC) status. Those on AC status may have a cellie, they have access to their full commissary, and they are allowed visits, though these are noncontact and take place in the same visiting rooms where we conducted many of our interviews. In the jails where we conducted our research, prisoners on AC status were allowed access to tablets where they could download books, music, and even email which allowed them to stay connected with their family and friends. Prisoners on AC status are also allowed phone calls from their cells. COs wheel a portable kiosk with a phone and a tablet connection to cell doors. The officer then opens the wicket and the person incarcerated in the cell can make a phone call or download email on their tablet right from his cell. Those with enough money could purchase a TV, which costs around $200, and a cable hookup with the full complement of cable channels including ESPN and HGTV for $17 a month. All of that being said, prisoners on AC status often lived for years in solitary confinement, where they were still subjected to strip searches every time they left their cells, limited human interaction beyond their cellies, limited exercise time, showers, and no opportunity to work. Quite obviously, because prisoners on AC status had more privileges, AC-status and DC-status prisoners could not be celled together.

Given the tradeoffs, it wasn't hard to understand why a transgender prisoner or a convicted police officer would prefer solitary confinement to general population, especially given the fact that they could retain most of their privileges. What was surprising for us to learn is that some people incarcerated in solitary confinement on DC status deliberately broke rules or "caught misconducts" on purpose so that they would be sent to solitary confinement. As we will discuss in more depth in subsequent chapters, some people engaged solitary confinement, even DC status, with limited commissary, no TV, no tablet, and few if any phone calls or visits, as a strategy for solving another problem, such as a debt or in the hopes of being assigned to another unit or even another facility in the state.

The literature and "history" of solitary confinement suggest that it was first imagined as a way for men to be "in solitude" and, through careful introspection, to be redeemed. Later, in the middle of the twentieth century, the purpose of solitary confinement was focused on its capacity for rehabilitation. Today, solitary confinement is used as a tool of punishment.[12] Through the lens of prison administrators and those assigned to work in solitary confinement units, solitary confinement is, most importantly, a prison management tool designed to control incarcerated people who are adjudicated as being unable to live appropriately or safely among others in general population. This includes people who are "known" to be affiliated with gangs, even if there is no evidence that they are actively engaged in gang activity. Though this is rarely spoken about, solitary confinement is also a tool that re-creates racial hierarchies and, in so doing, reinforces racial stereotypes. As in any setting, not only do racial hierarchies and the reentrenchment of racial stereotypes harm the individuals who are confined and work in solitary confinement, but they have the potential to stoke racial antagonisms throughout the communities where prisons are located, where they are the only job in town.

We argued in our book *Policing Black Bodies: How Black Lives Are Surveilled and How to Work for Change* that mass incarceration is a tool for removing Black bodies, particularly those who are poor, from the social political economy. Plantation prisons and the convict leasing system were a response to emancipation and the formal end of slavery. Mass incarceration, which is largely fueled by the policies and practices associated with the War on Drugs, was a direct response to the protests of the civil rights movement as well as to the additional freedoms guaranteed to Black people through civil rights legislation like the Voting Rights Act, the Fair Housing Act, and the Civil Rights Act, By the early 1970s, Black people had gained more and more freedoms, and they began to increasingly be seen as a threat to whites. One way to manage that threat was to enact drug laws that appeared to be race neutral but are, in fact, not, which led directly to the hyperincarceration of Black bodies. Additionally, as the economy became increasingly less reliant on the types of low-skilled labor that Blacks were relegated to, and as much of this type of labor was obtained overseas or offshore, an "underclass" of Blacks, as William Julius Wilson refers to them, emerged in both urban and rural ghettos. Erik Olin Wright, the recently deceased sociologist who contributed significantly to the development of neo-Marxist theory, argued:

> In the case of labor power, a person can cease to have economic value in capitalism if it cannot be deployed productively. This is the essential condition of people in the "underclass." They are oppressed because they are denied access to various kinds of productive resources, above all the necessary means to acquire the skills needed to make their labor power saleable. As a result they are not consistently exploited. Understood this way, the underclass consists of human beings who are largely expendable from the point of view of the logic of capitalism. Like Native Americans who became a landless underclass in the nineteenth century, repression rather than incorporation is the central mode of social control directed toward them. Capitalism does not need the labor power of unemployed inner-city

youth. The material interests of the wealthy and privileged segments of American society would be better served if these people simply disappeared. However, unlike in the nineteenth century, the moral and political forces are such that direct genocide is no longer a viable strategy. The alternative, then, is *to build prisons and cordon off the zones of cities in which the underclass lives.*[13]

Solitary confinement as it is conceived of and implemented in the landscape of mass incarceration serves a similar and equally racialized function: it removes (mostly) Black and brown bodies from general population, where prisoners have significantly greater access to "freedoms," and locks them away in the hole, physically and metaphorically removed so far out of sight that they become not only invisible but forgotten.

CHAPTER 3

Ideal Types

ACROSS THREE SUMMERS, we personally interviewed nearly one hundred prisoners and staff who were confined to or working in solitary confinement units. The interviews with incarcerated people lasted anywhere from thirty minutes to an hour. They took place in a variety of settings, including in the noncontact visiting rooms, but also in other spaces, including in rooms with the doors shut, to ensure privacy, with the prisoners locked in strip cages to ensure our safety.

Following in the footsteps of many talented ethnographers who came before us, we employed both ethnographic observation and ethnographic interviewing techniques.[1] Unlike surveys, which we also conducted, ethnographic methods focus not on representative samples that are generalizable but "on purposeful sampling, which is based on the premise that seeking out the best cases for the study produces the best data. . . . Therefore, it is important to be strategic when sampling in order to find 'information-rich cases' that best address the research purpose and questions."[2]

In our case, this meant being deliberate at two stages: the choice of the prisons in which to collect data and the cases we selected to present to you, the reader. The prison system where we conducted our research was really less about choosing and more about being chosen. Access to solitary confinement units is extremely rare, especially for researchers and those not studying mental health. We conducted our research where we could, in a system that allowed us inside. Why would officials let us into the invisible space of solitary confinement? What we believe is that at least at the uppermost levels, officials and administrators were interested in having their approach to solitary confinement evaluated. They wanted to improve the conditions in solitary confinement and had taken several important steps that they believed, though this was highly debated by both prisoners and officers, improved the "experience" of solitary confinement for the incarcerated people. For their part, many COs believed that their own experiences as the workforce in solitary confinement had gotten worse under the implementation of these new policies and procedures, an issue we explore in subsequent chapters. In short, officials and administrators wanted to know if the changes they had implemented were working. We are grateful to our colleague Professor Danielle Rudes for negotiating with prison administrators to gain nearly unfettered access to solitary confinement units. We strongly encourage you to read her book, *Surviving Solitary: Risk, Rules, Relationships, Reform and Reentry while Living and Working within Restricted Housing Units*, in which she provides significantly more detail regarding the strategies she employed to gain this unprecedented access.

The ethnographic method allowed us to better understand the daily life of the staff and prisoners embedded within the racially antagonist solitary confinement units. The strength of our methods was enhanced significantly by the incorporation of face-to-face interviews. When it came to interviewing individual prisoners, staff, and officers, we talked to anyone who would talk to us. As with anything, this approach has its drawbacks, but it also has its benefits, and they differed when it came to incarcerated people as opposed to staff and officers.

Incarcerated people have nothing but time, and staff and officers have everything but time. In other words, many incarcerated people that we and other members of our research team interviewed agreed to be interviewed for the simple fact that it bought them an hour out of their cells, despite the invasive strip searches they had to endure in order to come out. Many of them hoped that we could help them with their legal cases. We could not, and we were clear with every incarcerated person who we encountered that we could not. The majority of them wanted their voices heard anyway; we encountered very few incarcerated people who when invited to participate refused to be interviewed. Their voices become those that build the narrative of the remaining chapters in the book. They shared deeply insightful thoughts and perspectives on life behind bars in solitary confinement units. We tell some of their stories here.

Staff and correctional officers often didn't want to talk with us and reluctantly agreed only after we offered to chat with them while they worked. Some of their interviews were conducted in private spaces like offices, but others took place while we followed them on rounds, chatting in the in-between spaces that filled their days, or while we hung out in their offices. Officers who sought us out are like students who evaluate our teaching on RateMyProfessors.com or diners who leave reviews on Yelp: they were either very happy or very angry. They had something to say that they felt we needed to hear.

It's important to note that though we interviewed seventy-five incarcerated people but only twenty-five staff, our time with incarcerated people was limited to a single thirty-to-sixty- minute interview with each participant in a highly controlled environment. In contrast, though we conducted formal interviews with staff that often lasted a similar thirty to sixty minutes, we also had the opportunity to observe them in their work, eat meals with them in the chow hall, and hang out with them. Thus the data we analyze and present here reflect these different types of interactions. The data on staff are richer, the descriptions thicker, because we had significantly more time with them.

Some of the people we interviewed are treated as cases: their interviews told a specific story about their circumstances, and we identify them by pseudonyms we chose. Other times we heard more or less the same comments from several different people, often in group discussions or in passing conversations, and in those cases we combine their perspectives together, attributing them as if spoken by a single person, a strategy Weber refers to as developing "ideal types."[3]

One of the challenges of conducting research in solitary confinement units, and prisons more generally, is the need to protect the identities of those whom we interviewed. Research ethics are maintained by what are termed Human Subjects Review Boards (HSRBs) or Institutional Review Boards (IRBs). Our research protocol was heavily vetted by the university's HSRB and also the Department of Corrections' HSRB. HSRBs designate prisoners as a protected and highly vulnerable population for research. Though we gained prisoners' consent for each interview, the consent process is complicated by the fact that as a general principle, incarcerated people, and even more so those in solitary confinement, have constraints on their ability to give consent. Despite these constraints, we are confident that the incarcerated people we were privileged to interview were honest with us when they agreed to participate. All of the incarcerated people we interviewed seemed to genuinely want to tell their stories. They wanted to be heard, to be visible.

Other concerns for incarcerated people who participate in research include the fact that COs will know which incarcerated people participated and which didn't. This is particularly the case for incarcerated people housed in solitary confinement units. Because prisoners had to be escorted by COs to the interview rooms, everyone in the unit, including staff and other prisoners, knew who had participated in an interview. Though we have no evidence that there was blowback for participating in an interview, we have no way of knowing for sure. Perhaps, after we left and the lights went down, COs punished those prisoners who had participated in an interview. We are reassured by the fact that we made multiple trips to the same prisons and prisoners were always willing to participate. So if there was blowback, either it was not that significant or it was worth the risk.

Among the many protocols we practiced with vigilance was to be extremely careful about what we shared about prisoner interviews with COs. They would often ask us, "Didn't I tell you he would have stories!" in an attempt to get us to share some of the details of the interviews. We always responded in very generic ways: "Yep, you were right!" We were acutely aware that any small detail we might inadvertently share with a CO about our interview could lead to trouble for the prisoner later.

Similarly, though COs and other staff are as free to give consent as is any other adult, they are highly vulnerable as well. In their interviews they shared their perceptions and experiences of working in one of the most hidden,

invisible, and yet volatile places on the planet: deep inside solitary confinement units in maximum security prisons.

Though there are hundreds of staff who work in each prisons, a very small
number work in solitary confinement units. At each prison where we conducted research, the solitary confinement unit had no more than, say, thirty to
forty COs total working across three shifts, seven days a week. Each unit has
just two lieutenants (LTs) and two sergeants (SGTs), one for first and one for
second shift. Each unit may have only two "psych staff." Thus it would be
extremely easy to identify individuals if we were to associate them with a specific prison. And it would be even easier if we identified those who were in the
minority, for example, Black SGTs. We met only one.

In order to protect them, we present their data without indicating which
unit (some of the prisons had multiple solitary units) or which specific prison
they work in. If their racial or gender identity would make it easy to identify
them, we leave those details out as well.

As far as the integrity of the data goes, our first priority was to protect the
people who trusted us and shared what were often deeply personal aspects of
their lives. Our second priority is to provide a rigorous analysis of the data.
That being said, having spent close to three weeks in seven different men's
prisons and one women's prison, which we will discuss at length in part 5, we
found few differences across prisons, and certainly none that rise to the level
of extreme importance. Thus, when we quote from our informants, both
incarcerated people and staff, the reader can be comfortable knowing that the
specific location of their work or their cell did not impact in any significant
way their experiences. On the rare occasions when it did, for example, when
incarcerated people talked about different prisons as being "more or less racist," we note this. As we described in the previous discussion, all of the prisons
are built on the same architectural plan; all of the units look exactly the same;
there is nothing unique about the individual units such that treating them as a
single case in any way reduces the validity or reliability of the data. We refer
to the prisons where we collected data with a single name: "SCI-Wannabee."

Similarly, with only one exception, the communities where we conducted
research were also remarkably not unique. They were rural, economically depressed,
predominantly white, voted overwhelmingly Republican in the 2016 and 2020
presidential elections, Rust Belt counties that had experienced prison building
as part of the economic recovery plan. Each of the men's prisons we visited was
built between 1992 and 1996. In order to tell the story of the counties where
prisons are located, we examined census data for each county. When we refer
to the demographics of the counties and towns where we conducted research,
we exclude the one relatively urban community. All of the rural counties are
nearly identical in terms of demographics, and the only variations were not
significant in terms of the issues we explore and analyze here. Therefore, in order
to protect the specifics of the people we encountered and observed and also to

protect the identity of the individual prisons, we refer to the county where SCI-Wannabee is located as "Larrabee."

We are grateful to the people who allowed us into their lives. Some shared experiences with trauma. Others share deep personal experiences about their lives outside of the prison walls and the impact those experiences had on their time in solitary confinement, as both prisoners and employees. Some allowed us to follow them around for days, observing their work but also likely disrupting it at times. All of the staff we met were incredibly generous and gracious. As we detail in the book, the work of solitary confinement is extremely difficult and demanding, and it was made more so by our presence. We added to their work each day, each interview with a prisoner requiring an additional escort both to and from the designated interview space.

At the end of the day, despite every action we take to diminish the costs to those who participated in our research, the enterprise is a one-way street in which we, as the researchers, have all of the power, and we gain the majority of the benefit while the people we interviewed, both incarcerated people and staff, took the most risk. This book will likely benefit us financially, not so much in royalties, though there will be some, but in merit raises at the University of Delaware and honoraria for speaking engagements. This book will build our reputation in ways that will offer us professional exposure and increased opportunities for research and possibly even to write other books.

In contrast, the benefits for those we interviewed are small and mostly inconsequential. We believe that in some cases the interviews were in a small way therapeutic. In others, they helped someone pass the time. But mostly, the only thing we can offer is a commitment to those who trusted us to tell their stories to give them voice and to render them visible.

Finally, ethnographers are not "truth seekers." We weren't interested in settling a disagreement, but rather in finding those spaces where COs and incarcerated people saw things the same way and the places where they held very different truths.

We interviewed both incarcerated people and staff, including correctional officers, because we were interested in the perceptions that people on both sides of the bars had about their experiences in solitary confinement. As ethnographers, we approach the field with the understanding that there are multiple truths; for the truth lies in the perceptions of the individuals involved. We analyze these perceptions in relation to each other, and in doing so, we uncover the relationship between prisoners and officers. As Matthew Desmond, author of *Evicted*, argues: "Ethnography involves studying fields rather than places, boundaries rather than bounded groups, processes rather than processed people, and cultural conflict rather than group culture. While this approach comes with its own set of challenges, it offers an ethnographic method that works with the relational and processual nature of social reality."[4]

We are interested in understanding the processes by which the specific structures of solitary confinement shaped the daily interactions between white COs and mostly Black and brown prisoners in ways that produced and reproduced white racial resentment. More specifically, how did CO Travis and so many other officers like him come to resent the prisoners they locked up, 23 hours a day, believing that they, not the prisoners, were Trump's "left behind?"

And this is where our story begins. In the in-between spaces.

PART TWO

Scholar's Story

It's like I watch CNN and they watch FOX all day long.

—Scholar

Solitary confinement units are the sites of some of the worst racism in prisons.

—Terry Kupers, *Solitary: The Inside Story of Supermax Isolation and How We Can Abolish It*

CHAPTER 4

Recruiting People Incarcerated in
Solitary Confinement

THE PROCESS OF GAINING access to prisoners to interview begins with our recruiting them at their cell door. Typically on the first day at the prison, after the usual "orientation," a tour of the prison grounds and a meeting with the "important" people, a lead investigator for our team would ask, very nicely, a "white shirt" to create a list of all the incarcerated people, by name, ID number, and cell number, who were housed in the solitary confinement unit that day.

"WOMEN ON"

Members of the research team, accompanied by officers and armed with one-page handouts, would enter each pod and walk cell to cell asking incarcerated people if they wanted to participate in an interview. Our arrival required, by PREA and the law, that our presence, as women, be announced. "Women on!"

Once on the pod, we approach each cell door, note the name(s) of the incarcerated people in the cell and ask to talk with the inhabitants about our project. The officers who escort us stay close enough to provide a sense of safety, but far enough away to maintain a small modicum of privacy. But this is the catch: the guards know which incarcerated people have agreed to an interview and which haven't. They often "suggest" that we interview certain prisoners because "they have a story to tell." Often the officers were right: the incarcerated people they recommended did have interesting perspectives. But we also wonder whom they might have *steered us away* from interviewing.

For us, the benefit of recruiting cell to cell was getting access to the pods and cells so that we could observe the conditions. However, this strategy created a set of vulnerabilities for those people there. The safest way to talk to the prisoner is through a small crack between the cell door and its window. The crack is just wide enough to slide a piece of paper through to the occupant, which we did, offering them a handout with information about the study, but not wide enough for them to pass through anything unwanted like urine or feces back out. Thus, talking through the crack was a much safer strategy than using the wicket. The crack was also a conduit for noise, which facilitated our recruitment discussion. What that meant for the prisoner, however, was several things. First of all, their "home" was on full display for us to see. We could see their laundry hanging, a book on their desk, pictures on their cell walls. It meant that we sometimes observed men who were not clothed. Admittedly that's exactly what some of the them wanted, and they often baited us to look. But for others it can be experienced as an invasion of privacy, especially when the recruiters are all women. In order to hear, we had to yell, which meant that every other person incarcerated on the pod could hear the content of the conversation. Everyone knew who had signed up for an interview and who hadn't. And sometimes why. During the recruitment phase, prisoners often thought that by participating in an interview with us, we could advocate for something they wanted or needed. Many used the recruitment "conversation," yelling through the space in the glass, as an opportunity to start advocating. "Interview me, the guards suck!" "Interview me, I haven't gotten my property!"

Participating in our research, as valuable as it was to us, provided only a short-term, hour-long, benefit to the prisoner, a benefit that came at a tremendous cost. We hope that by sharing their stories and rendering them visible, more people will begin to understand what solitary confinement is really like and advocate for reducing its widespread use in the United States. This would ultimately benefit those we interviewed, but certainly the wait for this benefit is potentially as long and indeterminate as a sentence to solitary confinement.

After taking note of the inhabitants of each cell, we talked briefly with each about our study, emphasizing that their participation was voluntary, that our conversation would focus on their experiences in solitary confinement, and that we could not guarantee that even if they agreed to participate that they would be included. We learned early in our field research that there were all kinds of reasons why we might not be able to interview everyone who volunteered: sometimes we simply ran out of time, we had too many volunteers and too few interviewers, and sometimes there were circumstances that stopped our interviews altogether.

For example, one day we had passed into the visiting area of the solitary confinement unit and "set up shop" to begin interviews when there was an unplanned use of force by officers. In their version of the story, a person incarcerated in the unit was being noncompliant and the COs had to extract him from his cell, nearly dislocating his arm when they pulled it through the wicket. The unplanned use of force meant the prisoner, once extracted, was moved to a special observation cell. We never heard his side of the story—one of the most common features of solitary confinement. Another case we heard about took place in the women's prison the day before we arrived there and involved an inmate throwing urine on an officer when the CO attempted to collect her breakfast tray through the wicket. Unplanned uses of force are obviously disruptive because they are unplanned. No one knows they are coming, not the

COs or the prisoners. And like any change in the hyperroutinized day in solitary confinement, they cause chaos. Incarcerated people get agitated by the event, and they see their daily privileges slip away as the unit is put on lockdown. Appointments, phone calls, even shower or yard that they were supposed to get that day are canceled.

Sometimes the "use of force" is planned. A planned use of force takes place when there is a situation that the white shirts deem must be addressed and the only way to address it is to use force on the prisoner. For example, we heard about cases in which incarcerated people refused to bathe, for months. One person we were told about also refused to shave or cut his hair, and he spread feces on the walls and door of his cell. At some point the smell got so bad and the prisoner was in such poor physical condition that the white shirts decided he must be extracted from his cell. In cases like this, the use of force is planned. Everyone knows when it will take place; the prisoner has been given, according to the COs, plenty of advance warning; and the unit is put on lockdown in order to create a "safe" environment for the use of force.

Just as a "use of force" is disruptive for those incarcerated in solitary confinement, there are also impacts on the officers. Not only is there a heightened sense of anxiety, as uses of force are dangerous, they also generated tons of paperwork that kept the officers busy for hours. Every detail must be carefully documented in case a prisoner files a lawsuit.

As such, because of the unplanned use of force that particular day and the unit being put on lockdown, we sat for most of the day in a single room waiting, unable to conduct any interviews. That day we learned the importance of pre-warning prisoners who we were recruiting for interviews that they might not get selected despite their interest in volunteering. We didn't want anyone to feel badly when circumstances were out of our control.

Once we had a roster of incarcerated people who were willing to be interviewed, we worked with a white shirt to develop a plan for pulling prisoners for interviews. We negotiated where the interviews would take place, utilizing as many spaces as we could for greater efficiency, and any preferences for the order in which incarcerated people were pulled. For example, because one of the members of our research team was focused on the impact of changes in the DTU (the diversionary treatment unit for people with severe and controlled mental illness), we made every effort to interview every inmate from the DTU who was competent enough to give consent. Other than that, we were dependent on the officers to determine which prisoners to pull and in which order. Often they would tell us that they couldn't pull certain prisoners because they were in the shower or at yard. And we have no reason not to believe them. We did wonder, however, if sometimes they didn't pull a prisoner they thought would accuse them of mistreatment or tell us a story they didn't like or pontificate about the conditions of incarceration more generally and solitary confinement specifically. And we will never know.

In total, our team spent more than 1,700 hours in solitary confinement units and conducted thirty- to sixty-minute interviews with 329 incarcerated people and seventy-nine staff. We personally spent more than 200 hours in solitary confinement units conducting nearly one hundred interviews, about seventy-five with incarcerated people and twenty-five with staff. We compared our data, using the constant comparative method, to ensure validity and reliability, but our analysis herein includes only the data from the interviews we personally conducted. That allowed us to analyze not only the statements made by COs and prisoners but also our observations of them during the time we spent with them.

CHAPTER 5

Fox News or CNN?

EVERY TIME A PRISONER leaves their cell, including to go to the yard, to the shower, to the noncontact visiting room, to a therapy session, or to an interview, they are subjected to a series of actions that officers argue are security measures but many prisoners perceive as humiliating. Among the most controversial of these actions is the strip search, which as we noted in our previous discussion, was considered by many officers to be a matter of routine business, simply part of the security measures necessary in the maximum security space of solitary confinement and by my prisoners as a form of sexual harassment and a violation of the Prison Rape Elimination Act (PREA). Despite having to endure the strip search in order to participate in an interview with our team, most of the incarcerated people we spoke with said it was worth it in order to be able to get out of their cells and have a conversation with another human being for an hour. As researchers, we need to be constantly mindful of the burden our work places on participants, asking, do the costs to participate outweigh the benefits or vice versa? There are reasons why the institutional review boards (IRBs) consider prisoners to be vulnerable populations, and so we are grateful for the burden these folks bore in order for us to learn about their daily lives.

In addition to the strip search are the shackles. Though the protocols varied from prison to prison, and sometimes there was variation within units inside the same prison, when incarcerated people were escorted to the interviews (or to the showers or the yard), they were handcuffed, typically behind their backs but sometimes in the front. Around their waist they wore a belt or "belly chain" to which their handcuffs were locked. Sometimes, though not always, the COs attached a leash to the back of the belly chain. To us, it seemed humiliating, to have a human being on the end of a dog leash. COs told us it was a critical too for maintaining security: if the prisoner started to move "inappropriately," the CO could jerk the dog leash to get the prisoner back into line, just like you might do when walking a dog or riding a horse. Though this is how incarcerated people were routinely moved inside of the solitary confinement units, to the shower, to the yard, to therapy sessions, and maybe they had grown used to it, we never did. The sound of the shackles rubbing against each other or dragging on the floor, the image of the prisoner tethered by a dog leash, haunt us today, many years after we first bore witness to the humiliation people are subjected to when they are incarcerated in solitary confinement. Scholar arrived to his interview just this way.

Scholar is a Black man in his mid-thirties who is incarcerated in solitary confinement. He is dark-skinned and wears his hair in dreadlocks. He is tall and muscular, his body barely able to fit in the cage where we interview him. The solitary confinement unit at SCI-Wannabee has a "law library." It's the only library we have ever been in that doesn't have any books. We don't know the history of the law library, but we can speculate that as part of a lawsuit it was determined that even people locked in solitary confinement should have access to legal documents and legal resources, and thus each solitary confinement unit designated a room to be the law library. The law library has a small table, a plastic chair, and a cage. Presumably an incarcerated person could also meet their attorney in the law library: the lawyer sitting on the plastic chair, writing at the desk, the prisoner handcuffed and shackled in an orange jumpsuit in the cage. This is exactly how we interviewed Scholar. We pulled in an extra chair and rather than sitting at the desk, which faced the wall, we pulled the chairs up to the cage in an attempt to create a more trusting environment. The cage is almost the same height as the room, but it is very narrow, less than 3 feet wide and 3 feet deep. Inside the cage is a plastic chair, on which Scholar attempts to fold his tall and lanky body. It is difficult to sustain eye contact through the holes in the cage but we do our best.

Scholar has been in prison since he was seventeen years old. We look up his case after we leave the prison and learn that as a teenager he ran with a gang, and he and his "affiliates" stabbed a man to death when he resisted as they tried to steal his wallet. As a juvenile he was sentenced to life without the possibility of parole, one of more than 2,500 men in the United States serving this type of sentence, a disproportionate number of them in the state where we conducted our research. He admitted that his adjustment to prison was difficult; he spent most of the first five years in the hole. But as he has aged, he has learned how to navigate prison and he has dedicated his life to being a good role model for younger prisoners. We call him "Scholar" because he is a prolific reader, consuming everything from Shakespeare to Ayn Rand to Michelle Alexander's book *The New Jim Crow*. Reading has opened a door for Scholar to learn about systemic racism. Scholar looks forward to the day when they will allow tablets into SCI-Wannabee so that he can download and keep more than one book at a time. Talking about books we have all read and hearing his perspective, it's easy to forget that Scholar has taken a life and that he will spend the rest of his life in prison. When we interviewed him, Scholar was serving a nine-month sentence in solitary confinement for allegedly being involved in gang activity. It's not part of the purpose of our research to ask about or adjudicate sentences to solitary confinement, so we don't talk about it. We wonder later if it's true, or if he has been caught up in a sweep; perhaps he has a birthday card from a known gang member sitting in his cell. In any case, Scholar says that SCI–Wannabee is "one of the most racist prisons. They have no problem calling us 'n——.' "

According to Scholar, one of the reasons that SCI–Wannabee is "one of the most racist prisons" is its location in a rural county. "Inmates are more diverse than COs, not just in terms of race, but where they come from. Inmates come from [urban centers]. . . . COs are all from the local area. It's like I watch CNN and they watch FOX all day long."

Scholar aptly observes the demography of the prison: the people incarcerated here come mostly from the major cities in the state, which are racially diverse, whereas the correctional officers come primarily from Larrabee County or adjacent rural counties, which are more than 90 percent white, and which voted overwhelmingly for Trump in both 2016 and again in 2020.

As an educated man who chooses his words carefully, he didn't say "I watch CNN and they watch ESPN all day long", the implications of his statement offer insight into CO Travis' reference to being Trump's "left behind." Even though we interview both Scholar and CO Travis in the summer of 2016, during the dawn of Trump's presidency, it is already widely known that Fox is the outlet for mainstream white nationalist rhetoric.

Scholar, living deep inside the hidden world of solitary confinement, comes to the same conclusions we do, that the structures of solitary confinement and the siting of prisons in rural, white communities contribute to racial antagonisms and the maintenance of racial hierarchies.

CHAPTER 6

Racism in Solitary Confinement

IT IS WELL documented that the criminal legal system is one of the most racialized institutions in the United States, and solitary confinement is no different. And, it's not just Scholar's observations that tell the story of a racialized solitary confinement, the statistics on race and solitary confinement confirm our observations.

As the data in Figure 4 reveal, even among a population—those incarcerated—that is disproportionately Black, prisoners incarcerated in solitary confinement are even more likely to be Black than the prison population,[1] let alone their representation in the population of the United States.

The data in Figure 5 compare the number of men, by race, in general population to those in solitary confinement by *state*. With very few exceptions, which are of course interesting, in the vast majority of states, Black men are disproportionately likely to be incarcerated in solitary confinement compared with their representation in the state prison. Without revealing the name of the state where we conducted our research, a condition of our access to solitary confinement, we note that in the state system where we conducted our research, Black men are *significantly* more likely to be incarcerated in solitary confinement than in general population.

Our eyes did not deceive us. SCI-Wannabee incarcerates Black men disproportionately in solitary confinement, whereas white men are underrepresented in solitary confinement compared with their representation in the prison system.

Across the United States, in pretty much every jurisdiction, Black men are overly policed. Despite engaging in similar rates of crime, Black people are more likely to be stopped, they are more likely to be arrested, and charged and prosecuted, they are more likely to be convicted and they receive longer sentences.[2] And, there is no reason to assume that solitary confinement is any different. And, as the data in Figures 4 and 5 reveal, in fact, it's not. So, if it's not necessarily the case that Black men in general population are more likely to commit misconducts that result in their being sentenced to solitary confinement, what accounts for the racial disparities in the data?

Solitary confinement is not just a punishment strategy, it can also be used as a "bed management" system. Solitary confinement units are built to maximize isolation. On this point everyone agrees. Staff and administrators also

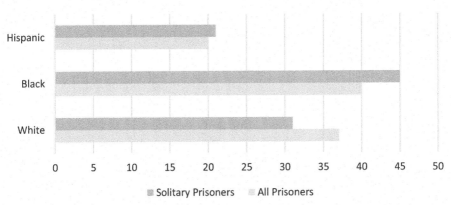

Figure 4. Race in Solitary Confinement.
Data source: Yale Law School, "Reforming Restrictive Housing: The 2018 ASCA-Liman Nationwide Survey of Time-in-Cell" and the related report, *Working to Limit Restrictive Housing: Efforts in Four Jurisdictions to Make Changes.*

argue that they are built to maximize security. Out of sight, out of mind. Because of the structural design of solitary confinement, it's not possible to simply "switch out beds." Solitary confinement beds cannot become general population beds and vice versa. Thus, it's possible to imagine a situation in which there are too many people in one unit and empty beds in another. Part of the morning routine we observed in SCI-Wannabee was the discussion of the "kick list." The kick list refers to those people incarcerated in solitary confinement who are to be sent back to general population sometime that day. Typically prisoners on the kick list have maxed out their sentences in solitary confinement, and they are automatically released back to general population. Sometimes, though, a unit manager like Steve or SGT Tom must move a prisoner out of solitary confinement in order to accommodate a new arrival, someone who caught a misconduct the night before and is sitting in the strip cage waiting to be assigned to a cell. What we observed is that the unit manager or white shirt would look at their roster board and identify someone who was just about to max out, who had not been in trouble while in solitary confinement, and "kick" them back to general population in order to make space in a cell.

Because the nature of our research was to learn more about being incarcerated and working in solitary confinement, we had almost no contact with officers who were working in general population, other than that we would see them when we came through the metal detector each morning or when we exited each afternoon or when we ate lunch in the dining hall. We didn't talk with them or observe their work. Reading Mary Buser's discussion of officers in general population being "forced" to write tickets in order to move prisoners into solitary confinement, thus freeing up beds in general population, made us think back to many of the interviews we conducted with prisoners, and it did make us wonder.

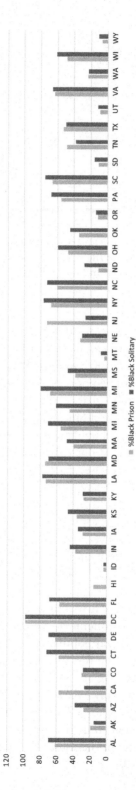

Figure 5. Race in General Population and Solitary Confinement by State.

Data source: Yale Law School, "Reforming Restrictive Housing: The 2018 ASCA-Liman Nationwide Survey of Time-in-Cell" and the related report, *Working to Limit Restrictive Housing: Efforts in Four Jurisdictions to Make Changes.*

Mary Buser writes about a conversation she had with a CO named Smitty.

The inmate's protest, *I didn't do a thing!* made me wonder. Several days earlier, a friendly officer nicknamed Smitty had stopped by my office for a cup of water and a quick break. As he was leaving, he pulled out his infraction pad and revealed something stunning. "I've got to go write up tickets. The way they're loading up the island [Rickers], they're scrambling for beds. With five hundred beds in the Bing [the slang for the solitary confinement unit on Rikers], they can't afford to let one of them sit empty. Every time somebody goes into the hole, a GP [general population] bed opens up. We have our orders: 'Write 'em up! Write 'em up!' Let me go find some poor schmo. See you later, Miss B." Now I wondered if the person in this cell was one of those poor schmos.[3]

In our previous book, *Policing Black Bodies,* we analyze the Department of Justice reports that followed on the heels of the deaths of Mike Brown in Ferguson and Freddy Gray in Baltimore and the ensuing protests. The reports revealed that, among other things, police officers targeted Black communities where they wrote traffic and other kinds of tickets—for activities like loitering, selling single cigarettes, and so on—in order to build the coffers of the police department. In this context, the practice that Buser describes seems all too familiar. Perhaps Black men in general population are written up more often, for insignificant infractions, as part of a bed management system.

For example, in one of the prisons in our sample a huge percentage of prisoners housed there, more than 25 percent, are in solitary confinement. Because the solitary confinement unit is so large, it made sense for us to spend more time at this prison than any other we visited. Not only did we visit this prison twice, but we conducted a significant number of interviews there and spent many hours observing the unit. This prison holds approximately 1,800 prisoners, 500 of whom are in solitary confinement. If a warden has to balance 1,800 prisoners using 1,300 general population beds and 500 solitary confinement cells, it's *possible* that COs in general population accuse prisoners of minor misconducts in order to send them to solitary confinement for a few days or weeks until the bed space in general population is back in equilibrium. And, that the prisoners they target for ticketing are disproportionately Black. This may seem like a far-fetched idea, but as Mary Buser reveals, it is documented as having taken place on Rikers Island.

We certainly interviewed a lot of prisoners who said they hadn't done anything or they reported being charged with extremely minor infractions: too many books or honey buns in their cells. Scholar argues that because there doesn't seem to be any rhyme or reason as to which infractions get people sent to hole, the beds in solitary confinement must be like a quota that has be filled. "This program [Scholar is on a step-down program for prisoners who are believed to be associated with a gang that takes, on average, nine months to complete] pulls you out of the loop and you disappear for a year." Perhaps one way to get to solitary confinement is simply to be a schmo. The stop-and-frisk equivalent in solitary confinement.

★   ★   ★

Martin Luther King Jr. used to say that the most segregated hour in America was Sunday morning worship.[4] Perhaps only solitary confinement is more segregated.[5] Solitary confinement units, and prisons more generally, are not just racialized in terms of those incarcerated. The vast majority of staff working in solitary confinement units are white men. It is not surprising, then, that racism is expressed and exercised in these spaces. As noted, we spent time in several different prisons in the same state system, and the levels of racism we heard about and observed for ourselves varied. Interestingly, the prison in which we heard the most racist language and observed the most racial segregation was identified by people in solitary confinement as "one of the most racist prisons. "They have no problem calling us 'n———,' Scholar said.

When we asked incarcerated people about their experiences with race, Black prisoners reported that the COs told racist jokes, one Black prisoner told us he was forced to cut his dreadlocks, and others simply stated: "White inmates are treated better than Blacks and Spanish [the term prisoners commonly used to refer to Hispanic or Latinx] inmates." Others referred to the racism they personally experienced as part of a larger system of racism in the prison system.

For example, one incarcerated person we interviewed, Pitiful, was in solitary confinement for fighting. He claimed he was defending himself from being raped. We call him Pitiful because that's the language he used to describe his circumstances: they were "pitiful." Pitiful, who is a light-skinned Black man in his early twenties, with a slight build and close-cropped hair, told us that he has been gang raped ten times in general population. He blames the COs for not protecting him. When we asked him what the COs were doing that contributed to his being such a frequent target of rape, Pitiful replied: "In general population there is only one CO for over 200 prisoners. Guys [prisoners] are all wearing uniforms. The COs say 'Black guys, they all look alike.'"

But it's more than the "all Black guys look the same" defense. The prison uniform renders the individual invisible, nameless, faceless, devoid of humanness. One Black prisoner is indistinguishable from another in the sea of Black faces on the prison yard.

In the words of Ralph Ellison, he is just another invisible man.

CHAPTER 7

The Cell Assignment

RACE IS THE *FIRST* CONSIDERATION

WE HAD HEARD rumors that race was a factor in cell assignments, and as luck would have it, or more likely because we spent so many hours in staff offices that it was inevitable, we were hanging out in the office when a CO came in to alert the unit manager, Steve, that a new prisoner had arrived and was waiting in the strip cage for his cell assignment. We asked if we could watch the process of cell assignments. Steve enthusiastically invited us to observe the entire process.

Unit Manager Steve's office was, like so many staff offices, small, cramped, and overflowing with stuff. The office was a square, approximately 10 feet by 10 feet. In addition to the door, the wall to the right of the door has a large window that allows Steve to see, from his desk that faces the window, anyone and everyone coming into the unit. On the wall to the left of his desk is a set of shelves filled with envelopes and bags and boxes. We learn later that these envelopes and bags and boxes are the property of prisoners that has yet to be delivered to them. When prisoners arrive in solitary confinement, their property has to be inventoried and searched for contraband and items that are not allowed in solitary, such as extra books and honey buns, before it is delivered to them in their cells. And, according to the inmate handbook, property is to be delivered within seven days of placement in solitary confinement. While we were hanging out with Unit Manager Steve, a CO came in to deliver a complaint. One of the prisoners, who had been in the solitary unit for more than a week, was complaining that he hadn't received his property yet. Unit Manager Steve laughed and said to the CO, "What's the rush, guy's gonna be here ninety days." Neither Unit Manager Steve nor the CO did anything we could observe to resolve the matter. As far as they were concerned, the prisoner can just wait. What else does he have to do anyway?

Above the door to Unit Manager Steve's office, just behind his desk, is a file cabinet. On top of the file cabinet is a video monitor. The monitor gives Unit Manager Steve a view of the strip cage. Every prisoner, including the honor prisoners who come in and out the day we are there to help staff change out asbestos panels in the bubble, must be stripped on their way in and out of the unit. The monitor not only allows Unit Manager Steve to observe the strips but also records the strips in case an inmate claims a PREA violation or that contraband an officer finds during the search was planted.

Unit Manager Steve doesn't seem to pay much attention to the monitor, but on the way to lunch that day, he makes a totally unsolicited comment to Hattery: "Black guys don't really have bigger dicks."

Why did Unit Manager Steve feel compelled to make this comment? Why did he feel compelled to make the comment when he and Hattery happened to be walking alone, a few steps behind the rest of the group?

If prisons aren't racialized, if solitary confinement units weren't racialized, if race didn't matter, why make this comment?

Because race does matter, and every day, in fact thousands of times a day, white men are in close, intimate contact with Black men, and each and every instance creates an opportunity for stereotypes to be confronted, be they stereotypes about bodies or stereotypes about behaviors: Black men are violent; they are thugs; they are angry; they are lazy.

In solitary, everything is racialized, including cell assignments.

Behind Unit Manager Steve's desk is a wall with a big white board that is marked with grids and letters and numbers and prisoner ID cards. This board tells the story of every man locked in solitary confinement: who is in which cell, whether they can eat pork or not, whether they are on AC or DC, whether there is a razor restriction, and their projected release date from solitary confinement. The board allows Unit Manager Steve or really anyone, including us, to easily get a "snapshot" of the unit.

The wall serves another essential function. It is the primary tool Unit Manager Steve uses to make cell assignments.

When we asked Unit Manager Steve how he makes cell assignments, he said that race was his *first* consideration. We asked why. Unit Manager Steve said: "The white guys wouldn't live with Black guys and vice versa." We, of course, have no way of knowing if this is true or if this is just the perception of the staff. However, prisoners we interviewed also confirmed that very, very rarely were prisoners celled with those of other racial or ethnic identities. White guys were celled with white guys and Black guys were celled with Black guys.

INTERVIEWER: "Is religion also something you consider when making cell assignments?"

UNIT MANAGER STEVE: "Yes."

Ahh, we thought, so there is religious bias as well.

UNIT MANAGER STEVE: "You can't house Muslims and Christians together."

INTERVIEWER: "Why not?"

UNIT MANAGER STEVE: "Because the Muslims have to get up before sunrise and pray 5 times a day, they want a mat to face Mecca, and they eat different food. Christian guys don't like to be disturbed by the praying and they don't like smelling the food. . . . I've had many Christian guys say they won't go in a Muslim's cell and they don't want a Muslim in their cell."

So what else matters in cell assignments? As we learned from Unit Manager Steve, but heard many times over in many different units, in addition to race and religion, there are very practical factors that dictate cell assignments. You can't house prisoners on AC and DC together. This seems obvious because the different statuses offer a different set of punishments and privileges. If you house someone on AC with someone on DC how would you know if the person on AC shares a book or a honey bun with the person on DC? That would be highly problematic.

You can't house two people who are charged with fighting each other together. That makes sense; you wouldn't put two kids who were fighting in the same timeout chair.

Relatedly, you also can't house two people with rival gang affiliations with each other, as they might take a hit out on each other.

You can't house lovers together. This was not common in the men's prison, but in the women's prison, women who were in relationships with each other but who were on different cell blocks in general population would sometimes commit misconducts as a way of trying to get to solitary and either cell together there or request to cell together when they were released. This was yet another reason why someone might "choose" solitary.[1]

Despite all of these practical considerations when making cell assignments, as Unit Manager Steve noted, race was his first consideration.

CHAPTER 8

It's "Culture" not "Race"

WE SPENT SEVERAL DAYS in a specialized solitary confinement unit that housed known gang members who were considered high threat. This is where we met Scholar. As we wandered around the unit, we came across a room that had two small tables, a desk with a computer that looked like something from the late 1990s and definitely didn't connect to the internet, and the same kinds of boards we saw in Unit Manager Steve's office.

The difference in these boards is that they were organized by gang affiliations. Perhaps to keep their privacy, perhaps for some other reason, the columns weren't labeled, but when you got up close you could see that the prisoner ID cards also indicated gang affiliations. So, for example, there were columns and columns of pictures of Black people. On each card, in addition to their picture, was their name, ID number, and race. Scrawled on the card was their "believed to be" gang affiliation, for example, "Crips" or "Latin Kings." We should note that every prisoner we interviewed in this special gang unit claimed they weren't in a gang, but they did talk at length about the importance of having "friends" and "associates." One of the people we interviewed, Leroy, who is Black, when asked about his identity (which was a very open-ended question and did not necessarily mean gang affiliation), noted: "Associating is a big part of my life. . . . It's a Brotherhood."

Leroy, who had been incarcerated in the Deep South, including in New Orleans and at Parchman Farm, the notorious Mississippi State Penitentiary, argued that "the COs treat people differently, but not so much because of their race as because of their gang affiliation. . . . In the south in NOLA [New Orleans] and Parchman, inmates were segregated by race but 'up here' they are segregated by gang affiliation, which isn't always completely about race. . . . Here, we don't self-segregate, but down south, inmates do self-segregate. Here people hang out with their gang associates."

After our interview with Leroy, we return to the board in the gang unit, and we notice there is some racial "slippage." In other words, there are some pictures of men who are identified as "white" whose card denotes an affiliation with a Black or Latinx gang, men with Latinx names like "Rodriguez" are listed with affiliations that include Black gangs, and so on. What we do not see are any men who are Black or Latinx listed as being associated with

Aryan Nation or other White Supremacist gangs. The slippage seems to be a one-way street.

When we talked with officers and other staff about their perceptions of race in solitary, what was most striking was the different responses from white and Black staff. White officers did their best to avoid the question, but when they couldn't, they offered what sociologists refer to as a "symbolic racism response." For example, in conversations with COs in the gang unit, they offered statements that contradicted Unit Manager Steve. They said that they don't consider race as much as gang affiliation when making cell assignments or any other decisions about the people incarcerated in solitary confinement. *Yet, despite a bit of slippage, gang affiliation serves as a pretty accurate proxy for race.*

Other staff indicated that it wasn't about race, it was "culture."

One afternoon we were sitting in LT's office and there were five or six COs standing around shooting the breeze. It was around 1o'clock in the afternoon and their shift was about to end. They had worked a long day and they were taking a break after hours of being on their feet. The office was relatively small and very crowded, like so many are. On this point the COs are right: the prison isn't designed for their comfort. There was a desk against the wall, where LT sat doing paperwork, but it was clear to us that he was also listening to what his officers had to say. There was a table with three or four chairs where we sat alongside a couple of officers. There were a couple other chairs by the door, where the unit manager, Sam, sat. Other officers stood in the doorway, pulled in by the conversation. Behind LT was the board that displayed the organization of the unit, just like the board in Unit Manager Steve's office, only much bigger because this unit can incarcerate hundreds of men in solitary confinement. Names, pictures, ID numbers. Most of the faces are Black, some are "Spanish," a few are white. In stark contrast, all of the COs in the office were white and all were men. We don't remember how the conversation started, but the interviews and much of the conversations from the previous days leading up to this afternoon had focused on changes in solitary, the COs' views on punishment (they all believed solitary confinement had become too easy to do, too generous for the prisoner), and their own experiences being in solitary confinement eight to sixteen hours a day. Perhaps they were just primed.

CO Bunker is standing in the doorway. At first he seems reluctant to join the conversation. We didn't interview CO Bunker; he didn't want to be interviewed. But it's clear once he starts talking that he has a lot to say. And when he talks, others listen. CO Bunker is white, and he's medium height, in his thirties or early forties. He has dark, brown, curly hair and a thick moustache and beard. Before coming to work in the prison, he was in the military. He was deployed several times to Iraq and Afghanistan.

CO Bunker makes it clear that he thinks that solitary confinement is not harsh enough, that the prisoners get too many privileges. "What about the victims? They're not coming back. Their families will never see them again.

What about them? The system has forgotten about the victims." This statement gets lots of heads nodding in agreement.

The unit manager, Sam, is sitting by the door next to where CO Bunker is standing. Like most of the unit managers we meet, he is a civilian. He is a white man, in his forties or early fifties. He has brown hair that he is losing. He's tall and lanky and he's wearing khakis and a button-down, long-sleeved shirt. His ID is clipped to his front right pants pocket. He chimes in: "I used to run a mentoring group. I thought that if the guys could see that someone had believed in them that they might turn their lives around, live for something bigger than themselves. I asked the guys, 'Think of someone you would consider a mentor,' and they were all like, 'What's a mentor?' See, they come from a different culture from us. Their culture is different from ours. I stopped running the group after that."

We argue that many of the COs we interviewed spoke about race, at least in our presence, in similarly coded language. They spoke, for example, about "cultural" differences between the prisoners and themselves. Not only is "culture" often code for "race," but in the carceral spaces where we conducted our research nearly all of the COs and staff were white and the majority of the people incarcerated in solitary confinement were Black or Latinx. What else could their comments have been meant to convey?

Eduardo Bonilla-Silva's framing of symbolic racism explains the ways in which racism is expressed in the climate of political correctness. White families, at least in many parts of the country, no longer agitate or protest against integrated schools, instead they advocate for neighborhood schools. Because housing segregation remains nearly as persistent and deeply entrenched as it was fifty years ago, neighborhood schools will produce what legal scholars refer to as "de jure" segregation. Is it any less racist to express a desire for neighborhood schools that will all but ensure the same level of racial segregation as the schools white southerners protested to protect from school integration movements in the 1950s and 1950s? Bonilla-Silva's research suggests that the tone may be different, but the desires and the outcomes are the same. Specifically, he argues that "In contrast to race relations in the Jim Crow period, however, racial practices that reproduce racial inequality in contemporary America (1) are increasingly covert, (2) are embedded in normal operations of institutions, (3) avoid direct racial terminology, and (4) are invisible to most whites."[1]

The COs and staff are all white. The majority of people incarcerated in solitary confinement are Black. Just as gang affiliation is a proxy for race, it's impossible to interpret the staff's comments about culture as anything other than statements about race.

There were very, very few Black staff of any rank working in any solitary confinement unit at any of the prisons where we conducted research. In order to protect their identities, we cannot individuate them. The few Black staff who work in solitary confinement units were clear that they experienced racism working in rural prisons like SCI-Wannabee. Before working in SCI-Wannabee, each of the Black staff we interviewed or talked with had previously been employed in large urban jails and prisons. This makes sense because there are literally no Black people living in Larrabee County, so the only route to working at SCI-Wannabee was a transfer from another jail. When we asked them about the differences they observed when it came to race in rural versus urban prisons, they talked not about the prisons themselves, but about the counties in which the prisons were located. "I can relate [to the experiences of the Black inmates]. . . . I'm aware of the racism in this place [SCI-Wannabee]. . . . I'm not going to act like I can't relate. I understand this is [Larrabee] County."

In urban jails, they said, the majority of the staff live in the urban area. As a result, their life outside the prison is far more integrated. They grew up going to integrated schools, they played on integrated sports teams in high school, they had "normal" interactions with people of other races. All of the Black staff we interviewed continue to live in the urban city and commute out to SCI-Wannabee. They would rather spend three hours a day commuting to and from work than live in rural, white, Larrabee County. This decision speaks volumes about the sacrifices they are willing to make to avoid living in a rural, all white, pro-Trump county.

We asked the Black staff whom we interviewed about their experiences working in the racially segregated world of solitary confinement, Black faces behind bars and almost entirely white staff, other than themselves. "Everything we are taught [stereotypes] is reinforced. White officers don't know the culture of the community they are policing."

White men who have few if any normalized interactions with Black people spend eight to sixteen hours a day arguing and fighting with Black men in cages. Black men, some of whom have committed horrible crimes. Black men who are angry that they are locked in cages. Black men who sometimes behave in terrible ways, like throwing feces and urine on the COs.

This Black staff's observation "Everything we taught [stereotypes] is reinforced" couldn't be more profound. The racial segregation of solitary confinement confirms, over and over again, day in and day out, all of the racial stereotypes we associate with Black men: that they are angry, that they are criminals, that they have no respect for authority, that they are violent.

Black staff also face their own set of challenges. White COs and white prisoners regularly accused Black staff of taking the side of Black prisoners. And Black prisoners accuse Black staff of being racial turncoats. "Black inmates tell me I must help white inmates. . . . They say 'You side with the oppressors.'"

This comment once again underscores the very real racial hierarchy in solitary confinement where those behind the bars are more likely than not to be Black and nearly the entire staff, from administrators to white shirts to officers to civilian staff—unit managers and psych staff—are white. Those with power are white. Those without it are Black.

White COs and white prisoners also made assumptions about Black staff, one of whom remarked: "White guys assume I help the black guys because we share common ground . . . the hood. . . . I'm not from the hood, I have a master's degree!"

Fred, who is incarcerated on death row, when asked why there are no Black officers, concurred: "As soon as they get any time in the institution they are removed. . . . They are seen to be too friendly with the Black inmates."

The experiences of the Black staff in SCI-Wannabee mimic what we see in professional work environments as well, including in law firms and hospitals, as our colleague Adia Harvey Wingfield reveals.[2] In her research on the invisibility of Blackness, Adia Harvey Wingfield shares the insights of Black professionals whom she interviewed:

> I was coming off the elevator, and this female partner, who's on my floor—who's freaking two doors down from me—was getting off the elevator. I allowed her to get off the elevator first, which I always do, and I was coming behind her to get in the door on our floor, and she waved her badge and she literally tried to close the door to keep me from getting in. And I had to show her my badge, like with my picture on it that [shows] I work here, for her to let me in. First of all, I had on a suit. I didn't have on a tie, but I had on a suit. I mean, what do you think I am? Let's assume you thought I was the copy guy; still, why are you—she's acting like a—she's literally closing the door! Maybe she thought I was going to hurt her. I don't know what she was thinking. But that kind of stuff, those types of things happen, and you have to be mindful. Every day, I have to think, okay, well, how's this person perceiving me? They haven't seen me in court. They haven't seen any of the briefs I've written. They haven't seen me interact with a client. So, they don't know my abilities as a lawyer. All they see is the black bald guy who, if he was stuck in traffic that morning, has an angry face or—so I don't know what it's going to be. So those types of things make it uniquely hard for black men. And so when you don't have people that look like you who've been around for a while, [but] they know that white men are lawyers, it's kind of hard.

The point that the lawyer is making is that Black men are simultaneously both invisible and stereotyped as violent. Being rendered invisible, his female, white colleague doesn't really see him and therefore can't distinguish him from other Black male bodies that she encounters at work or on public transportation or walking through the local park. In the encounter he describes, the fact that she has never really seen him results in her lumping him in with all of the other images of Black men she has seen, and of course most of those images portray Black men as violent. This account sounds eerily similar to that of Pitiful, who blamed the gang rapes he experienced on officers' inability to tell the Black men in identical prisons jumpsuits apart.

Symbolic and overt racism are "baked" into solitary confinement. Race determines the likelihood that one will be sentenced to and confined in solitary confinement, thus shaping the complexion of those behind bars. It also shapes who works in solitary confinement units. Locating prisons that house incarcerated people who are primarily from urban, diverse communities, in counties like Larrabee that are more than 95 percent white, produces a racial hierarchy of power. Though they often feel disenfranchised themselves, as we will explore in much more depth, the COs and other staff, who are almost entirely white, have all of the power, and the incarcerated people, who are disproportionately Black, are on the receiving end of extreme and dehumanizing behavior.

The first step in dehumanization is "othering." By defining Black bodies as less than fully human, the removal of even the most basic human rights from Black people who are locked in solitary confinement, determined first by a court and second by an internal hearing board, labeled in many cases as violent animals, becomes not only palatable but easy. COs convince themselves that not only do prisoners deserve the treatment they receive, but the treatment they receive is better than the conditions under which the COs themselves labor and work.

PART THREE

CO Porter and Dr. Emma

Most of us are here because of choices we made in the past, both the guards and the inmates.

—CO Tom

CHAPTER 9

Locating Prisons in Rural Settings

PRISONS ARE SITED in many different kinds of communities, from large urban centers to very small towns. In most states in the United States, there are jails in large urban centers and the majority of the prisons are "upstate" (or downstate, depending on where the urban center in the state is geographically located). Let's consider New York as an example. Rikers Island is the largest jail in the country, incarcerating up to 15,000 men and women on any given day; more people are incarcerated on Rikers than are incarcerated in the entire state of Utah. Rikers Island is located on a literal island in the East River between Queens and the Bronx. If you have ever flown into La Guardia Airport, you have flown directly over Rikers Island. There are, however, no prisons in the five boroughs of New York City. Instead, the state prisons in New York are all located "upstate" in places as distant and remote as Cayuga and Alden, New York. Seven of the state prisons that constitute the New York State Department of Corrections are located within an hour's drive of Canada, both Montreal and Toronto.

What may come as a surprise to many readers is that though big cities like New York, Chicago, and Los Angeles have enormous jails, the vast majority of prisons, operated by state departments of correction as well as the federal government, are located in rural communities, which, unless they are in the Deep South, are predominately white.

We conducted our research in just such communities.

The state Department of Corrections, or DOC, as it is known, the letters emblazoned on the back of every prisoner's jumpsuit and jacket, where we conducted our research is not particularly unique. According to the Prison Policy Institute website, just less than 1 percent of state residents in this state are incarcerated on any given day. Comparatively with other states, this state's incarceration rate is in the middle of the pack. So, in many ways this state is typical.

The state DOC consists of twenty-four state prisons, twenty-two for men and two for women. There are also many federal prisons in this state, but because they are such a different type of prison, we don't include them in our discussion here.

Prior to 1987, this state had six prisons. Then, like many states that took advantage of the funds available through a variety of federal programs that were associated with the War on Drugs and then President Clinton's "The Violent Crime Control and Law Enforcement Act of 1994," this state built eighteen new prisons. Thirteen new prisons were built during a single decade, between 1992 and 1996. The state, like most other Rust Belt states, experienced a prison boom. Along with the prison building boom came an incarceration boom; currently there are just fewer than 50,000 people incarcerated in this state prison system. The steep rise in the incarceration rate trickled down to the hole as well. On any given day, thousands of people in this state are locked up in some form of solitary confinement.

During the height of the industrial revolution, this state had one of the biggest economies in the United States. It is still ranked among the top ten, in large part because of the coal that was discovered and mined in the mountainous part of the state. Coal has been mined in this region for nearly 300 years, and many, many communities thrived as a result, both in this state and in neighboring states. But as demand for coal declined, so did the number of jobs. According to a report, 1993 marked the greatest decline in coal production since 1885.[1] That same year, 1993, the state DOC opened five prisons. Coincidence? Many of the COs whom we interviewed and spent time with talked about the history of coal in their communities. They spoke of their fathers and grandfathers who had worked in the mines. Even they understood clearly that prisons became the preferred economic development strategy to bring jobs back to struggling communities.

As we sat in the reception area at SCI-Wannabee waiting to be cleared, Unit Manager Steve gave us a mini-lecture on the history of prison building in the state. According to Unit Manager Steve, the prison boom in this state was financed in part by federal funds that were earmarked for economic development. Counties like Larrabee that were rated as economically depressed could apply for federal funds and build a prison. In this way, Larrabee was also not unique. Twelve other counties in this state had taken advantage of the same federal prison-building programs.

Sociologists and criminologists have spent the last two decades analyzing piles of economic data in order to make a case for or against the economic impact of prison sitings.[2] Based on our conversation with Unit Manager Steve, it seems that the practice of siting prisons in economically depressed communities was common knowledge for people who live and work there.

In an opinion essay published in September 2019 in a progressive local newspaper, the writer describes the reaction of state representatives from one local county upon learning that the prison there was being closed by the DOC.

The department's announcement had barely landed in reporters' inboxes before the complaints from legislators *from both parties* and both chambers of the General Assembly began, all from [the] County. Their underlying argument: Closing SCI-[County] will adversely impact the economy of the region. Legislators go to [the state capitol] to advocate for their constituents, and defending jobs that pay well and include strong benefits fits squarely in that lens. And this wasn't the first time an announced prison closure elicited such a reaction. State legislators from western [state] were similarly outraged when the department announced another prison closing a few years ago. But their message couldn't be more transparent, or appalling: *[State] needs to incarcerate as many people as possible to provide jobs for other people.* In the eyes of these legislators, *keeping people in cages is necessary for economic sustainability.*[3] (emphasis ours)

We pause to note that in the highly divisive, "tribal" political climate of this decade, rarely do lawmakers of different parties agree. But in the case of prisons as economic development, they do. This alone speaks volumes about both the importance of and support for prisons as economic drivers in economically disadvantaged white communities.

After the collapse of coal mining in the rural counties, tucked away in the Appalachian and Allegheny mountains, the Department of Corrections began to acquire land and build correctional facilities in these same rural, predominantly white communities. The expansion of prisons (nine federal institutions and twenty-eight state facilities) was driven by a confluence of factors, including the impetus to expand prison industries, as well as to bring jobs to economically depressed counties. Though it is impossible to make a cause-and-effect argument, the prison building boom corresponded with a 132 percent rise in the incarcerated population. As in most states, the majority of people incarcerated here are from the major urban areas, and the majority of prisons are in rural counties with predominantly white populations. All of the prisons where we conducted interviews were located in counties just like this.

CHAPTER 10

Prison Town—Larrabee

LIKE MANY PRISONS, SCI-Wannabee is located in a rural, economically depressed region of the state. What used to be coal country is now prison country and Trump country. Larrabee County, where SCI-Wannabee is located, is 94 percent white, and the median household income is $45,535. Fourteen point eight percent (14.8 percent) of residents live in poverty and 40 percent of female-headed households with children live below the poverty line. In 2016, 70 percent of the residents of Larrabee voted for Donald Trump, and support for Trump jumped to 74 percent in 2020.

According to the Prison Policy Institute, the incarcerated population of SCI-Wannabee, which mirrors that of the United States, is 46 percent Black. In a county with between 35,000 and 40,000 residents, at least 33,000 of whom are white, more than 1,000 Black men "live" there as prisoners at SCI-Wannabee.

As we walked each day from the solitary confinement unit to the staff cafeteria, we passed through the yard while the thousands of men incarcerated there were moving from their cell blocks to the "chow hall." It was a sea of Black men's bodies. They were all dressed in brown, marked with the letters DOC on their backs. As we moved through the local community, eating in local restaurants, checking in and out of the hotels where we stayed, our team of researchers included *the only Black faces we saw.* Is it any wonder people were wont to ask us what we were doing in "their" community.

Larrabee is a community where coal used to be king, and the king has left the kingdom. Not surprisingly, the very same people who used to work in the coal mines now work in SCI-Wannabee. Just as fathers and sons worked alongside each other in the same coal mine, today fathers, and increasingly mothers, and their children work alongside each other in SCI-Wannabee.

SCI-Wannabee is located in a very small town that used to be a coal town and is now a prison town. Interstate highways crisscross and collide with exits that are crowded with fast-food joints and midrange hotels like the Comfort Inn and Microtel and Motel 6 that may have been great in their heyday but all of which look from the outside like they need remodeling, and if the other hotels at the exit are like the one where we stayed, they need a serious remodel inside as well. Driving through Larrabee and surrounding towns, one sees blocks of boarded-up businesses along Main Street and house after house that is in disrepair. As many as a dozen pizza places vie for attention, and the only other businesses that are open are liquor stores and convenience stores. "President Trump" is painted on old buildings, barns, and billboards, even a year or two after his election.

During our first trip to SCI-Wannabee, Hattery took an early morning walk before heading to SCI-Wannabee for the day. She wanted some fresh air and natural light as she anticipated the eight to ten hours they would be "locked up" that day. There was one problem: it was difficult to find a good place to take a walk; the hotel was just off an interstate "interchange," which meant that the only roads accessible to the hotel went directly off of or back onto the highway. So, she decided to simply walk laps in the hotel and adjacent fast-food restaurant parking lots. Even a good playlist wasn't enough to relieve the boredom.

Before she went out for her walk, Hattery dropped by the breakfast room to scope out the offerings and there she noticed the woman who "hosted" the breakfast engaging in easy banter with the early morning coffee and tea drinkers that suggested a familiarity, that they knew each other, as least as acquaintances. During one of Hattery's many laps through the parking lot, she noticed that the same woman who "hosted" the "free" breakfast was standing outside taking a smoke break. Hattery paused the playlist on her iPhone, and her walk, for a chat. The hotel employee was a tired-looking white woman, who was probably forty but looked fifty-five. She needed dental work. Her shift starts at 5 A.M., but she gets there at 2:30 A.M. so she can "get her floors done before people get up." When there is a snow or ice storm, she sleeps at the hotel. Having noticed her earlier in the breakfast room, Hattery decided that the woman must know something about the other occupants of the hotel and decided to ask her what she knew about the trucks and utility vehicles that filled the parking lots. The woman said that she wasn't sure exactly what the guests of the hotel do for a living, though the boot tracks on the floors she rushed to work to clean suggest they do utility poles or road construction. She added that most of these guys have lived here for at least nine months.

We returned to SCI-Wannabee in late autumn the following year. This time it was cold enough to need a jacket or sweater not just outside, but inside the prison as well. It felt surreal to return to Larrabee County. It's weird to feel so familiar and so not.

This time we stay at a nearby hotel that had been recently remodeled. Once again there are trucks in the parking lot. Some of the trucks have trailers with construction equipment. Most have license plates from Florida and Texas.

Hattery remembers the walk in the parking lot the year before and seeing all of the trucks and wondering why so many had out-of-state license plates. After a conversation with an SGT in another prison a few counties over, we now know that it's all part of the larger fracking operation, a modern technique that releases natural gas buried deep in the same mountains that have been stripped of their coal. Not only do many of the men we encounter in the hotel, in the parking lot, and in the diner, where we eat breakfast on days when the "free" hotel breakfast just didn't seem sustaining enough for a long day at SCI-Wannabee, work in fracking, they are also responsible for building the infrastructure necessary to get the natural gas that they capture during the fracking process out of the community and into refineries and ultimately distributed to consumers. Although fracking takes place in many parts of the United States, the efforts in this region of the country have resulted in the United States becoming the leading exporter of oil and natural gas. What we learned from the SGT at the other prison a few counties over, which is also deeply embedded in fracking country, is that the gas and oil companies bring their own employees from Texas and Florida to do the work. These are the men we see in the hotel, who the staff says have lived here for months. Turns out that all the environmental destruction and degradation associated with fracking isn't even providing economic development to these economically depressed coal towns, Trump communities. Instead, the local communities rely on prisons for jobs that pay decent wages.

Entry-level correctional officers, or CO1s, working for the DOC earn an average of $39,000 annually. When supplemented with overtime, many CO1s earn closer to $75,000 a year. Additionally, because staff at any prison in the DOC system are categorized as state employees, their benefits, which include health and retirement, are quite generous and affordable. Most COs we met talked with glee about retirement, which they could take after putting twenty-five years into the system. Additionally, because of policies that preference veterans in hiring, those who had served their country before coming to the DOC confirmed that they could "port" or get credit for five years of their military service toward their twenty-five years. Most COs we interviewed noted that this was a major factor in their decision to work in the prison. The prison provides the highest-paying, best-benefited job to a person, more often than not a white man, with only a high school education, either a diploma or a GED.

CHAPTER 11

Dr. Emma and the Professional Staff

IN OUR INTERVIEWS, we asked each staff, from COs to white shirts, "Why this job?" "Why do you work here?"

CO Tom responded: "I didn't go to college like I was supposed to, when I was supposed to."

CO Tom talked at length about prison being the end of the line for men who made bad choices. From his perspective, which is actually not that far from what the data indicate, both COs and prisoners end up in prison because they made bad choices, including not going to college when they were "supposed to." CO Tom made the point quite clearly: "Most of us are here because of choices we made in the past, both the guards and the inmates."

We know that for Black men in particular, prison is an almost foregone conclusion if one doesn't graduate high school; 70 percent of Black men who drop out before earning a high school diploma or GED go to prison. Likewise, white men growing up in rural, Rust Belt communities, where jobs for men without high school diplomas were plentiful across the most of the twentieth century, find that today, prisons are "the only game in town."

When we asked professional, civilian staff this same question, we generally got responses that focused on wanting to make a difference, being intrigued intellectually by the set of challenges that incarcerated people face in terms of mental health, and so on.

On one visit to SCI-Wannabee, we had the opportunity to observe the delivery of mental health services to men in a variety of solitary confinement units, including those on AC and DC status as well as those in the DTU, which houses men suffering with severe mental illness. We followed Dr. Emma on her rounds, observed her conducting group therapy sessions, and interviewed her in the cramped office she shares with another civilian staff. Dr. Emma, as the prisoners call her, is in her late twenties, is white, and has long, brown hair that is either naturally straight or flat-ironed. She wears jeans that are a bit more "close fitting" than we instruct our students to wear, a cami, and a loose-fitting button-up shirt. She wears her wedding ring but no other jewelry. Her ID badge is clipped to the front hip pocket of her jeans. We spend most of one entire shift with her.

Dr. Emma recently completed her PhD in psychology and has always wanted to work in a prison. "I always wanted to work for the DOC. My dad was a CO [at another SCI] and I was always fascinated by the stories he told about what he had to do. I got my MA, which is required to be a counselor, psychological services specialist. I got my first job at a rehab facility and less than a year later I started at the DOC. At the behavioral health job, I worked with kids and I didn't like it. I wanted to have 'life conversations.' I'm interested in how the mind controls behavior."

In order to advance in her career, after beginning her job at the DOC she enrolled in an online program to earn her PhD.

When we asked her about the skills she needs to do her job well, Dr. Emma said:

> Most of my work is doing crisis calls and groups. It's difficult to do any *real* therapy with twenty to forty prisoners on my caseload . . . and they are all supposed to have an hour out of cell with me per week. I have to ask every one of them every week if they want an hour out . . . but I don't offer to see them individually. If I did I would do nothing but see clients all day every day and not get anything else done. They know they are entitled to it [an hour out each week] as part of the policy. When they see something they can control . . . they may not need mental health services, but they know they are entitled so they can control that and so they ask for it.

We are, of course, impressed by Dr. Emma's commitment to serving an underserved population that has significant mental health needs.

But why solitary confinement? Why would a young woman with so many skills, so much interest and training, choose to work in a solitary confinement unit? Dr. Emma said these are the people who need the most help, who need her the most: "That's why they are down here. . . . They are scared and vulnerable."

For part of a day we shadowed a unit manager, Brenner, who is also a civilian staff. He is a white man, in his forties or early fifties. He was wearing khaki pants and a short-sleeved button-down shirt. He has a bachelor's degree in criminal justice and elementary education. During a conversation we are having in the hallway, we asked him about working in the prison: "Can you advance without security [CO] experience?"

Unit Manager Brenner remarked: "They were impressed by my communication skills. . . . The major doesn't have a security background. It's all about communication. . . . It's a mess down here. . . . They need new leadership. . . . My job is to get everyone on the same page . . . move out the old gulag and into modern times."

Civilian, professional staff had earned college or advanced degrees. They were interested in psychology and mental and behavioral health. They saw working in solitary confinement units as both a challenge for their skillsets and a place they could make a real difference, despite, as Dr. Emma notes, spending most of their time doing crisis intervention and group therapy.

Most of the "white shirts" we interviewed and shadowed also expressed pride in their jobs. In the carceral state, in solitary confinement, the job structure mimics both law enforcement and the military, and "white shirts" occupy a sort of middle management position. Their jobs are primarily to supervise the COs, coordinate with the psych staff, and liaise with those in upper administration, the major, the deputies and warden.

Many of the SGTs and LTs we interviewed extolled their ability to get along well with others. Many of their staff described them as great team leaders, who were responsible for building the culture of the unit.

Some also saw themselves as being responsible for assembling and managing a coherent message for the unit; they were the protectors, if you will, of the unit. One day we are hanging out in the hallway just outside LT's office waiting for prisoners to be escorted down for their interviews. The student researchers were back in the visiting rooms waiting, so it's just us and the staff. COs are busy moving prisoners, honor prisoners who are assigned to work in the solitary confinement unit are sweeping the hallway, and SGT Jack is sitting alone at his desk. We pop our heads in to chat with him. SGT Jack is a big man, over 6 feet tall and over 250 pounds. He is in his mid-thirties, white, with brown hair and a beard. He has an easy way about him. We can imagine him dressing up as Santa and entertaining kids during the holidays. Like so many of the "white shirts" with whom we spend time and interview, he's both jovial and sharp-tongued at the same time. "White shirts" tell us that part of their job is to ease the tension of the COs, deescalate the situation, but they also establish rapport by talking a lot of shit.

SGT Jack is very busy doing paperwork. There are piles of paper on his desk and he is busy logging things into the computer.

WE REMARK: ["Wow, you have lot of paperwork."]

SGT JACK: "Yes, I do all the paperwork."

INTERVIEWER: ["Do you like that? 'Cause we hate paperwork. . . . What's the worst part of your job? We'll tell you ours: grading."]

SGT JACK: "No offense, but my work is important. . . . It matters. . . . I write up all of the reports for the COs. . . . That way we have the record straight and they just have to sign it."

INTERVIEWER: ["They must appreciate that. . . ."]

SGT JACK: "Yep, they do. . . . If they type up their own paperwork, they miss things; I have to fix it anyway. . . . There's a lot they don't know [pointing to LT's office and Captain's office]."

SGT Jack views his work as important for several reasons. First, he must ensure that the paperwork that comes out of his unit, under his watch, is consistent. In several unrelated conversations with COs, they frequently mention that they appreciate working with a SGT who manages the paperwork. On the one hand, most of the COs we interview find their way into their profession via the military, and most tell us that they went into the military because they weren't good at school. So it's reasonable to assume that many view paperwork as "school work," the very thing they left and meant to avoid when they took a job in a prison. Second, though prisons, and solitary confinement units in particular, are bureaucracies that are buried in paperwork, in solitary confinement, "paperwork" usually references the reports that must be submitted because of an incident, an unplanned use of force, a prisoner "refusing" a meal, pepper spraying a prisoner in their cell, a PREA complaint, or in the worst case, finding someone who has "hanged up" or killed themselves. "Paperwork" can mean legal action, disciplinary hearings, litigation. Paperwork must be carefully *managed* to protect the unit, and SGT Jack is that gatekeeper. As he noted, "There's a lot they don't know," suggesting that he is also protecting his bosses, laying the groundwork for plausible deniability should a prisoner's family file a lawsuit alleging a violation of their loved one's rights when COs deny them meals, stream tear gas into his cell, or use force to extract them.

SGT Jack is a professional who is proud of his work.

But even the "white shirts" reveal that they work in the prison because it is "the only game in town."

Though nearly everyone we met who works in solitary confinement said they took this job because "it's the only game in town," civilian and "rank" staff took pride in their work. Though they looked forward to retirement, they didn't express disdain for their jobs.

Correctional officers, COs, on the other hand, ranged from resenting their jobs to hating them. They expressed these feelings both in interviews and in the ways we observed them talking to each other. During shift changes or when we would come into the units each morning, people would greet each other, "How's it going?" and COs would respond with comments like "Just six more to go," meaning six more hours on their shift, or six more years to retirement. We heard these kinds of exchanges constantly, and though they might be part of a habit, a preestablished pattern of communication, they are also communicating something important: COs are counting down the time they have left in solitary confinement, just like the people they guard twenty-four hours a day, seven days a week.

CHAPTER 12

The Hotel

When we first rolled into Larrabee, we drove around looking for a place to buy tonic, to add to the gin we have brought with us, a part of the comfort we'll enjoy after a long day in prison, and we end up at Rite-Aid. It seems as if there is no actual town here; it's just a stop on the highway, hotels and fast food, built almost entirely, it seems, for the purposes of housing and feeding the employees the fracking industry has brought to town and people coming to visit relatives and friends at the prison. An entire town whose sole function seems to be to support these industries.

The hotel has been renovated since our last visit. It's early December, and the staff have put up Christmas decorations. Stockings with names hang from the check-in desk. A Christmas tree is in the corner of the lobby and a "runner" with lights and a "Christmas town" is on display on the front window sill, greeting guests as they enter. There is a Christmas tree near the elevator (and ice machine) on each floor.

When you first walk in the door of the hotel, there is a basket tree with three tiered baskets and a sign that reads: "Muddy boots. Boot covers." Being greeted by a basket of boot covers tells us much about the guests at the hotel, it confirms what we learned on our first trip to Larrabee: the town functions as a staging ground for the nearby fracking operation. Because a picture is worth a thousand words, we decided to take one on Hattery's iPhone (see Figure 6).

We imagine that was devised by someone like the woman we met last year who arrives at 2 a.m. each day to clean the floors. The boot covers must cut down on the time she spends mopping and buffing each morning. Perhaps this allows her to catch a few extra minutes of sleep each night.

We checked into the hotel around 6:15 on a Monday night, and there were many "long-term" guests in the breakfast area eating dinner they had picked up from a local restaurant or had delivered. They were dressed casually, in jeans, t-shirts, and hoodies. Having shed their construction boots, they wore tennis shoes. Some talked to each other. Mostly they scrolled through their phones and watched the community TV.

When we checked in, we asked the manager about food. She says: "There aren't really any restaurants here . . . but there is a good, local pizza place and

Figure 6. Shoe cover basket from Larrabee. (Photo by Angie Hattery.)

they deliver." There is no restaurant in the hotel, though they do sell frozen dinners that can be microwaved in one's room as well as a variety of beer and mini bottles of wine, and microwave popcorn and ice cream. We wonder how many nights men and the few women we saw come in from fracking are too tired to eat anything other than the snacks they can grab from the cooler behind the desk and microwave in their rooms. Their dinner is only slightly more nutritious than the meals the COs eat during their shifts in the prison.

In the morning, on Tuesday, the breakfast area is full of people, almost all men. All white. Sitting quietly inhaling food. Contemplative or bored or anticipating a day they aren't looking forward to.

Everyone is wearing boots. Some wear green vests like those worn by people who hold the STOP/SLOW sign where road construction is taking place.

Hattery gets up from breakfast and goes to the desk to get change for a $20 bill so she can buy a Diet Coke at lunch. She asks the woman at the desk, a young, white woman with a name tag that announces her as "Kelly" whose nails have been recently manicured, with polish and glitter, to make change. "We're going to the prison and the machines won't take big bills."

"I'm familiar," she remarks.

Perhaps because she visits someone in the prison. Perhaps because families who are visiting loved ones at the prison stay at the hotel. We assume that's the case, because the hotel is so close to SCI-Wannabee that we can see the tower and sections of the buildings and razor wire from our room. To be any closer to SCI-Wannabee would be to be incarcerated or working there.

CHAPTER 13

It's Either This or the Coal Mine

THE DRIVE ACROSS miles and miles of rural, mountainous landscape on the way to Larrabee County is beautiful, especially in the fall when the trees are in full color, their leaves signaling the changing of the seasons. After our very first trip, we vowed never to plan research trips during the winter, because covered in snow and ice, these windy, steep roads would be much too treacherous to traverse. As ever present as the glorious scenery are the warehouses. Whether we are cruising a major highway or navigating local roads, we see huge warehouses, pole barns, made of steel siding with steel roofs, one story, painted gray or tan, with huge parking lots and often dozens upon dozens of eighteen-wheelers backed into loading docks, their bellies filled with packages waiting to be delivered across the Northeast.

According to Amazon, there are more than one hundred fulfillment centers in the United States, dozens of them in the Mid-Atlantic and Rust Belt states where we travel to conduct our research. Each fulfillment center employs hundreds of staff. Employment ads posted on Indeed.com list these positions as paying between $10 and $13 per hour. In contrast, COs, even those just beginning their careers, make on average $17 to $18 per hour. Unlike Amazon, where pay raises are slow, with overtime, COs can expect to double their pay after their first five years. As most COs we interviewed indicated, it was not just the pay, but the benefits: generous health benefits, vacation time, and most importantly a pension they can live comfortably on, able to retire by age fifty-five.

In every interview with every CO, we posed the question, why this job?

"If I could work somewhere else and make the same pay and benefits [state benefits] I would."

COs came to work in the prison for one of two reasons: because it was the only job in town, or because they didn't want to relocate after losing a job or leaving the military.

We interviewed a woman CO who worked in SCI-Wannabee. There are very few women who work in men's prisons, and those who work in solitary confinement are even rarer, as they are considered to be a burden to the solitary team. When we first met CO Cat, we were hanging out in the COs' office observing their work and talking with them. Though we conducted formal interviews, we often found that COs were the most relaxed and forth-coming when they were in their own space. It was in these casual interactions, while they were doing paperwork or shooting the breeze with each other, that they were the most honest. CO Cat was sorting the mail. CO Cat is a young white woman, probably in her twenties, with a lean, athletic build and a crew cut. While she was sorting the mail, we asked CO Cat why she decided to come work in the prison, and her response was typical:

"I used to work at the Harley dealership but someone told me about this job. I make better money here and get better benefits."

Another officer described a typical pathway to working in a prison. He was laid off from his job and he was a military veteran. CO John was a machinist for ten years. He made riveters that are used in every conceivable type of equipment. He seems very proud of this. He loved his job. He was in the national guard for twenty-two years. Two deployments.

INTERVIEWER: ["Why did you start working at SCI-Wannabee?"]
CO JOHN: "Guys in the national guard all worked at SCI-Wannabee and encouraged me to work here."
INTERVIEWER: ["Do you like your job here?"]
CO JOHN: "I love it and I hate it."

CO Mark came to work at SCI-Wannabee from another SCI.

"I used to work at another SCI . . . until it closed. . . . I put in a transfer and now I'm here."
INTERVIEWER: ["That's a long commute,"]
CO JOHN: "It is what it is. . . . Gotta go where the work is. . . . I put in for a transfer but this is the only place they would move me."

Many officers we interviewed who were veterans came to work at SCI-Wannabee after they were discharged. Some, like CO John, sought employment in the DOC because that's what their friends had done and they were encour-aged by them to pursue this pathway. Others returned from military service to the communities where they had grown up, married, and wanted to raise their own kids, and prisons were the only job in town that paid a living wage.

Finally, in addition to getting preference in hiring, many veterans talked about the similarities between the military and the work of a CO that made the transition easy.

A "white shirt," LT House, whom we interviewed in his office, also while he was doing paperwork, said:

"I started working in the jail at age twenty-five after the military."
["Tell us about the transition."]
"The transition was easy; it was the easiest transition. The structure of the jail is the same as the structure of the military."

["We've heard about buying back time."]

"Yes, I bought back my military time and I can retire five years early. . . .
   When I came back [from the military] there were no jobs around. The
   prison was built while I was in the military. . . . When I got back it had
   opened and back then jobs were mostly word of mouth. It's the best-
   paying job around and has great benefits."

["What other kinds of jobs can people do around here?"]

"Manual labor, construction, teachers, nurses, doctors."

For others, the transition between the military and working in a prison
was more straightforward. It was as simple as the clocks.

CO Chipper is sixty-one. He served for eight years in the military, and
when he came home he worked for many years in manufacturing. When the
plant where he worked closed he came to work in the DOC. He's worked for
seven years in SCI-Wannabee, five of those years in solitary confinement. We
interviewed CO Chipper in the COs' office in B Pod. His story reveals much
about the impact of working in solitary confinement on COs' lives as well as the
hardships they face in their lives outside of work. Hardships that drive them to
working a job they often hate, even when they are in their fifties and sixties.
When we asked CO Chipper about coming to work in the prison, he said:

"I didn't care so much about the military buy back. . . . my job went under
   [making solar panels]; we couldn't compete with the Chinese market . . .
   so we got the Obama plan."

["What do you mean?" We're thinking he's going to talk about Obama care.]

"When jobs were lost to the Chinese, Obama had a plan that required
they help you find a new job or go to school. . . . At fifty I was too old to go
back to school . . . so my VA Rep recommended this place. . . . They have
international clocks like the military, so I'm used to it."

Many of the COs we spent time with have had difficult lives, but like for
CO Chipper, the transition to working in prison was easy. It was all about the
clocks.

For some officers, the connection extended into law enforcement as well
as the military. Both CO Nick and SGT Josh said that when they were growing up they wanted to be state troopers. According to SGT Josh, he got into
too much trouble in high school—his father was an addict and his mother
died of cancer—to be admitted to the police academy. "The military came to
my high school . . . a guidance counselor, maybe the principle, seen the good-
ness in me . . . loved on me."

SGT Josh served for ten years in the military, and when he returned, he
began working as a CO at another SCI before he was transferred to SCI-
Wannabee. He's been with the DOC for seventeen years, steadily rising
through the ranks from CO to "white shirt."

Though CO Nick's pathway to law enforcement and ultimately the military was somewhat different, the general theme is the same: "I wanted to be a state trooper and I thought this would be a foot in the door. Then I found you can't be a state trooper if you have visible tattoos." (He has visibly tattooed arms.)

CO Nick went into the military at age seventeen, right after high school, because "I didn't like school. Plus there's military in my family, so I felt an obligation."

After being discharged and finding himself back in his home community, he was attracted to employment at SCI-Wannabee because it offered both a well-paying stable job and an easy transition. "The philosophy . . . regimented, organized . . . being a CO is a lot like being in the military."

Like many of the COs we interviewed or spent time with, he "bought" time from the military . . . and he also got a big signing bonus, which "I blew on a truck. . . . I don't even have it anymore. I wish I had it now!"

We spent many hours with many different staff at SCI-Wannabee and the other facilities where we interviewed COs, just listening to them talk about work and their jobs. The work of a CO is extremely difficult, and it's even more demanding for those who choose to work in solitary confinement. Men described hating their jobs. They complained constantly about the prisoners and the working conditions, as well as the upper administration whom they considered out of touch. Their eyes only lit up when they talked about when they could retire or what they were going to do with their upcoming time off. Most of them talked about the outdoors, about camping and fishing and hunting. And it's no wonder—they, like the prisoners, are locked in solitary confinement eight to sixteen hours a day; a space devoid of natural light, breathing stale air.

When we first started our interviews, it seemed natural to ask men who hated their jobs why they didn't look for something else. We realized after several conversations that even the question itself reveals class privilege. We live in a world where mobility is common, both occupationally and geographically. Between us, we have worked at ten universities in six different states. Each move was prompted by a better professional opportunity. And we are far from unique. Gone are the days when professionals start at a company or firm in their twenties and retire from that same firm in their sixties. Many professionals in all types of careers work not just in multiple firms but often in multiple careers across their lifespan, and often these career moves require moving to new communities.

This is not the case for men who work in prisons. They are not mobile, in part because they have limited education and skills and in part because many expressed a strong desire to live in the communities where they grew up. They were willing to take the best job they could in those communities rather than move to places with more occupational opportunities. And once they began working in a prison, as CO Nick said:

"Now, it's hard to leave."
["Why?"]
"They pay a lot for very little work."

Why work in solitary confinement?

Beyond just working in the prison itself, we were intrigued by the choice COs and "white shirts" made to work in solitary confinement. Solitary confinement is a difficult place to be, and the work is among the most dangerous in the prison. In another chapter we will take a deeper dive into what it's like to work in solitary, but here we explore the reasons—which range from the extremely practical to those that are more substantive—that COs and "white shirts" say they choose to work in solitary confinement.

We should begin by noting that very, very few COs began their careers working in solitary confinement. Everyone agreed that in order to be successful in solitary confinement, a CO must first have some experience working in general population. Having spent time ourselves in solitary confinement units, this makes perfect sense. In our observations and in conversations we had with COs, they pointed to several qualities that make someone suitable for a bid in solitary confinement. In solitary confinement, a successful CO must be able to de-escalate. Being locked in solitary confinement twenty-three hours a day, seven days a week for weeks and months on end makes those incarcerated there restless, and tensions can arise over simple things, like someone changing the channel on the pod TV. A seasoned CO has the experience to de-escalate the tension and devise compromises and solutions that ultimately reduce the likelihood of violence and an unplanned use of force. There is widespread agreement that working in solitary confinement also carries additional sets of risk for violence, being the target of urine and feces being thrown through the wicket on the cell door as well as the violence that can occur during an escort or a cell extraction.

When we talked about the reasons they chose to work in solitary confinement, every CO we interviewed was able to compare their work experiences in solitary confinement with their experiences, however brief, in general population.

One of the things we heard over and over again from COs and "white shirts" in solitary confinement was that the nature and the structure of the work both created and necessitated a family environment that many of them found appealing: "It's more of a family down here, a team; you depend on each other more than any other part of the jail and it grows on you."

So what makes solitary confinement units "feel like family" for the staff who work there? First, there is the structure of the work. In general population, COs are assigned to work either in large dormitories or in the yard. A single CO may be responsible for "guarding" 200 prisoners. For the most part, the COs assigned to general population work alone, and they interact with other officers only at meal breaks and shift changes. Many of them live in the same communities and commute to work together, either in their own cars or in DOC van pools.

In contrast, in solitary confinement units, the unit manager and LT assemble a team that *they choose*. As noted, there are typically eight to ten officers on each shift, plus the "white shirts" who are serving meals, escorting prisoners to showers and yard, delivering mail, even escorting prisoners off the unit for medical appointments or to the visiting room to see their lawyers or a family member or, in our case, a researcher. Because the rules stipulate that COs must double up when escorting prisoners, they spend much of their days working in teams. This structure is critically important in the development of the family-like atmosphere among staff in solitary confinement. Some COs went so far as to say that they felt closer to their coworkers than to anyone else, including their families, an obvious consequence of the nature of the work.

We interviewed two COs at another SCI who have been part of a team for several years. Interestingly, their team is gender integrated (the prison is a women's prison, where this is more common). We asked them about how they deal with the stress of work. Just a few days before, both had had urine thrown on them by the same inmate.

CO Sam said, "[Sarah] is like my work wife." They said that they "know how to handle each other" and "when the other person needs a break." When CO Sarah had urine thrown at her, Sam told her to "take a break," meaning leave the unit and take a walk. CO Sarah returned the favor when CO Sam was the target of the same prisoner's aggression. Both agreed that trust between them was critical to doing a good job and not taking work home. For CO Sam and CO Sarah, and many other COs we spent time with, the family atmosphere in the unit was a critical element to successful strategies for leaving work at work.

Some of the COs and "white shirts" we interviewed indicated far more practical reasons for working in solitary confinement. Many COs talked about the pace of the work in solitary. The flip side of the difficulty of the work was that time went faster. "Benefits of working in the RHU [solitary confinement]? The day goes faster." For people who hate their jobs, having time go faster is a huge benefit. Perhaps the most practical reason was provided by LT House:

"My carpool."
["Your car pool?"]
"My carpool was working in the RHU [solitary confinement] and I would always have to wait on him at the end of my shift, so to make it easier, I transferred to the RHU."

LT House pursued work in solitary confinement because of the potential to carpool with friends.

Despite the difficulties of work and the rules that "required" staff working in solitary confinement to "rotate out," many people we interviewed had worked for years in solitary, without the "required break," preferred it, and had no intention of leaving anytime in the near future.

CO Bezos sums it up. He has worked at Wegmans and at an Amazon warehouse, and this is the best job he's ever had: "I could warehouse boxes or warehouse people; people are more interesting."

True.

CHAPTER 14

CO Porter

"SOMETIMES I SLEEP IN MY CAR"

CO PORTER IS A WHITE MAN in his early sixties who, like CO Travis, was very anxious to talk. CO Porter is far more memorable for what he said than for his physical presence. He is medium height, medium weight. If anything describes him physically, it is "rumpled." His hair is dark with wisps of gray, and thinning, though it seems it was never thick. It's messy, as if he just took off a hat and didn't have time (or a mirror) to comb it.

CO Porter has worked in the DOC for seven years, five of which he has worked in solitary confinement. When he came into the office and we asked if he wanted to talk, he jumped at the chance. The interview took place in the CO office in A Pod. One of his jobs that day was to do the rounds, which are done every hour. Perhaps because of a lawsuit in which a prisoner had died or hanged up and no one noticed for hours, COs who do the rounds carry a stick that they tap on a sensor at the end of every tier recording that the round was in fact completed. That way, if someone complains, the prison has a record to demonstrate that at least every hour a CO walked both tiers in each pod and looked into the cells to check to see if everyone was still alive. Our interview was interrupted twice while he went on his rounds, but it flowed well and like old friends we just picked back up where we left off.

In hindsight, though we could have anticipated the impact that working in solitary confinement has on one's mental health, we didn't think so much about the impact on the COs' physical health until we spent weeks observing them.

The second summer we conducted research in prisons, Hattery was also in physical therapy dealing with osteoarthritis in her right knee, which she discovered after a run on a treadmill that left her in excruciating pain and on crutches for a week. In retrospect, she ended up on crutches by not paying attention to her body and seeking the services of a physical therapist. After a few weeks in physical therapy, Hattery became very well acquainted with the ways that people walk when they have knee pain. Watching or walking with COs in the hallways or climbing the stairs in the tiers of solitary confinement units, she noticed many COs whose gait suggested that they had some sort of lower body pain, in their knees, feet, or hips. At one prison, she observed, across several days, a CO who was always carrying a bottle of water. She made an off-handed comment to him one day about how he sure was staying hydrated, and he remarked that he had suffered a bout of kidney stones. Though we didn't go into the details of his medical history, having spent so many days in solitary confinement, it is easy to understand why COs and staff would not be adequately hydrated, as one consequence of hydration is frequent urination. Urination requires access to a bathroom and the time to use it. For COs working the first or second shift, time can be a precious commodity. Delivering and picking up trays at each meal can easily take two hours, as can showers and taking prisoners to the yard. There is rarely time to sit down, let alone use the restroom. If there is an emergency, if a prisoner throws feces or urine through the wicket or refuses to comply with an order, which often leads to a cell extraction and the use of pepper spray, every CO on the unit must be ready to respond. As a result, many COs as well as other staff don't adequately hydrate, and this can lead to all kinds of urinary tract disease, including kidney stones. As CO Travis put it: "When you sit down, you're still thinking. There are no breaks at work."

Certainly these physical ailments are not limited to the job of the CO. They are also associated with many other types of manual labor, including construction work or road work. But we agree with Lisa Guenther that when coupled with the mental stress of the work of guarding people through constant surveillance, including strip searches, at the risk of having feces or urine thrown on you, or worse yet, being physically harmed, the work is dehumanizing. COs often live with other invisible stresses as well.

CO Porter has a lot of difficulties in his personal life. He is raising three stepkids, each of whom has a different biological father, since they were little, in his words, "for as long as they can remember." They are fifteen, thirteen, and twelve. Their mom, his ex-wife, left him a few months before our interview for a twenty-seven-year-old drug dealer. He thinks she is bipolar. He knows she is a drug addict.

One morning, a few weeks before our interview, CO Porter's ex-wife left the house at 6 A.M. and didn't return all day all the while leaving her kids unattended. CO Porter had left for work a few hours earlier at 4 A.M. and was unreachable because staff are not allowed to have their cell phones with them in the jail. When the kids came out of the house and complained about being hungry and alone, a neighbor called Child Protective Services. Ultimately, a judge awarded CO Porter sole custody of his stepkids.

CO Porter is currently living with his parents. He pays their mortgage. This way, the kids have a safe place to live, and in exchange, his parents take care of the kids while he is at work. He rented his own house to his brother-in-law. The rent his brother-in-law paid allowed CO Porter to cover his own mortgage—until his brother-in-law stopped paying rent. CO Porter lost the house and had to declare bankruptcy. On top of paying his parents' mortgage and monthly expenses, CO Porter pays $650 a month on his bankruptcy settlement.

CO Porter works four overtime shifts per pay period in order to be able to make his monthly expenses and the bankruptcy payment. It's December when we interview CO Porter, and he says: "I've told the kids, Christmas will be different this year."

We asked him about this and how hard it must be. He said he does have some control and only takes overtime when it doesn't conflict with his kids' sports and other events. He feels a sense of control because he chooses it; it's not mandated like it was when he was a trainee, though he admits: "I wouldn't work overtime if I didn't have to."

Though working overtime helps CO Porter pays his bills, it creates additional stresses in his life.

"Overtime means I work 6 to 2 and then 2 to 10 and then I have to be back at 6. . . . Since I live an hour and a half away, I wouldn't get home 'til midnight and I'd have to be up at 3, so when I work overtime I sleep in my car."
["Where?" we ask.]
"In the parking lot [of the prison]."
["Don't they care?"]
"No, as long as you get your body to work the next day, they don't care."
[It was pretty cold the night before, so we said, "Wow, you must get pretty cold."]
"My kids gave me a big blanket."

CO Porter sleeps in his car when he works a double shift, four times per pay period, or four times every two weeks. He can't afford the $65 a night it would cost to stay in the hotel where we stayed, the hotel that is so close to SCI-Wannabee that you can see the tower and the razor wire from the windows in our room.

CO Porter understands clearly the impact that working in solitary confinement has on both his physical and mental health, and yet he does it because it's the only job he can get, especially at his age, that pays so well. Well enough to take care of the children he is raising. But is it worth it?

When CO Porter works a double shift and sleeps in his car only to return to the unit a few hours later, he is admittedly irritable. Who wouldn't be? He has problems of his own that no one really knows or cares about, least of all the people incarcerated there. Yet, from his perspective, they spend all day whining and complaining about things that are insignificant to him, like which channel the community TV is tuned to. He may not be locked in a cage for twenty-three hours a day, but from his perspective, his life circumstances aren't much better. He sleeps in his car two nights a week, for gosh sakes, even in the winter. When we stand in his shoes, it's not hard to understand how CO Porter and CO Travis and CO Bunker and so many others come to resent the prisoners they guard twenty-four hours a day, seven days a week, at a job they hate. In the context of the prisons like SCI-Wannabee and Larrabee County, that resentment can become racialized.

PART FOUR

Fifty's Story

If they only touch you when you're at the end of the chain, they can't see you as anything but a dog. Now I can't see my face in the mirror. I've lost my skin. I can't feel my mind.

—Arizona State prisoner, quoted in
Legal Slaves and Civil Bodies

Many prisoners find themselves stuck within a present that seems to go nowhere, with little to lose and little to look forward to, waiting for a future release that may never come or that, when it does, might not deliver the longed-for sense of freedom. They find themselves haunted by a past that cannot be undone and that may return obsessively to dominate the present and drain the future of hope. This lack of control in the present can extend itself indefinitely into the future for inmates serving multiple life sentences, subject to strict rules and sometimes arbitrary judgments of prison authorities, in a world where even the release from prison does not guarantee a job, a home, meaningful relationships with others, or anything else that distinguishes freedom from the mere absence of constraint. If hope for the future is to be anything more than a fantasy or cruel joke—if it is to be a source of empowerment rather than self-deception—then the future must have an effective, dynamic relation to the present.

—Lisa Guenther, *Solitary Confinement:*
Social Death and Its Afterlives

CHAPTER 15

Dehumanization

HAVE YOU EVER SEEN a movie or a YouTube video in which a wild animal chews off a paw to escape a trap? A quick Google search will yield dozens of these heartbreaking videos.

The notion that human beings can be locked in cages for twenty-three hours a day, given only an hour out, if they are lucky, to shower and "exercise" is in and of itself a construction rooted in dehumanization. After being locked in solitary confinement for even a few days, many human beings will begin to respond like the wild animal whose paw is caught in a trap. The more we treat human beings like animals, the more they engage in behaviors none of us think we ever would. They will cut themselves, they will bang their heads against the wall until they bleed, they will spread feces on their walls, they will attempt suicide, they will do anything to get out of the cage.

Everything about solitary confinement is dehumanizing.

And, yet, for some people solitary confinement is a choice they make because the alternative is even worse. In the previous chapter we heard from COs who choose to work in solitary confinement, in spite of the ways in which they are dehumanized by it. Fifty's story, the focus of this chapter, allows us to explore and interrogate the tensions around the choice some incarcerated people make to serve out their sentences in solitary confinement, even when it is their last stop toward freedom.

The vast majority of people who are incarcerated will one day come home, at a rate of nearly three-quarters of a million each year. And some percentage of them, perhaps as many as 20 percent (or 150,000 people), will have served at least some of their time in solitary confinement cells in either a jail or a prison.

Rick Raemisch was appointed executive director of Colorado's Corrections Department in 2013 shortly after the murder of his predecessor Tom Clement, who was shot and killed by a former prisoner in the Colorado Department Of Corrections. The man who murdered Clement had been released directly from solitary confinement to the streets. Though his actions are an exception to the rule, and should be understood as such, the fact that incarcerated people like this man and a prisoner we interviewed who we call "Fifty" can be released directly from solitary confinement to the streets surprised us and is a practice that is worthy of further study. Rick Raemisch thought so too. He decided to undergo an experiment that involved being locked in a solitary confinement cell in the very prison system he oversees. In his twenty-hour stay in solitary confinement, he experienced twitching and paranoia. He quickly learned that locking an individual up—even those who have committed violent crimes—isn't the way toward rehabilitation since, at least in Colorado, 97 percent of those incarcerated are returned to their communities.[1]

Across the many, many hours we spent in solitary confinement, we observed processes and structures that are designed to dehumanize, but we also witnessed rules and practices that seemed unnecessarily dehumanizing. We could find no rationale for them when it comes to security, the primary mission of solitary confinement. Practices such as limiting a person incarcerated in solitary confinement to one book a week seems unnecessarily punitive; it seems to fly in the face of the purpose of solitary confinement as conceived of by those who developed it in the mid-nineteenth century as a period for self-reflection and intense introspection. Wouldn't reading be an important part of introspection and self-reflection, books being a tool that can actually facilitate this process?

It wasn't just the people incarcerated there who experienced solitary confinement as dehumanizing. Many of the COs did as well. Correctional officers are also locked up eight to sixteen hours a day in dehumanizing conditions. The work that they do to dehumanize the prisoners also dehumanizes them.

As others, including Lisa Guenther have noted, in discussions of solitary confinement, it's important to resist the urge to focus only on extreme types of dehumanization. Though extreme actions of dehumanization, like pepper spray and cell extractions, inarguably impact both the prisoners and the COs, they are much less frequent than everyday acts that dehumanize. Here we consider both the extreme actions and those that occur daily.

The hole is dark. Everyone expects it to be quiet, which one would think would be a necessary condition for introspective self-reflection. But it's not quiet. It's loud. Prisoners holler at each other and at the COs constantly. They bang on their cell doors. Anytime the COs are moving prisoners to shower or to yard, one hears the clanking of the chains and the closing and opening of the doors. The air is heavy. The floor is littered with trash. It's not someplace anyone wants to be.

Rationalizing the use of conditions that are no better than an animal shelter, in some cases even worse, is believing that the people who are incarcerated here deserve it. That their behavior or even their very person is so bad, so deeply flawed, so offensive that they deserve these conditions. To treat someone the way we treat people who are incarcerated in solitary confinement is to first and foremost render their humanity invisible at best and nonexistent at worst. The first step is to dehumanize, to treat people who are incarcerated as less than fully human. Nearly every person we interviewed who was incarcerated in solitary confinement proclaimed: "They treat us like animals!" "We are like dogs in cages!"

And it's true. Though there were moments of compassion and empathy that we observed, most often in interactions that involved psych staff, or between COs and women who were incarcerated in solitary confinement, these moments were relatively few and far between. The many hours we observed in solitary confinement units were filled with dehumanizing behavior and language.

Some people in solitary confinement have done horrible things, either on the inside or on the outside. We met at least two dozen people who have killed someone, often brutally. We met prisoners who treated COs, each other, and even themselves in terribly dehumanizing and often violent ways, including prisoners who assaulted COs and were sent to solitary confinement as punishment and those who threw urine and feces on COs or on each other while in solitary confinement. It's actually fairly easy to discount an incarcerated persons' humanity in solitary confinement. In many ways it's not hard to transport yourself into the shoes of a CO. That's the whole problem, just how easy it is, and the transition from seeing the humanity in people to treating them as less than fully human, as animals, is facilitated by the very conditions of solitary confinement, some of which the COs inherit and some of which the COs design.

CHAPTER 16

Language

LANGUAGE CAN BE DEHUMANIZING. Language is an expression of othering. Of creating hierarchies. Of us versus them. One need look no further than the development and deployment of racial or ethnic slurs. When white people use the n-word, they are invoking a language of hierarchy, of dehumanization, of citizenship, of stereotypes. Invoking the n-word communicates that you are less than, that you don't have a right to be in this space.

There are debates in the policy and advocacy communities about the language we use to talk about people who are incarcerated. We acknowledge the broad trend as well as the insistence by advocates to use "first person language," for example, "people with disabilities" instead of "the disabled," or referring to people who are incarcerated as "residents" instead of "inmates" or "prisoners," phrases that denote the *status* of the person, not the person themselves. Admittedly we struggle with the appropriate language. We understand and are sympathetic to the perspective of advocates who argue that calling someone an "inmate" or a "prisoner" implies that is all that person is, whereas using terms like "person who is incarcerated" focuses on the person's humanity. And we agree. And, throughout the book we do use this language.

However sometimes the language is cumbersome. And, furthermore, sometimes we want to use language deliberately to reinforce the point that when a person, a human being, is sentenced to jail or prison the state effectively controls and rescinds many of their civil and human rights. Lisa Guenther and others refer to this as social death. Furthermore, we want the reader to be constantly reminded that the people we interviewed who are incarcerated in solitary confinement are not free to leave, they do not have many of the civil and human rights we take for granted, they are not full citizens, their citizenship is, in fact, held by the state. Therefore, we chose to use the term "prisoner" for several reasons.

First, we use the term "prisoner" rather than "inmate" because "inmate" is the term used by the state, and formerly incarcerated people we consulted sought to resist and reject the language of the state.

Second, and of equal importance, there is a long history of Black people being targeted as enemies of the state and incarcerated as prisoners of the state. Members of the Black Panther Party are one example, as are Angela Davis, and a prisoner you will meet in the final portion of the chapter; Freelimo; and our colleague Claude Marks. The term "prisoner" denotes the status of a person who is controlled by the state.

Third, as we hope we have demonstrated throughout this book, we will not sanitize or "whitewash" the experience of prisons. The vast majority of people, including many staff in jails and prisons, do see the people they guard as less than fully human. As prisoners. How else could they treat them the way that they do? Dehumanizing them is central to the strategy of incarceration, and even more so in solitary confinement. Though we do not want to reproduce this dehumanization, for we see the people who agreed to spend time with us as fully human, we don't want to in any way soften their experiences as people who are *seen* as less than fully human. There are many examples like this in our work. Here's another. Rather than describing prisoners as being "housed" in solitary confinement, we prefer the phrase "incarcerated in solitary confinement." "Housing" is what we do with students who live in dormitories on campus; we "house" them. Prisoners are incarcerated. The differences could not be more profound. Depriving people of their liberty is the most serious legal and social action we, as a society, can take against another citizen, and we don't want to minimize the impact.

Finally, despite all of the human rights debates among both scholars and activists, the truth of the matter is that although people who are incarcerated are physically alive, they suffer both civil and social death. Prisoners have almost no legal rights, save those that are guaranteed by the Constitution, and those are few and very far between, often secured only through hard-fought lawsuits. Prisoners in solitary confinement have even fewer rights, justified by the fact that they have committed infractions or caught misconducts that landed them there. They are removed so far from view that other than to their loved ones on the outside and those charged with their "care, custody, and control," they might as well be dead. That's how they are treated.

Mary Buser makes a similar observation based on her time working on Rikers Island.

Back at the clinic, I prepared to do battle with the MHAUII (Mental Health Assessment Unit for Infracted Inmates). The removal of a Bing [the solitary confinement unit at Rikers Island is referred to as the "Bing"] inmate came in two parts: our decision that he should come out, and the MHAUII's agreement to accept him into one of their specialized cells. Since their small unit wasn't only for Bing inmates but also for high-profile and otherwise odd cases, their eight cells were never empty. The arrival of a Bing inmate meant that an occupant of one of these cells needed to be relocated. For the MHAUII staff, these bumps were disruptive and time-consuming. Sure enough when I reached out the MHAUII chief had a different take on things. "Smearing feces is the oldest trick in the book. You can't let him manipulate you." "Listen," I countered "it's over 100 degrees in there, he's naked and he's covered in shit. He needs to come out." "This isn't life or death. If you give in every time these Bing monsters act out, then you're going to wind up with five hundred empty cells." *Bing monsters!* There it was again, and from our own staff! Though I heard dehumanizing terms every day, I never got used to them. It seemed to me that when you can call someone a *monster* or a *skel* or a *body*, then it suddenly becomes okay to do whatever you want to them because they're not really human beings.[1]

Language is indeed part of the overall and deliberate process of dehumanization in solitary confinement.

CHAPTER 17

Studies with Monkeys

HARRY HARLOWE WAS A PSYCHOLOGIST of the mid-twentieth century who was interested in the impact of social isolation on humans. He arrived in Madison, Wisconsin, where Hattery did her graduate work, in the 1930s to pursue his PhD in psychology. He set up a colony of rhesus monkeys in a park that would later become the Henry Vilas Zoo, a popular spot for families and their young children. Hattery took her kids, Travis and Emma, there often, including every October for the highly anticipated Haunted House at Henry Vilas Zoo.

Harlowe began a multidecade study that transformed the way that psychologists think about isolation. In his first set of experiments, Harlowe took infant rhesus monkeys away from their mothers and put them in cages with either a "wire-cage mother" who dispensed milk when the babies crawled in her lap or a "soft mother," essentially the same wire-cage mother but wrapped in blankets, who did not dispense milk. Harlowe hypothesized that the baby monkeys would prefer the "wire-cage mother" who provided milk over the "soft" mother who offered no milk. Much to his astonishment, not only did the monkey babies prefer the "soft mother" who had no milk over the "wire cage" mother, but when he tried to remove the baby monkeys from the cage with the "soft mother" they clung fiercely to her, desperate for physical contact with her.

Harlowe then began a series of experiments in which he removed baby monkeys from their mothers and housed them in isolation cages. They were offered food, but they were not offered any contact with a human or monkey. Food was dispensed to them multiple times a day through a set of feeding tubes. Harlowe's original research design laid out a twelve-month protocol. But Harlowe stopped the study after only a few months.

No monkey has died during isolation yet. When initially removed from total social isolation, however, they usually go into a state of depression, characterized by . . . autistic self-clutching and rocking. One of six monkeys isolated for 3 months refused to eat after release and died 5 days later. The autopsy report attributed death to emotional anorexia. . . . The effects of 6 months of total social isolation were so devastating and debilitating that we had to get the experiment rolling, but we soon assumed initially that 12 months of isolation would not produce any additional decrement. This assumption proved to be false; 12 months of isolation almost obliterated the animals socially.[1]

Ultimately the scientific community, and Harlowe himself, concluded that his experiments amounted to animal cruelty and they were never repeated. If solitary confinement can have that type of impact on a monkey, what is the impact on human beings of sustained isolation and lack of any meaningful human contact? It is nothing short of devastating. As we have said over and over again, 80,000 to 100,000 people are incarcerated in solitary confinement every single day in the United States. Some spend only a few hours or days, but many, many, many are incarcerated in long-term solitary confinement for months, years and even decades. For those who want to learn more about the psychological impact of isolation on people, we recommend the work of our colleagues, including Terry Kupers author of *Solitary: The Inside Story of Supermax Isolation and How We Can Abolish It*, and Craig Haney, author of "The Science of Solitary: Expanding the Harmfulness Narrative" published in the *Northeastern Law Review*.

Sadly, some of the people in the United States who are incarcerated in solitary confinement are children. Kalief Browder was arrested just a few days before his seventeenth birthday, in May of 2010. He was charged, but never convicted, of stealing a backpack. The court refused to allow his family to post bail, and for three years he was incarcerated on Rikers Island, an adult prison, while he awaited a court date. Browder spent nearly two years in solitary confinement. He was finally released in 2013, the charges dropped. Sadly, just two years later, just after turning twenty-two, he committed suicide. According to the documentary produced by Jay-Z, *The Kalief Browder Story*, he struggled with severe mental health issues including depression and anxiety that are attributed to the time he spent, *as a child and young adult*, in solitary confinement.

Khorey Wise was sent to prison in 1989, having been wrongfully convicted of the rape and brutal beating of the "Central Park Jogger," Trisha Meilli. Wise was the oldest of the "Central Park Five." He was sixteen at the time of his conviction, and the only one of the five to be incarcerated in an adult prison. Wise spent nearly fourteen years in prison before his exoneration in 2002, most of it in solitary confinement. Award-winning documentary filmmaker Ava DuVernay devotes the entire fourth episode of her film *When They See Us* to Wise's experience in solitary confinement. It is devastating to watch. Difficult to get through. And, yet, watching a docudramatic portrayal of Wise's years in solitary confinement is nothing compared to what it was actually like for him.

The impact of long-term isolation is clear and not debated. The UN Commission on Human Rights argues that it should be used sparingly, and never for more than fifteen consecutive days.

If a baby monkey can't live for a few months in isolation, what is the impact on humans? Including *children* like Kalief Browder and Khorey Wise? Though we assign it in our classes, most students can't make it through the fourth episode of *When They See Us*. It's just too excruciating to watch. What is it like to live in longer isolation? That is one of the questions we hoped to find answers to when we spoke with men and women who did.

CHAPTER 18

Hygiene Products

IN THE 1960s, sociologist Erving Goffman conducted ethnographic research in what were then referred to as "insane asylums." This research led him to coin the term and the concept of the "total institution." The most common features of total institutions include de-identifying or de-individualizing, total control, a system of rules and privileges, and modalities for adaptation. Total institutions are, by design, dehumanizing.

One of the first things that happens when one is remanded to the custody of the state and sent to prison is the assignment of an inmate number. As soon as prisoners actually enter the facility where they will be incarcerated, they are stripped and handed a uniform. Much like prisoners in Auschwitz who had their identification numbers tattooed on their arms, prisoners are often referred to by their inmate numbers. In reality, we saw staff routinely refer to the prisoners by their last names, but in all formal, institutional communication with they are referred to by their number. In SCI-Wannabee we learned early on that everyone goes by their last name, including COs, "white shirts," psych staff, and people who are incarcerated there. The argument for this practice is that it keeps things professional. In reality, it also contributes to the dehumanization or at least de-individualization of everyone in the prison, including staff, who are "white shirts" or "COs," not Travis or Porter or Emma.

Similarly, the prison uniform, for both prisoners and staff, is highly regulated. People who are incarcerated wear a jumpsuit, the color dictated by their status in the prison. Every article of clothing is highly controlled. Prisoners are allowed to wear only those items that can be ordered from the DOC commissary catalog. A highly regulated uniform serves to both dehumanize and de-individuate, but it also creates a black market for sewing. Because uniforms come in only a few sizes, prisoners who are shorter or taller than average often seek out other prisoners who have sewing skills to alter their uniforms for a better fit. For a price of course, paid in commissary items or contraband. Staff uniforms are equally regulated and ordered from the DOC staff catalog. Staff appearance is also regulated through regulations on hair styles and piercings. For example, during some of the time we were conducting research, Hattery had purple or pink highlights in her hair. Many of the staff commented that such a thing would never be allowed for staff. Nor would visible piercings of anything other than one's ears. Hattery violated this regulation as well. Thankfully no one required her to take out her many piercings.

If prisons are total institutions, then solitary confinement units are total institutions on steroids. In solitary confinement, prisoners on DC status have additional limits imposed on them. For example, though everyone has to wear the same uniform, prisoners on DC status are only allowed to have three jumpsuits and three pairs of underwear and socks in their possession at any one time, even if they can afford to own more. The "logic" behind this is that they can then have a clean change of clothes on shower days, Monday, Wednesday, and Friday. But really? Is it that much of a security risk to have an extra pair of clean clothes? Or is this the kind of rule that Goffman describes, the kind of rule that is about control and dehumanization, not logic?

Similar rules apply to shampoo and soap and even toilet paper.

Shaniqua is a slight woman in her late thirties who came to prison in her twenties. We would identify her as Black, though when we ask her how she identifies racially, she says: "My race is indeterminant. In here I feel less than a human, I don't know who I am any more."

She is short, around 5′ 3″ or 5′ 4″ and petite. We had originally met her in the yard, and she was by far the most boisterous of all the women. In the yard, she tells other prisoners that they should talk to us, imploring: "They want to hear from you! You need to tell them what's going on in here." She has easy rapport with the unit manager, Mike, and the counselor, Tom. She is complaining to them about something that we don't overhear. We get the sense that she banters with the staff on a very regular basis, and her interview, which takes place in a cage in the law library, feels like a continuation of that banter. She is there to complain more than to tell her story. Shaniqua sees herself as an advocate for other prisoners. She sees herself as a broker. And this makes sense, because she is serving a long sentence and she is an "old timer" in the sense of how long she has been in SCI-Women. She is a regular in solitary confinement. She knows all of the regulations, and several times during the interview she cites details from the inmate handbook. She is smart and attentive to detail. We wonder what she might have done had she not been in prison. She would make a good lawyer. She would make a good social worker.

Shaniqua has been in prison for fifteen years. She has served almost all of her sentence, fourteen years, in SCI-Women. She has nine more years to serve on her sentence. She has a daughter who is twenty-six and going to a local community college.

When it comes to the rules and regulations, Shaniqua says:

It's the little things that matter: COs control the TV. They control the toilet paper. . . . We get three rolls of tissue a week. You have to charge back the brown tubes. They give out two rolls on Sunday and one on

Wednesday. If you come in [to solitary confinement] on Wednesday, you might not have enough till Sunday. If you didn't have a brown tube. We fish, especially when new people come in so that everyone gets tissue . . . and other stuff, too. You only get two jumpers a week and not on Sunday. You don't get a new jumper just because you get a shower. You have to shower and put your dirty jumper back on.

Is toilet paper a significant risk to safety and security, or is it a rule that the COs establish in order to demonstrate their total control over the prisoner? By creating a climate in which toilet paper is a scarce commodity, COs can turn toilet paper into a commodity that can be traded on. An article in the *New York Post* describes both men and women COs demanding sex in exchange for extra toilet paper.[1] What the *New York Post* article does not describe, but we can imagine, is that the same CO who trades sex for toilet paper can turn around and write up that same prisoner for having extra toilet paper, an offense that could lead to time in the hole. As the saying goes: "Absolute power corrupts absolutely."

But even those locked deep in the hole demonstrate agency and resistance. As Shanique reports, they fish toilet paper, juice and other commodities. In the hidden world of solitary confinement "fishing" allows prisoners to share small items with each other by using a system of strings, often pulled from their bedsheets and the seams of their clothing, which they attach to the item they want to fish, along with a weight, perhaps a small bar of soap which allows the fisher to have some limited control of the line. From under their cell door, they cast their line, like one might in a trout stream, from one cell to another sharing and bartering toiletries, food, and of course contraband. And, COs are well aware of the fishing in their units. Most told us they are willing to tolerate it by ignoring it as long as it doesn't "get out of hand." In other words, as long as they believe they are still in control of the unit. In this environment, innovative strategies, such as fishing, provide some limited agency even for the most powerless.

If anything is true of solitary confinement, it is the rigidity of the rules. Showers are on Mondays, Wednesdays, and Fridays. Clean jumpsuits on Sundays and Wednesdays. The same with toilet paper. No exceptions. Even when the temperature in the cells goes above 100 degrees.

Though we understand the shower restrictions from a management standpoint, escorting prisoners to and from their showers takes hours and hours of CO time each day, often consuming an entire shift, we can't help but wonder about the inhumaneness of the restriction. It may not matter every day, but there are circumstances that are all too common in which it does. For example, on one of our visits to SCI-Women, it was summertime, mid-August and very hot. There is no air conditioning in the dorms in general population, and so some women told us that people who are incarcerated there committed infractions and caught misconducts the week before so that they could get to solitary confinement, where there is air conditioning. Ironically, the days we were there, the AC was also out in the solitary confinement unit. The cells were excruciatingly hot and it was very humid. We wanted to take a shower as soon as we left and got back to the hotel where we were staying. Wouldn't the people incarcerated there also benefit from a shower? Perhaps they wouldn't be so irritable or tense if they could rinse off and put on a clean jumpsuit. Wouldn't that increase safety and security?

Similarly, deindividuation also means no special treatment. Just because you got your period unexpectedly in the middle of the night on Wednesday and bled through your underwear and jumpsuit doesn't mean that you can get clean laundry on Thursday. Or Friday. Or Saturday. You simply have to wait until Sunday, because that's laundry day.

Shaniqua explains: "You won't have any trouble getting [menstrual] supplies, but you have to wash out your underwear and your oranges in your sink. They won't take them to the laundry with blood on them. . . . You can't get clean ones if you don't turn in a pair. . . . It's gross."

In other words, prisoners have to hand-wash bloodstained underwear and jumpsuits in their steel sink-and-toilet combination with only the small, hard bar of soap that not even the Motel 6 would put in its rooms. No Tide or Dawn dishwashing soap allowed.

What exactly, we wonder, are the safety and security risks around clean underwear?

Of course there are none. The vast majority of the rules and regulations we observed in solitary confinement were simply tools of dehumanization and punishment.

While we were writing an early draft of this book, Hattery was recovering from serious foot surgery. The recovery involved more than six weeks in a cast and zero weight bearing allowed on the impacted foot. She wasn't terribly comfortable on the crutches; she was terrified, actually, that she would fall and hurt her foot. Thankfully she had a knee scooter to give her enough mobility to get from the couch to the bathroom. For six weeks, Hattery was restricted to living on the main floor of their townhouse . . . sleeping (and reading and writing) on the couch. Restricted from the shower, she relied on sponge baths and washing her hair in the sink to meet basic hygiene needs. Even though she had some idea of what to expect, as this was her second surgery on this foot, she often found herself discouraged as she struggled with these significant restrictions on her life. She missed her daily walk to the gym on campus followed by a thirty-minute cardio or weight workout and then the walk home. She missed the luxury of running errands or going to the mailbox to get the mail she knew was piling up.

One day, as she was washing her hair in the sink, hair that is more than long enough to go down the drain with the food waste washed off the dishes, she reflected on the experiences of the people she had interviewed in solitary confinement. Though her life was not nearly as restricted as those of people confined to a 10×12 cell, nor was it even as confined as the solitary confinement simulation assignment we asked our students to participate in, it was surprising to her how quickly she became discouraged. The usual task of washing her hair in the shower was a ten-minute activity at best; in the sink, it took more like fifteen minutes. And then there was the sponge bath to take. She found that she restricted her fluid intake, especially later in the day, so as to limit trips to the bathroom, which involved transferring from couch to knee scooter to toilet, and back again, an activity made more difficult in the grogginess of sleep. The first week after surgery, though she could smell her own body odor every few days, changing into somewhat cleaner shorts and a t-shirt didn't seem that important. Incarcerated people we interviewed complained a lot about restrictions on their hygiene in solitary confinement. Only two changes of clothes and three showers a week. All other "washing up" was restricted to that which could be done in the sink of their steel sink-and-toilet combination. Washing clothes while they waited for a new set was managed similarly, in their steel sink-and-toilet combination. Hung to dry on a line strung from their desk to the toilet. Why only two sets of jumpsuits per week? Why only three showers a week, even in the heat and humidity of the summer? The answer, of course, is that it takes too much labor for the COs and is therefore too expensive. The other answer is that most of us believe that the people locked in solitary confinement are there because they have done terrible things and therefore they are entitled to only the most basic of human needs. Three showers a week. Two changes of clothes. Monday seems a long time from Friday . . .

We asked Candy, an incarcerated person who we interviewed in solitary confinement in SCI-Women about access to feminine hygiene products, and she said: "Tampons have gotten better. Sunday you get two rolls, [of toilet paper] and Wednesday you get one. Some officers will let you get more when you come in, some won't. As far as tampons, you get a certain amount and then you have to buy the rest. You get one bar of green soap a week. . . . When you come in you get an intake bag: toilet paper, tampons, soap—the COs are supposed to give it to you, but sometimes they refuse."

In solitary confinement, Candy says: "Commissary is a privilege; you can't get things like ChapStick and decent deodorant. I mean, ChapStick, c'mon, is that something that should be a privilege?"

Apparently ChapStick is ruled a matter of security and safety.

But it's not just ChapStick. It's also soap and shampoo. And for those who menstruate: tampons and pads, Restricting access to personal hygiene products is a form of punishment for those serving DC time in the hole.

At some level we can understand the restrictions on commercial soap and hair products because they may contain substances that can be distilled for misuse, to make drug or alcohol substitutes. Yet the commissary catalog contains only the *approved* personal hygiene products for the prison. So why add restrictions on the amount of shampoo and soap for those incarcerated on DC-status but not those incarcerated on AC-status. It's obviously not the risk associated with the products. So it can only be for punishment.

Time in solitary confinement denies people access not only to civil rights but also to basic human rights, including the most basic personal hygiene.

CHAPTER 19

The Mirror

ONE OF THE MORE CONTROVERSIAL restrictions in solitary confinement involves the mirror.

People incarcerated in solitary confinement, are not allowed to have mirrors in their cells. The mirror in the shower cage is nothing more than a shiny piece of metal that allows one to see a distorted image of oneself. Because the mirror is small, about the size of an 8 × 10–inch piece of paper, all you can really see is your face.

We can understand the concern about mirrors. The glass on the mirror can easily be broken and used to hurt oneself or another person.

Yet, a mirror is an important part of personhood. Mirrors are used in literature and poetry to describe the window to ourselves. Sociologist Kjerstin Gruys spent a year without looking at herself in a mirror. She wanted to understand the role that mirrors play in our self-esteem. What she learned is that she felt better about herself and was less judgmental of her body and beauty when she couldn't see herself in the mirror.

But what happens when you go years without seeing yourself in the mirror? And what happens when the absence of a mirror takes place in the larger context of not getting any feedback about yourself, certainly none that is positive?

Kjerstin Gruys did her experiment during the year leading up to her wedding, which was both a bold move and her motivation. She found that while shopping for her wedding dress and constantly surveilling her body in full-length mirrors, she became hyper-self-critical. During her year without mirrors, however, she had plenty of friends and family, including her fiancé, giving her feedback and praise on how great she looked. Folks could not believe how beautifully she did her hair and makeup without a mirror!

For people incarcerated in solitary confinement, no one is providing positive feedback, making the absence of the mirror even more significant.

Interestingly, in our interview with Shaniqua at SCI-Women, she raised the issue of the mirror organically. We hadn't mentioned it, though we had been giving it much thought since our first observation of the shower cage at

SCI-Wannabee. Other women at SCI-Women also spontaneously mentioned mirrors in their interviews.

Shaniqua said: "You need a mirror in your room. If you don't see yourself, your self-esteem gets low, it's like I'm an animal. . . . I've seen women so desperate to see themselves that they try to see themselves in the water in their toilet. . . . You look in the mirror and your attitude can change. . . . What do I have to look forward to? What might I lose? You lose you!"

Candy also talked about the mirror.

We interviewed Candy in a noncontact interview room in the solitary confinement unit. She is a white woman, twenty-six years old. She has been incarcerated for four years. She was originally sentenced to serve two to four years on a drug possession charge. She was released after two, but was arrested again about nine months before we interviewed her. She assaulted someone over $30 of crack, which violated her probation, so she's back in prison serving the remainder of the initial four-year sentence. By the time we interview her, she's spent a total of ninety-three consecutive days in solitary confinement; she caught a misconduct for "fooling around" with her girlfriend on the yard.

Candy is beautiful. She has long, dark hair that looks styled, even though she comments many times that she feels unattractive, that she can't take care of herself in solitary confinement. Candy seems eager to be interviewed. She breaks down crying several times during the interview. She had a difficult childhood. Her parents were both drug addicts and her father sexually abused her when she was a child. In response, she was removed from her parents' home and placed in the foster care system. As a "tween" or preteen, Candy began running the streets and using drugs to self-medicate.

We think of her and think of all the things that went wrong, and we wonder if there had been an appropriate intervention if she would have a different life. . . . She could be one of our students. She is the same age as our daughter.

Candy begins her interview, without prompting, by saying that she gets to shower only three times a week: "Hygiene shouldn't be a punishment. . . . You get no phone calls except PREA. No mirror. You go crazy if you can't see yourself. They are killing themselves in solitary confinement. . . . You have no one to talk to, they [COs] say they help people but it's not true. We have other people to see; we just don't see you. The only way to get help is to threaten to hurt yourself."

We wonder, what's it like to not see yourself for days, weeks, months, or even years? You may catch a glimpse of yourself in the polished metal square in the shower, but you don't really *see* yourself. Is your hair turning gray? You notice hair in the sink or when you brush or comb your hair, but are you balding? What does your hairline look like? Are you developing crow's feet around your eyes? And that's just your face. It feels like you've gained or lost weight, but what does your body look like? Is that bump you feel on your nose a pimple, or are you developing skin cancer? How much of how we see ourselves is what we see in the mirror? What is the impact on your mental health when you can't really see yourself? Shaniqua tells us that without being able to see yourself, you are like an animal. Or worse yet, as she suggests, you may lose yourself.

CHAPTER 20

Food

By far the most contentious issue in prisons, and in solitary confinement in particular, is the food.

In general, prison food is bad. Johnny Cash wrote a song about it. When people on death row are about to be executed, they are offered the opportunity to request even the most outrageous "last meal." When people are preparing to leave prison, one of the most frequently asked questions is, "What's the first thing you want to eat?"

None of this is by lack of coincidence. The food in prison is terrible, and the food in solitary confinement is even worse because prisoners in solitary confinement don't get to exercise any choice in what they eat other than to indicate dietary restrictions. No wonder there is such a market for honey buns.

The food is not only unhealthy, it tastes terrible, or in many cases has no taste at all. And for people incarcerated in solitary confinement, there isn't even enough of it. Prisoners in solitary confinement receive just enough calories to meet the minimum required by law. They complained: "What we get, it's not enough for a grown man; it's not enough for a seventh grader."

Shanique offered her own critique of the food: "Sometimes the trays are dirty. You know why we have rubber trays, right? Because they break windows and they cut [self-mutilate] with the trays and so they switched us out to rubber. We get rotten fruit, all the time. The food is cold. The portions are small. The bread is wet. . . . We fish coffee, juice. I don't drink my juice so I fish, give [another inmate] my juice; it made her happy."

We can personally attest to the quality of the food. Passing back through security is time consuming and not terribly efficient, and thus we ate our lunch each day with the COs and "white shirts" with whom we were working, accompanying them to the "staff dining room" or chow hall.

Typical of institutionalized food preparation, there are absolutely no spices, which results in very bland food. Similarly, the food is very basic. Think grade school lunch. Three times a day, 365 days a year. Chicken patties, pizza, powdered eggs, heavy on the starches and sparse on vegetables, the carrot/pea/corn mixture providing the only fiber on the menu. Fruits are limited almost exclusively to apples and bananas. White bread and peanut butter are the default.

It's not just the prisoners. The staff eat the same food. The only difference is the staff, like the people incarcerated in general population, get to choose from the offerings of the day and there is always a salad bar and white bread, peanut butter, and jelly if nothing looks appealing. Which mostly it doesn't. Staff and researchers in solitary confinement find that they rely as much on the vending machines for food and drink as the cafeteria. Again, think of a large public school, and you get the idea. Hamburgers that you can purchase with quarters from a vending machine and heat up in the microwave. Not exactly like a burger made on your backyard grill. This is the importance of our stop to get "change" at the desk in the hotel lobby, so that we could purchase food and drinks from the vending machine if we were desperate.

We find food to be one of the more dehumanizing aspects of prison for everyone who is incarcerated or works there. Food is punishment, not nourishment, not for the prisoners and not for the staff.

What's different about food in solitary confinement, as compared to in general population, is the food delivery. Obviously people incarcerated in solitary confinement don't go to the chow hall, as prisoners in general population do. Instead, meals for people incarcerated in solitary confinement arrive three times a day on a special cart that is supposedly moderating the temperature, keeping cold foods cold and hot foods hot. One of the most dreaded jobs of the CO working in solitary confinement is to deliver trays to each and every prisoner in the pod. The food cart is wheeled into the unit, and as a result it's relatively easy to deliver the trays on the ground floor, but for the cells on the upper tier, the CO must hand carry trays up the stairs and come back thirty minutes later to pick them up. If there are twenty cells on the upper tier, even the CO carrying two trays at a time must make ten trips up and down the stairs to deliver food and ten more to pick up the trays. One way in which the COs further the already dehumanizing aspects of the food is by punishing prisoners for the smallest infractions and denying them a tray. We heard over and over again, from both prisoners and staff, stories about the COs burning prisoners on their trays.

We heard from *both prisoners and COs* about specific and unnecessarily restrictive rules. For example, some COs require that in order for a prisoner to receive their tray, which is passed through the wicket, they must be standing at the cell door, clothed, with the light on the moment the CO approaches the door. One person we interviewed who is incarcerated in solitary confinement told us that he takes antipsychotic medication to treat his severe mental illness. He complained that one of the side effects of his medication is that it makes him drowsy and he often oversleeps the 6 A.M. call for breakfast. COs record his noncompliance as refusing his tray, and he has to wait another four hours for lunch, losing out on one-third of his daily caloric entitlement. Another person we interviewed who is incarcerated in solitary confinement, a white man in his mid-sixties who admitted to us that he is in a gang affiliated with the Aryan nation and who has white nationalist tattoos visible on his arms and face, is hearing impaired and wears hearing aids. Because the pod is so loud, he takes the hearing aids out at night so he can sleep. As a result, he often doesn't hear the CO enter the block for 6 A.M. count, and he, like the prisoner taking antipsychotic medications, misses breakfast. COs argue that it's too inefficient for them to wait on prisoners or circle back to be sure that everyone has a chance to receive their tray. People incarcerated in solitary confinement experience being burned on meals as another form of punishment and torture unique to solitary confinement.

What we observed is that food delivery is a source of deep tension and fuels racial antagonisms.

Chapter 21

Time

Time is perhaps the most dehumanizing aspect of solitary confinement. There is nothing, absolutely nothing to mark it. Except of course food.

Many people during the COVID-19 pandemic talked about losing track of time. As we were working from home, learning from home, in our sweats and t-shirts, days bled into one another. For academics like us, who can work any time of the day and any day of the week, often every day of the week, the weekdays become indistinguishable from the weekends. There is nothing to punctuate the time. Those of us in the free world can tell it's the weekend by the changing anchors on our favorite news channels. At least we have that.

For people in solitary confinement, there is even less to punctuate the time. With no natural light and only very small, if any, windows, dusk bleeds to dawn. Food becomes the marker. Breakfast is delivered at 6:30 A.M. Wednesdays are chicken patty days, and pizza is on Fridays. The thing people complain the most about becomes the only thing that reliably marks the time.

Scholar described time: "Today is commissary so all everyone is talking about is commissary. Tomorrow is movie night, so all everyone will talk about is what movie they will show. *Every day you spend waiting for the next thing.*"

There is something inhumane about not being able to mark time.

Perhaps it's because time is a human invention.

Time isn't real. But time becomes real because we make it real.

No wonder prisoners talk about "doing time." Time becomes something to do, to get through.

It's not just the prisoners who see time as something to get through; so do the COs. How much time is left in my shift? How many years until I retire?

Solitary confinement steals one of our most precious commodities: time.

In her book *Solitary Confinement: Social Death and Its Afterlives*, philosopher Lisa Guenther explores the concept of time, writing:

> What does it mean to serve time? To be at risk of having time *do* you, or even *do* you in? Every prisoner must face this question on some level. But time is an especially pressing issue for the supermax prisoner who is isolated from others and confined to a tiny cell for weeks, months, or even years.

Just as the security doors chop up supermax space, so too does the prison schedule chop up supermax time; the supermax inmate is subject to a rigid schedule of feedings, showers, and short sessions in the "dog run." . . . The constant repetition of the same makes each day blend into the next, such that time seems both to grind to a halt and slop away without incident or event. . . . Waiting to do nothing . . . reinforces inmates' dependence on prison authorities to receive even the most basic rights and privileges. Waiting for the arrival of something important—whether it is a meal, a bit of toilet paper, or a book from the prison library—both devalues the present and extends it indefinitely. . . . The prisoner is bound to negotiate with this asymmetrical structure, not only of power but of *power over time.*[1]

Officer after officer told us that solitary confinement is "hard time" because it is meant to be. COs who work in the hole take some pride in the fact that they are responsible for carrying out the punishment that prisoners are sentenced to endure. They see themselves as responsible for remembering the victims, often of truly heinous crimes: taking someone's life, molesting a child, raping a white woman. They see themselves as loyal: punishing the prisoner who assaulted an officer in general population. They see themselves as critical workers in a system of rehabilitation. If they have done their jobs in solitary confinement, no one will want to come back to it, and therefore the threat of solitary confinement serves as an effective deterrent. COs working in solitary confinement talk about themselves as a sort of recidivism specialist. If they do their jobs, the prisoners won't want to come back.

Once you construct the role of solitary confinement as simply punishment and not rehabilitation or a "pause" for introspection and self-reflection, then it makes sense to design the experience of solitary confinement not as a minimalist monastic retreat that the wealthy will pay hundreds or thousands of dollars to experience, but to be as brutal as possible.

But here's the catch: the majority of people incarcerated in solitary confinement aren't there for brutally raping or murdering someone or assaulting a guard. They are there for having too many honey buns in their cell or refusing to obey an officer's order, which might not have been that important to begin with. Absolute power corrupts absolutely. Sometimes the ability to control the prisoner becomes the end in and of itself, rather than a means to an end.

If you have ever raised a child, especially during their toddler or teenage years, then you have experienced this. Sometimes the disagreement, the "fight," is worth it. The child or teen wants something that is dangerous, and your job as a parent is to dig your heels in and say "no" so that you can keep your child or teen safe. Your child may really want to take the car out to pick up ice cream at 1 A.M. in the middle of a snow storm, but you know that the risks of driving after dark in a snow storm, especially if one is an inexperienced driver, are not worth it. Eat the ice cream we already have that's in the freezer!

But sometimes the fight between a parent and a child or teen becomes about winning for winning's sake. Parents often get pulled into these fights because even the toddler and especially the teen can see the truth. In many ways it's no different than relationships between COs and prisoners. Sometimes, and we would argue more often than not, the CO gets pulled into a disagreement or a fight that isn't over anything important. Winning becomes the only goal. And in the world of jails and prisons, winning is everything, precisely because it is a demonstration of power. Absolute power corrupts absolutely.

CHAPTER 22

Mail

THERE IS NOTHING, or at least very little, that COs can do about many of the dehumanizing elements of solitary confinement like personal hygiene products and food.

But like fighting with the toddler or the teenager, there are structures—procedures, policies, and practices—that the COs can and do control. And they exercise this control to intensify the dehumanizing nature of solitary confinement. Sometimes COs also bend the rules in order to create circumstances that are less dehumanizing. In the final chapter we explore some of the factors that can enhance the latter behavior and reduce the former.

We have a friend, Paul, who is incarcerated in the New York Department of Corrections. In a series of phone calls in the summer of 2020, Paul begged us to get an email account through JPay or Securis so that we could email him. Paul is in general population, but his story about email illustrates perfectly the ways in which COs manufacture rules in order to dehumanize prisoners.

A few weeks after we set up the email protocol, which by the way costs 33 cents per page of email, Paul called. (The phone calls, also run through Jpay or Securis, cost $5 per minute.) We asked him why he didn't return our last email, and he said, "The CO wouldn't let me go to kiosk."

In general population, just as in solitary confinement, at least for prisoners on AC status, the tablets they are allowed to use don't connect directly to the internet. Instead, they connect to a sort of intranet. We send an email to Paul. A CO reads the email, decides if it's OK for Paul to receive it, strips out any pages he doesn't want Paul to get, including in this case a PDF of the cover of our book *Policing Black Bodies*. Curious. And we still had to pay 33 cents to transmit the page even though Paul never saw it. Once the email message is sanitized and cleared, the CO transmits it to Paul's account and Paul can download it by plugging his tablet into a kiosk.

We asked Paul why the CO wouldn't let him access the kiosk. Paul replied, "He just didn't want to. . . . He just didn't want to."

He just didn't want to.

There is no policy that indicates that Paul can't access the kiosk. He's not in solitary confinement. The cell block isn't on lockdown. The CO just didn't feel like it.

We learned from our interviews as well as from Paul that communication, including phone calls, letters, and email, is one of the most important things that tethers the incarcerated to the free world. COs know this. In our interviews, many people incarcerated in solitary confinement talked about the ways that the COs controlled the mail. To spite them. To dehumanize them.

Shaniqua says, "They don't want to bring your mail. You might get mail at 9 [P.M.] and you get bad mail, and you need someone to talk to. Why not bring the mail earlier in the day so that if it's bad you can talk to someone about it?"

As Shaniqua points out, mail is the tether to the free world, to family, but it can also bring bad news. Though it's difficult to argue that COs intentionally hold bad mail and deliver it at night when they know the prisoner won't have anyone to share difficult news with or anyone to get support from, like the psych staff who work the eight-to-four shift, what we can say is that COs know the importance of mail. Whether they intentionally hold the mail or they push mail delivery down the list of chores for the day, ranking it of lesser importance, their control of the mail hurts people who are incarcerated in solitary confinement where it counts; it reminds them that *they don't matter. That they are out of sight and out of mind. That they are invisible.*

Tragically, COs also exert power and control by physically and sexually abusing prisoners. Why? Because they can, and they can get away with it.

CHAPTER 23

Choosing the Hole

IT TOOK ONLY a few minutes to confirm our expectations of the hole. Not only does the typical person not want to go to prison, no one wants to go to solitary confinement, or so we thought before we spent time there. Not only do some people who are incarcerated choose the hole for the obvious safety reasons that compel someone like Paul Manafort or someone who identifies in the LGBTQ+ community to request AC status, some people who are incarcerated intentionally committed misconducts in order to get sent to the hole. Why would a prisoner trade what little freedom they have, access to a tablet or TV, not having to put up with strip searches and showering in a cage, or being able to have as many honey buns as they would like in their cell for solitary confinement? Prisoners told us that they caught misconducts on purpose in order to hide or even as a strategy for being transferred to another prison.

We interviewed Jose during our first visit to SCI-Wannabee. Jose is a light-complected Hispanic man who refers to his ethnic identity as "Spanish." Jose is in prison for "financial crimes." He is a self-described entrepreneur. On the streets he sells drugs and weapons, which explains his twenty-year sentence. In prison, he "allegedly" sells contraband. Jose was sentenced to a ninety-day stint in the hole for running a store. "Allegedly" guards found $300 worth of commissary (food items) in his cell, which is more than four times over the "legal" limit of $70 in commissary. Of course Jose claims he is innocent. According to Jose, stores are forbidden not because of the exorbitant interest they extract but because of the resources a prisoner is able to amass. According to Jose, a store owner can become powerful, and this is threatening to the rules of the institution and especially to the correctional officers.

As Mary Buser learned from her conversation with Smitty, it's also possible that COs write tickets for too much commissary simply as part of a bed management system, a tool for moving prisoners out of general population and into solitary confinement in order to "free up" bed space in general population.

Solitary confinement can be a place to hide out if you owe a debt, perhaps to a store man like Jose. This didn't seem to us like a permanent solution to managing a debt, especially because one of the main disadvantages to being in the hole was not being able to work and earn money. Prisoners assured us that the "hide out in the hole" strategy could work because by the time you got out, if you served a long sentence of at least ninety days, other "associates" might step up and pay your debt, or the person to whom you owe the debt might himself have been sent to solitary confinement, even incarcerated next door to you, but without the ability to touch you. If you were released back to general population before him, you might be able to clear the debt. Or one or the other of you might even be transferred to another facility. For this strategy to work, prisoners carefully selected misconducts that would yield the desired sentence in solitary confinement.

As is documented by other researchers, incarcerated women sometimes use solitary confinement as a way to maintain the "family" structures they create as a strategy for surviving prison.[1] Some women might request to go to solitary confinement on AC status in the hopes of being celled with their "girlfriend," though staff assured us that they would not assign girlfriends to the same cell. Though Candy's girlfriend has already been released from prison, when we asked her why someone might choose solitary, she told us that some women commit misconducts in order to be sent to solitary confinement in the hopes that when they are released, they will be assigned to the same cell, or at least the same dorm or housing unit as their girlfriend. Being assigned to the same dorm in general population would greatly increase the amount of time two women in a relationship could spend together.

"Fifty" is a young Black man in his early thirties who identifies as "Puerto Rican and Black." He has caramel-colored skin. He is very thin and medium height. He wears his hair in long dreadlocks. When we interview Fifty, he is wearing his solitary confinement–issued orange jumpsuit, with a long-sleeved white undershirt, white socks, and white canvas slip-on tennis shoes, without laces. "DOC" is stenciled on the back of his orange jumpsuit. Fifty is dressed like every other person we interview who is incarcerated in solitary confinement.

We call him "Fifty" in honor of rapper 50-Cent, whose given name is Curtis Jackson. 50-Cent, the rapper, is known for his over-the-top style. Most of his lyrics are about alcohol, drugs, cars, and of course women. His stage name is meant to invoke both drugs and money. Fifty is also a rapper. He also has women. During the course of our interview, he repeatedly veered off course and wanted to show us the pictures he has of women. With his hands cuffed in front of him, propped on the narrow shelf on his side of the plexiglass in the visiting room, Fifty held up a stack of pictures as thick as a deck of cards. In order to keep Fifty on track during the interview, we would occasionally indulge him and look at his pictures. Some of the women he claimed were girlfriends or women who wanted to marry him. In some of the pictures, the women were naked. The stack of pictures was as worn as a well-used deck of cards or a dog-eared book. It's obvious he has spent many hours thumbing through them.

Like his namesake, Fifty also claims to have $75,000 in his commissary. We're not entirely sure that a person who is incarcerated can even have that much money in their commissary, and we would think if prisoner did have that much money, that they would be better off keeping it in free world bank accounts or even in an investment portfolio, but that's none of our business. Our business is to learn about Fifty's experiences in solitary confinement.

Fifty is, like his namesake, very entertaining. He has difficulty focusing on the interview questions and would rather talk about his women, which he does as he continuously flips through his picture pack, stopping every few photos to hold up a picture and tell us about the woman in the picture. He talks about his money. He rhymes and raps. Hattery considers ending the interview several times because it feels like Fifty is getting off having this chance to be so close to a woman, and because it feels like Fifty is just bullshitting. We trust very little of what Fifty says other than the details of his confinement.

Fifty has been in solitary confinement for about a year. Fifty chose solitary. Fifty told us that he engaged in behavior that caught him a misconduct with the goal of being transferred to a different facility. He was successful, and when we met him and we asked him what landed him in the hole, he revealed that he had deliberately committed a serious misconduct in a lower-security facility so that he would be transferred to maximum security at SCI-Wannabee, where we met him. His goal was to be housed in a different facility than the man who killed his brother. He feared he would kill the man if he saw him, and he didn't want to be tempted, and he didn't want to add any more years to his sentence. Other incarcerated people told us that this strategy was regularly employed by rival gang members or by prisoners trying to leave gangs.

We will return to Fifty's story in the last chapter, but one of the most compelling parts of his story, other than that he chose solitary confinement, is that he will complete his entire sentence while in solitary confinement. In fact, he was due to "max out" just a few weeks after we interviewed him. We confirmed with the COs that Fifty will be released directly from solitary confinement into the streets.

Fifty's story, as well as many others we heard, challenge our assumptions about solitary confinement, and they also force us to consider the bigger picture. If prisons, arguably the most secure institutions in the world, cannot keep people incarcerated there safe, and therefore they must subject themselves to all of the dehumanization and negative effects of solitary confinement in order to ensure their safety, we are failing at our mission. Moreover, despite all of the negative and dehumanizing elements of solitary confinement, the act of choosing, by either petitioning for AC status or committing a misconduct in order to be sentenced to solitary confinement on DC status, must be understood as an act of agency in an environment in which prisoners have very little power. In the framework of Robert Merton's strain theory, those who choose solitary can be understood as "innovators." Unable to achieve their goals, in this case

safety, or access to family, through traditional pathways (e.g., in general population), they choose solitary confinement as an innovative pathway toward
safety, avoiding a debt, or celling with a girlfriend or lover. The act of choosing
is, therefore, deeply significant. In Part 7, we will explore this tension and offer
a set of recommendations for reforming solitary confinement and prisons more
generally while making the case for significantly reducing the prison population and severely limiting the use of solitary confinement.

CHAPTER 24

Freelimo

THE SILENCING OF THE POLITICAL PRISONER

IN MANY WAYS, Fifty is a canary in the coal mine. If the safest place for someone in jail or prison is in solitary confinement, be that person a member of the LGBTQ+ community, a snitch, a police officer, or a pedophile, if we cannot keep that person safe in general population, then we must reform general population first. There is no world in which it makes sense to choose solitary confinement, even AC status, locked down twenty-three hours a day, showering in a cage, exercising in a dog kennel, with limited opportunities to see family members and loved ones, and never a contact visit unless you cannot be incarcerated safely anywhere else. So, we suggest, and we are indebted to Kevin Wright for this discussion, that first, we must continue to decarcerate, as we suggest in our book *Policing Black Bodies*. Second, we must ensure that everyone we incarcerate is provided maximum safety. We believe that once we have accomplished both of these goals, there will be no need for solitary confinement. It will have abolished itself.

That is, of course, unless the system of solitary confinement is not really about safety at all but rather is about removing Black bodies, especially those whose rhetoric shines a light on the racist foundation of the system of mass incarceration, not just from the social political economy but from any contact with the outside world. Rendered invisible. Socially dead. As was the case with a political prisoner we interviewed.

The process of interviewing Freelimo was fraught with controversy and tension. Everyone, including the members of the research team and COs and white shirts, agreed that Freelimo, a political prisoner serving a life sentence, who when we met him was housed on death row, had a story to tell. Freelimo had "status" as a violent Black Nationalist. COs considered him dangerous. They also said he was racist because he accused the white staff of being racist. He only agreed to an interview if that interview would be with Smith, the only Black man on the research team. We had to negotiate with the white shirts and COs about the best way to conduct the interview.

Adding to the complicated negotiations is the fact that Freelimo is confined to a wheelchair. COs and white shirts insisted that Smith be kept safe, and they strategized the particulars of the interview with this in mind. Unlike other incarcerated people, for example, Freelimo could not be moved to a noncontact visitor room because noncontact visitor rooms are not ADA compliant; in other words, his wheelchair couldn't be moved into a visiting room. Ultimately, they settled on wheeling Freelimo into a strip cage. Freelimo was under heavy escort. Instead of just the typical two-officer escort, four officers guarded Freelimo as they rolled his wheelchair into the cage where he was elaborately chained both to the wheelchair itself and to the cage.

Smith was, admittedly, a bit nervous about interviewing Freelimo.

After all this talk, Smith expected a big, hulky, threatening man. Instead, what he encountered is a man impacted by the passage of time and decades in prison. In fact, Freelimo was an older Black man, in his late sixties by the time we met him. He shared with Smith that his deteriorating physical condition, including his inability to walk and reliance on a wheelchair, is the result of a beating he received by correctional officers (COs).

In retrospect, this seemed like an awful lot of security for someone who can't walk.

Freelimo is not, in fact, someone to be afraid of. When he introduced himself he let it be known that he was looking forward to the interview because he has a story to tell.

And what a story it was! Freelimo recounted his recruitment as a teenager into the Black Panther Party. It was there, he said, that he was introduced not only to the ideology of the party but more broadly to Black Nationalism. According to Merriam Webster's dictionary, Black Nationalism believers are "members of a group of militant Blacks who advocate separatism from the whites and the formation of self-governing Black communities."[1]

Freelimo has been in prison for almost forty years. During this time, he has become an admirer of Mumia Abu-Jamal, a well-known political prisoner who was sentenced to death after being convicted of the murder of a police officer. After the moratorium on the death penalty, he was finally released from death row to serve out the rest of his life sentence in general population.

Much like Mumia, Freelimo identifies himself as a political prisoner.

In the course of the interview—which lasted approximately an hour—Freelimo discussed, using carefully worded language, the consequences for Black political prisoners like himself who have to struggle, on a daily basis, to gain and ensure some modicum of dignity in a prison world Freelimo argues is "built, fundamentally, on dehumanizing Black prisoners every day of the week."

He is rather proud, too, that he has gained a reputation as a "jailhouse lawyer" via the litigation and lawsuits he has managed to file on behalf of others. Not only is Freelimo a jailhouse lawyer, he is a prolific writer. He has a website that is maintained by friends in the "free world," and upon returning to our motel at the end of the day, Smith accessed the site. There, for all who enter, is his work: his art and his writings.

Freelimo says he is not a racist. He also says that he is educated to the extent that he understands his punishment as revenge for his crimes.

As Smith prepared to end the interview and call for the CO's to unlock the room, he could see that Freelimo, looking very sad, had tears in his eyes. Freelimo asked Smith to promise not only that he would look at his webpage but that he would spread the word that prisoners like him were suffering, being suffocated, inside the prison with no real voices to speak on their behalf.

People don't often think about the fact that solitary confinement takes place in all kinds of jails and prisons, including federal prisons that predominantly house those convicted of white-collar crimes, people like Bernie Madoff and Michael Cohen. But all jails and prisons have some capacity to house incarcerated people in segregation cells. In his memoir, *Disloyal: A Memoir; The True Story of the Former Personal Attorney to President Donald J. Trump*, Cohen describes his two stays in solitary confinement, both a result of COVID.

In his memoir, Cohen recounts the summer of 2020 and his experiences in solitary confinement. Because he was rated by the New York Bureau of Prisons as a nonviolent, low-risk inmate and because he has several underlying health conditions that constitute COVID comorbidity, Cohen was selected to be released early from prison and to serve his final months on home confinement. In preparation for his release, he was required to quarantine in solitary confinement, where he spent thirty-five days. He writes about the ways that COs burned him on things like refusing to allow him to use the hot-water tap to make coffee. This may not seem like such a hardship when compared with the dehumanization incarcerated people told us about, but in the context of a minimum-security federal prison, it certainly serves as an example of the tension between rights and privileges that is constantly negotiated between COs and people incarcerated in solitary confinement.

Ultimately, Cohen was released and offered the opportunity to serve out the remainder of his sentence in his midtown Manhattan apartment. However, not long after he was transferred to e-carceral custody, his home confinement status was revoked. Summoned to the courthouse to meet with his probation officer, he was presented, according to Cohen, with a set of conditions that he would have to agree to in order to finish serving his sentence from his home. If he did not agree to the conditions, he would be returned back to prison to serve the remainder of his sentence. Cohen writes that the first condition of his e-carceration would have prevented him from earning a living. Specifically, it would prohibit him from having any contact with the media or engaging in any writing projects. Just prior to this meeting, news had leaked that he was writing his memoir. Cohen is convinced that these specific conditions were developed by then attorney general William Barr and were nothing short of an attempt to use the power of the White House to silence him. When Cohen refused to agree to these conditions, he was not only returned to federal prison but once again confined in solitary. He argues that he was, in fact, being held a political prisoner in an attempt to silence him as a very high-profile and vocal critic of the sitting president.

So, you might be saying to yourself, but Michael Cohen is white. Yes, he is. And, some of the prisoners we interviewed in solitary confinement were also white. Just because COs burn white people who are locked in solitary confinement does not mean that the system isn't rooted in white supremacy or that the system doesn't produce racial antagonisms. As Chris Hayes argues in *A Colony in a Nation*:

"The Colony is overwhelmingly black and brown, but in the wake of financial catastrophe, deindustrialization, and sustained wage stagnation, the tendencies and systems of control developed in the Colony have been deployed over wider and wider swaths of working-class white America. Maintaining the division between the Colony and the Nation is treacherous precisely because the constant threat that the tools honed in the Colony will be wielded in the Nation; that tyranny and violence tolerated at the periphery will ultimately infiltrate the core. American police shoot an alarmingly high number of black people. But they also shoot a shockingly large number of white people."[2]

Whether you are a fan of Michael Cohen's or not, his story provides yet another testimony that confirms both the ways in which COs engage in behavior that exacerbates the dehumanizing conditions in solitary confinement and the ways in which solitary confinement is used against political prisoners.

CHAPTER 25

Extreme Violence

THE USE OF FORCE, either planned or unplanned, begins with the COs donning their cell extraction suits, preparing for a cross between a moon walk and war in Iraq. In full riot gear, COs approach the cell of the prisoner who will be the target of the force. Based on what we observed and were told by both prisoners and staff, the typical use of force involves pepper spray and/or a full cell extraction. We interviewed many people incarcerated in solitary confinement who had either been sprayed or been in a cell nearby when someone else was. Being sprayed is a bit of misnomer in that the CO doesn't spray pepper spray through the wicket and into the face of the person incarcerated in the cell. This would be difficult if not impossible to do without extracting the person from the cell, which is the purpose of spraying: to avoid having to do a cell extraction. Rather, COs fog bomb the cell with a canister of pepper spray. Without any ventilation other than the wicket, which is closed, the cell quickly fills up with gas that does more than burn the eyes; it burns the skin as well. Prisoners told us that COs would turn off the ventilation fan to the cell to prevent the fog from being cleared from the cell, intensifying its burn and lengthening its impact. One person who had been gassed in his solitary confinement cell told us that the smell of the gas stayed in his braids for months. Other people incarcerated in solitary confinement told us that they experienced collateral or downwind impact if their cell was anywhere near the cell of the person being sprayed.

Prisoners argued that COs used pepper spray to punish those they viewed as too demanding or whom they didn't like. We interviewed people incarcerated in solitary confinement who provided accounts of themselves and other incarcerated people being sprayed because they demanded their property or other rights such as access to their legal paperwork. Shaniqua told us that she had been sprayed for her attempts to advocate for the rights of a transwoman incarcerated in the unit. She remarked: "The COs don't need to get permission anymore to use pepper spray."

One afternoon, we observe an interaction that provides some support for Shaniqua's claim. We are sitting in LT's office at SCI-Wannabee when a SGT walks in and begins talking with LT about some kind of event. Perhaps because we are there or perhaps because they are simply using shorthand to refer to something they all know about, they don't reveal any of the details about what the event is. SGT says to LT: "[Inmate] Smith called me to his cell door and says he's going to do something unless he gets to see you." LT says he's not going to go to see Smith at his cell. SGT responds: "But he's going to do something."

LT's responds: "F-cking spray him, f-cking spray him, f-cking spray him and we'll deal with it later."

What's implied is that if the COs spray Smith and he files a complaint that the spraying was unwarranted, LT will "deal with it later." He will take responsibility on behalf of his team. Or, perhaps more likely, SGT will "fix" the paperwork so that any potential problem simply disappears.

For the most part, COs we interviewed believed that pepper spray was an important tool in controlling the behavior of people incarcerated in solitary confinement and maintaining safety in the unit. CO Lisa, a woman who works in the women's prison, sees it differently. CO Lisa says that she doesn't spray the women in the behavioral management unit (BMU) because it tends to escalate, not de-escalate, the situation. She says that newer COs, those with less experience, "follow the rules to the letter of the law" and they do use pepper spray. She hates having to work with them or work the shift after theirs because they are quick to escalate the situation, and that makes it harder for her to do her job.

To make her point, CO Lisa tells a story about a person incarcerated in solitary confinement who was on three-day restriction for self-mutilation. She says that if the prisoner does really well for two days, she will let them off the restriction a day early. In contrast, her colleagues will not only keep the incarcerated person on restriction for the full three days but spray her if she violates any of the terms of her restriction, including refusing to come out of her cell or take a shower. When her colleagues respond to this misbehavior by spraying a prisoner, not only will they be agitated, but in all likelihood so will all the other people incarcerated on the pod. Even if they are not directly impacted by the spray itself, the unit will be on lockdown and they will likely miss whatever privileges or activities they were entitled to that day, including showers or yard. The disruption in the highly routinized schedule of solitary confinement, the only way the person incarcerated there has to "mark time," tends to increase problematic behavior as well as complaints; prisoners may fight back by throwing urine or feces. CO Lisa, coming in to work on the next shift or even the next day, will face a steep uphill battle as she tries to de-escalate the situation and get things back under control. From her perspective, COs who are quick to spray make her job *more difficult, not easier.*

Cell extractions are perhaps the most severe form of punishment in solitary confinement units. As Terry Kupers describes, often cell extractions occur when officers escalate rather than de-escalate, as CO Lisa recommends:

Almost all prisoners in supermaximum security units tell me that they have trouble focusing on any task, their memory is poor, they have trouble sleeping, they get very anxious, and they fear they will not be able to control their rage. The prisoner may find himself disobeying an order or inexplicably screaming at an officer, when really all he wants is for the officer to stop and interact with him a little longer than it takes for a food tray to be slid through the slot in his cell door. Many prisoners in isolated confinement report it is extremely difficult for them to contain their mounting rage, and they fear losing their temper with an officer and being given a ticket that will result in a longer term in punitive segregation. Eventually, and often rather quickly, a prisoner's psychiatric condition deteriorates to the point where he inexplicably refuses to return his food tray, cuts himself, or pastes paper over the small window in his solid metal cell door, causing security staff to trigger an emergency "takedown" or "cell extraction." In many cases where I have interviewed the prisoner after the extraction, he confides that voices he was hearing at the time commanded him to retain his tray, paper his window, or harm himself. The more vehemently correctional staff insist the disturbed prisoner return a food tray, come out of his cell, or remove the paper from the cell door so they can see inside, the more passionately the disturbed prisoner shouts: "You're going to have to come in here and get it (or me)!" The officers go off and assemble an emergency team—several large officers in total body protective gear who, with a plastic shield, are responsible for doing cell extractions of rowdy or recalcitrant prisoners. The emergency team appears at the prisoner's cell door and the coordinator asks gruffly if the prisoner wants to return the food tray, or do they have to come in and get it? While a more rational prisoner would realize he had no chance of withstanding this kind of overwhelming force, the disturbed prisoner puts up his fists in mock boxing battle position and yells, "Come on in, if you're tough enough!" The officers barge in all at once, each responsible for pushing the prisoner against the wall with the shield or grabbing one of his extremities.[1]

After the prisoner is forcibly removed from the cell, they are placed in an observation cell. They are stripped and put into a straitjacket, which is called a "security smock," and given nothing other than a security blanket. What makes a blanket a "security" blanket, you might ask. It's not because it brings a sense of security as a child's "blankie" might. It is named for the fact that it is sewn in such a way that it can't be torn or dethreaded. It can't be used to harm oneself or an officer, nor can it be used in any way to commit suicide. [Or for that matter to fish.]

The prisoner is "secured" rather than "secure."

Once in the observation cell, people are typically incarcerated there, under constant video surveillance, for twenty-four hours, even longer if they are extracted on a Friday afternoon and there is no psych staff to conduct an evaluation until Monday. During this time they are entitled to, but might not always receive, a "safety meal," which is limited to finger foods only. When we asked prisoners to describe the infamous finger food diet, they told us that it was limited to only foods that can be eaten without utensils. COs denied that there was such a meal.

Cell extractions are violent and brutal. Prisoners are often injured during the process and the safety risk is high for COs as well. Cell extractions are extremely disruptive to others incarcerated in the pod as well. Yet many COs told us that cell extractions were the best part of their job because conducting a cell extraction is what they were trained for. The implication here is that they were not trained to deliver and pick up trays or escort prisoners to showers or yard. They were trained to maintain safety and security. They were trained for the war. Perhaps this is why so many COs grew to deeply resent the routine work that they did over and over again, hour after hour, day after day. The sensory deprivation of the routine was dehumanizing to the COs as well, and in ways that brought even greater harm to the incarcerated people they are charged to protect.

Like their counterparts in the free world, police officers who use excessive force on unarmed citizens, corrections officers carry out brutality against prisoners with impunity.

Several people we interviewed who were incarcerated in solitary confinement told us about the beatings carried out against them, but none of the experiences they shared with us matched the story of our friend Paul who is incarcerated in the New York Department of Corrections.[2] On October 28, 2012, Paul Henry was attacked by a gang of twelve corrections officers and was "beat . . . to the ground [and] repeatedly kicked . . . with steel toed boots to his upper body, groin area, head and both of his legs."[3]

Henry was hospitalized for eleven days in an Albany, New York, hospital (Albany Medical Center) for the injuries that resulted from the gang attack. The injuries were horrendous. Based on the medical report obtained from the family, he suffered at least nine cracked ribs and a collapsed lung. Henry's facial injuries included lacerations all across his face.

Mary Buser describes observing a beating in a hallway on Rikers Island as she was returning to her office one night:

> On a stretch of corridor common to the men's jail, our conversation was interrupted by angry shouts. To our left were long rows of bars, and on the other side empty patches of darkened space. Behind the bars, four or five COs were surrounding a male inmate. "No, man! I didn't do nothin'!" shouted the inmate. "Shut the f-ck up!" They were pushing the young

man into a corner where a set of bars intersected. All we could see of him were his jeans and sneakers as his legs were being spread apart—"Nooh!" he shouted. Just then, a white shirted captain coming down the hall spotted us. "Move along!" he ordered. No smile, no "good evening" nod. We hesitated momentarily. "Keep moving!" We did just that. As we neared the end of the corridor, Wendy said, "They're going to beat the crap out of him."[4]

COs, like many police officers, feel empowered to do anything they want to people who are incarcerated, who are defined, by law, as less than fully human, as prisoners of the state. And why wouldn't they? For COs and police officers alike there are very few countermessages, and there is rarely any accountability or consequence.

The murder of George Floyd by Minneapolis police officers was unconscionable.[5] But no less unconscionable is what Forsyth County, North Carolina Jail corrections officers Sarah Poole, Lavette Williams, Edward Roussel, Antonio Woodley and nurse Michelle Heughins did to John Neville resulting in his death.[6] In the video that was released in response to public pressure, Neville is shown on the floor of his cell apparently suffering from a medical condition. The four officers and nurse put a "spit mask" on Neville and in the video they can be seen trying to lift Neville and get him into a restraint chair. In the process of trying to lift Neville, the officers fold his legs upward behind him. He is then put in the restraint chair. According to an article in the *New York Times*, Neville is complaining that he can't breathe and the officers remove him from the restraint chair—though this takes several minutes because no one can get his handcuffs off—and lay him on the ground. Much like the murder of George Floyd: "In the second video, Mr. Neville is being held face down by several officers. They struggle to remove his handcuffs as Mr. Neville cries out, "I can't breathe." At one point an officer says, "You're breathing cause you're talking" and "You need to relax."[7]

The officers leave Neville on the ground, and the nurse peers through the window and reports that he looked OK, but she couldn't tell if he was breathing. Shortly after that, she fails to be able to find his heart rate. John Neville died after fewer than twenty-four hours in custody.

Corrections officers' brutality extends beyond these aforementioned examples. The point to be made is that almost never are these officers held accountable for their violent acts. Like police officers in the free world, the corrections officers have protections, both from their unions, which according to our friend Claude Marks are extremely powerful, and from their ability to enact retaliation against those harmed as well as the witnesses. That is to say, prisoners who do come forward with their grievances are often disciplined—including by sending them to solitary confinement, extending time they will remain in solitary confinement if they are already there, or beating them, often nearly to death as was the case with Paul Henry. The same Paul Henry who now complains that the COs won't let him get his email from the kiosk. Coincidence?

These acts of violence and brutality are so common in prisons, and in solitary confinement in particular, that they hardly garner notice outside of reporters, journalists, and scholars researching and writing about issues of incarceration. But isn't it our duty to hold corrections personnel responsible—as we do police in the free world—for the safety of those in their care?

We are certainly not the first to write about the dehumanization that people incarcerated in solitary confinement experience. And there is no amount of space that is too much to spend talking about the dehumanizing conditions and arbitrary rules that COs invent to exacerbate what is already a punishment that is considered by many, including us, to be so extreme that it should only be used in the rarest of circumstances, and then only for the most limited amount of time.

What fewer people talk or write about are the ways in which the conditions in solitary confinement also dehumanize the COs, and the ways in which dehumanization creates a cycle of violence that both the prisoners and the COs participate in, even if not equally.

Let us be clear. We do not endorse the behavior that COs exhibit toward prisoners. We heard them and saw them treat human beings like animals. The entire premise of solitary confinement is predicated on a notion that we find fundamentally flawed: that it is acceptable to lock human beings in cages, in total isolation from other human beings, and deny them not just civil rights but basic necessities like food and clean water and toothpaste, human rights. Despite all of this, prisoners like Fifty *choose* solitary confinement.

We argue over and over in this book and elsewhere for accountability. But until the day in which the use of solitary confinement is significantly limited if not eliminated entirely, which we ultimately advocate for, as long as prisoners like Fifty *choose* solitary confinement as the safest place for them to serve out their sentences, understanding the circumstances that produce cruel and unusual punishment can provide insight into creating structures and circumstances that restore some modicum of humanity to life in solitary confinement, for both those incarcerated there and the staff. Additionally, lessons from solitary confinement can be translated to other places and spaces where inhumanity seems inevitable but does not have to be. Ironically, one of those places is the Behavioral Management Unit, a specialized solitary confinement pod where we spent many days, in SCI-Women.

PART FIVE

Marina's Story

"Do you think I'll die here?"

—Marina, prisoner in the BMU, SCI-Women.

And the answer is likely yes.

CHAPTER 26

Welcome to SCI-Women

WE FIRST VISITED SCI-Women in the summer of 2017. Given our research expertise in gender, we were particularly interested in the experiences of women in solitary confinement, both the people incarcerated there and the staff. Although we conducted interviews and observations in each of the different pods in the solitary confinement unit, by visiting SCI-Women twice (during the summers of 2017 and 2019) we had the unique opportunity to concentrate our observations and focus our interviews with staff and people incarcerated in a specialized solitary confinement unit: the Behavioral Management Unit (BMU). As a result, in addition to the many interviews we conducted across the various solitary confinement units at SCI-Women, we have many hours of ethnographic observation in the BMU as well as interviews with COs, unit managers, and counselors who work in the BMU and, of course, people who are confined in the BMU. Thankfully there are only a small number of women who are incarcerated there, but that also meant that we each conducted separate formal and informal interviews with some of the same women, two years apart. Marina's story is one of the most compelling.

The BMU is perhaps the saddest and most depressing place we have ever been. Yet we knew from our first visit in that summer of 2017 that there were important stories to tell and much more to learn about the BMU.

The BMU is an isolation or solitary confinement unit. In that way it is not unique. What makes it different is that the BMU functions as a specialized unit for prisoners who the COs argue can't live safely or be well managed in general population, and who the psych staff have determined have behavioral or personality disorders but not severe and unmanaged mental illness; thus they are not candidates for the diversionary treatment unit (DTU). In diagnostic terms, people incarcerated in the BMU may have psychological diagnoses that include borderline personality disorder, bipolar disorder, and especially attachment disorders, as many of the women we interviewed likely did. Despite not qualifying for the DTU, psyche staff recommend that some people with personality disorders and behavior management issues, particularly those who engage in severe self-harm, be incarcerated in the BMU where it is believed they would benefit from the additional programming available to them in this specialized, solitary confinement unit.

Walking into SCI-Women itself, through the visitor's gate, and even entering the solitary confinement unit, the tension that you feel at any of the men's prisons, especially SCI-Wannabee, is noticeably absent. COs and prisoners banter with each other. There is a support dog training program, and as you walk across the "campus," as they call it, to the solitary confinement unit or to the chow hall for lunch, you can see the people who are incarcerated here training their dogs or just taking them for a walk across the yard. There is a garden where incarcerated people who are so inclined can grow vegetable and flowers. We learn that some of the vegetables even make it into the food served in the dining hall. Inside the solitary confinement unit, security doors to the pods are often left propped open so as to avoid having to "bother" the officer in the bubble to buzz you in, something we never witnessed at SCI-Wannabee. Some women are allowed to roam around freely inside the pod where their cell is located. It's not a happy place, but it is much less tense than the men's prisons. Security seems to be less of a concern.

Prisons that house men and women are distinct in large part because of the people they house. For example, women are far less likely to be incarcerated than men, and though Black women are the fastest-growing group being incarcerated, there are fewer racial disparities in women's prisons than in men's. The vast majority of women who are incarcerated are locked up for nonviolent offenses, many related to their attempts to escape abuse and trauma. A report cosponsored by *Ms Magazine* and the Georgetown Law Center indicates that 85 percent or more of incarcerated girls and women were sexually or physically abused prior to their incarceration.[1] The percent of girls and women with trauma histories among the incarcerated is nothing short of extraordinary. Though there are women incarcerated for violent crimes, in the words of CO Lisa, "the rest are here for crimes related to leaving the abuse": drug use, sex work, passing bad checks, and things like that. So, even in a maximum-security prison like SCI-Women, the incarcerated population is very, very different from what we see in a men's prison, especially at SCI-Wannabee, the largest maximum-security prison in the state. And, this likely accounts for the relative lax security that we observe the moment we pass through the gates.

SCI-Women was built in the early twentieth century, as the first and only facility in the state to incarcerate girls and women. Today it can house 1,500 women, and on the days we visited it was at 92 percent of its capacity. In stark contrast to SCI-Wannabee, the road leading up to the gate is tree-lined, manicured lawns flanking both sides. The main administration building looks like it belongs on a boarding school campus, complete with a bell tower. Inside the administration building, the ambiance continues, solid hardwood floors, chandeliers—all of the trappings of a turn-of-the-century mansion. Looking more like a college campus than a prison, the grounds are beautifully manicured; housing units that look more like old dorms scatter the acreage. The Allegheny Mountains provide a resort- or spa-like backdrop.

It looks like a place you would want to stay awhile if it weren't for the electrified fences and razor wire.

The gatehouse is a little building that sits outside the fences and razor wire. Staff on their way to work pass through metal detectors in the house. So do researchers. We arrive, hand over our driver's licenses, pass through a metal detector, and are banded with a green wristband, and once we are cleared, we wait for our escort. Unlike the reception building at SCI-Wannabee, the gatehouse at SCI-Women is very small, about the size of a small convenience store at a gas station.

All of the other prisons where we conducted research have a very large reception room, with rows and rows of chairs, seating anywhere from fifteen to fifty, depending on the size of the prison. The reception room also has bathrooms and vending machines and machines for loading up the cards that can be used to make food and drink purchases in the visiting room on the inside. There are no vending machines or bathrooms or card machines in this gatehouse, which would be quaint if it weren't for the metal detector and view of the tower where COs stand at alert with pump shotguns.

Certainly the gatehouse at SCI-Women was built this way in order to remain consistent with the architectural design of the prison, but we also think about the small size. Comparatively few women are in prison—in most states women make up less than 10 percent of the overall incarcerated population—and perhaps there are fewer visitors, and so there is no need for a bigger space. Perhaps the gatehouse is meant to be less daunting, creating a more "natural" environment for children coming to see their mom.

On our short walk to the solitary confinement unit we notice a relatively large building, a set of small trailers, and a fenced-in playground. The playground has a brightly colored playset with places to climb and play and hide and slide. There is also a piece of play equipment that is reminiscent of the playgrounds of our youth—we are pretty sure it doesn't pass code. It's designed to look like a man (with a yellow head and a red hat) who is pushing a wheelbarrow. The man and the wheelbarrow create a space for children to climb and hide and play. The large building, which we do not go in, is the regular visiting room for families and friends who come to visit their loved ones.

The trailers, we learn, are part of an initiative called Project Impact. Project Impact allows incarcerated mothers and their visiting children to have intense visits meant to simulate time at home; children spend time alone with their moms in the trailer, with no staff or other adults present, where they can cook and play just like they might once they get home to an apartment or a trailer. We didn't get a chance to see Project Impact for ourselves, but when we listened to the women we interviewed talk about their children, we can imagine the difference it can make, easing the time not only on the inside but also as they transition home.

In order to access the solitary confinement unit one must pass through another locked gate which bounds the walkway to the solitary confinement unit itself. The pathway is one long, narrow cage, fencing and razor wire–lined rather than tree-lined. Gates open and close automatically, controlled by an officer deep inside the unit whose job it is to buzz us (and the staff) in and out.

We pass through a double slider directly into the visitor waiting room of the solitary confinement unit. To the immediate left is a strip cage and an office for the CO working in the visitor room. Unlike at SCI-Wannabee, it's not a bubble, just an office. Directly to the left past the COs' office is a conference room where we sometimes sit for a moment, furiously writing our ethnographic notes. We learn from the COs that this is also where disciplinary hearings take place.

There are two bathrooms, one marked "men" and one marked "women." Oddly enough, unlike at SCI-Wannabee, there is no mention of a Koala station. What's striking about the lack of a Koala station at SCI-Women is the fact that the vast majority of women (80 percent) who are incarcerated have minor children with whom they were living immediately prior to their arrest, twice the rate of incarcerated men (40 percent). So our initial reaction is one of surprise. This seems counterintuitive. Perhaps, though, this is indicative of the experiences of children of the incarcerated. When men go to prison, the vast majority of their minor children live with either the children's mother or their own mother. When women go to prison, their children either live with their grandmother or they are moved into the foster care system, which is the case for nearly 30 percent of all children of incarcerated mothers. Perhaps the Koala station at SCI-Wannabee is suggestive of the fact that mothers are far more likely to bring their children to see their incarcerated father, even when he is locked in solitary confinement on AC status, than grandmothers or foster parents are to bring a mother's children to visit when she is locked in solitary confinement, even on AC status.

The visitor room is very small, maybe 15 × 15, or the size of a very small post-office or bodega or convenience store at a rural exit off the highway. There are five noncontact visiting rooms (A, B, C, D, and E). There are five chairs, a table, and a toy for a preschooler. Unlike the visiting room at SCI-Wannabee, which is at least five times larger, there are no books or magazines.

We ponder the size and minimalist nature of the visiting room at SCI-Women, as compared with SCI-Wannabee. Perhaps it is because there are so few women, relatively speaking, incarcerated in solitary confinement, and thus there are few people to visit them. Staff tell us that the women sentenced to the hole serve short sentences, on average thirty days. Given that women on DC status only get one visit per month, perhaps their family members don't think it's worth it to visit, since unlike in general population, the visit will be limited to a noncontact conversation via a phone or by hollering through the Plexiglas in one of the noncontact visiting rooms. It just might not be worth the trouble. Perhaps the main reason is because the majority of women in solitary confinement are held in either the DTU or the BMU in long-term isolation and these women, who are suffering from severe mental illness or who exhibit severe behavior problems, aren't the kind of people who get visitors anyway. Staff tell us that for the women in the BMU, with one exception, they don't get visitors. They don't get phone calls. They don't even get letters.

Legal phone calls for all people incarcerated at SCI-Women, including those in general population, are held in the visiting rooms in the solitary confinement unit, and while we were there, many women came in to receive calls. By and large, incarcerated women pose much less of a security risk and the procedures, so different from SCI-Wannabee, are just another indicator of this. During our time in SCI-Women we observed, on many occasions, a prisoner coming from general population to the solitary confinement unit to receive a legal phone call. Unaccompanied by an officer, the prisoner is buzzed in, just as we were, into the solitary confinement unit. First they speak to the CO in charge, then sit, waiting alongside us, uncuffed and unshackled. When the lawyer calls to the front desk, the call is routed to a visiting room and the incarcerated person waiting on the call simply goes in, shuts the door, and has their phone call. We thought this set-up made some sense because it offers more privacy than a phone call taken on a pay phone in a day room or in the yard where others can eavesdrop. But the women who come to receive phone calls tell us they hate this procedure because solitary confinement is very near the front gate, which means it's a long walk from their dorms.

In the visiting room there is also a vending machine stocked with sugary and salty snacks and drinks, including Diet Coke, Dr. Pepper, and iced tea. Several of us purchase drinks the first day. Dr. Pepper is the most popular, though Hattery continues to prefer Diet Coke, and when we leave after the first day there is only one can remaining. When we return the following day, the Dr. Pepper has been restocked. We wonder who has been there overnight to ensure that we can purchase the drinks of our choice. Whomever it is, we are grateful for the vending machine in the visiting room not only because we have regular access to it but also because the vending machines in the staff dining hall only take prepaid cards that staff, like students on college campuses, can load up with funds to purchase everything from pop to chips to prepared foods like hamburgers and macaroni and cheese that can be warmed in the microwave if the food offered at a meal is less than satisfying. Which it almost always is.

The hole in SCI-Women is laid out much like the solitary confinement unit in SCI-Wannabee. There is a secure door into the actual unit, a long hallway with bathrooms, a library, once again without any books, staff offices, and four pods, A,B,C, and D. The bubble is above, with access through a secure door. Conveniently, the DTU is on D Pod and the BMU is on B Pod. Makes it easy to remember where you are going, we guess.

It's not just the lax security features that are notable in SCI-Women. The gender dynamics in men's and women's prisons are also complex and interesting. Overwhelmingly COs and many "white shirts" see prisons as a workplace best suited to men. This is not at all surprising given the strong influence of the military and law enforcement on the culture of prisons, two professions that are also highly gender segregated. Many men we interviewed at SCI-Wannabee told us in no uncertain terms that they resented women as coworkers, with the exception of psych staff, who are almost all women. Mental health was constructed as "women's work," but the work of a CO was men's work. This was especially true in men's prisons, where men viewed women COs as a burden. Specifically, the Prison Rape Elimination Act (PREA) mandated that all strip searches be conducted by same-gender COs, and thus women COs were defined "useless" because they couldn't perform some of the key duties associated with the job. The strip search is one of the most intimate and yet routine parts of daily life in solitary confinement. If women are not able to participate in such an essential function, then they are defined as useless. What's so interesting about the exclusion of women based on their inability to participate in the strip search in men's prisons is that men are not similarly excluded in women's prisons. Men believe they have every right to work in women's prisons and have devised a "work-around" that could just as easily be incorporated into the work in men's prisons. This fact alone tells us a great deal about the gender discrimination women face in the work of the CO, especially in solitary confinement units. Mixed-gender teams in women's prisons simply configure their work so that while the woman CO is conducting the "strip," the man CO stands off to the side of the cell or shower or strip cage, out of sight of the prisoner. Once the strip is completed, the man CO jumps right back into the work of cuffing or uncuffing the prisoner, attaching the dog leash, and escorting them to the yard, the shower, or the interview room. There is nothing inefficient or cumbersome about this process, and we observed it dozens of times. Yet, when we interviewed COs and white shirts in men's prisons, they exclaimed that a woman CO would be like working "one man down." Interesting. To read more about the gendered work of the CO in men's prisons, we invite the reader to check out our paper "Sex Logics."[2]

All of the staff we interviewed, including many who had worked in both men's and women's facilities, confirmed that working in a men's prison is very different from working in a women's prison. Unit Manager Tom, who is in charge of the BMU at SCI-Women, articulates what many other staff, including COs, expressed to us: "When you tell a man 'no' he follows your orders. When you tell a woman 'no' that's just the beginning of the conversation. She wants to know, 'Why?' She'll go and ask everyone else she can find to say 'yes,' she'll file seventeen grievances and tell seven other people."

Most staff said that if there were a men's prison closer, they would transfer there, that the only reason they worked in SCI-Women was because it was close to home. Yet, in the same breath they would say that they felt safer working in SCI-Women and for many, especially Unit Manager Tom, counselor Mark, and CO Lisa, all of whom worked exclusively in the BMU, they felt they were making more of a difference.

CHAPTER 27

The Women's Hole

JUST LIKE AT SCI-Wannabee, our visit to SCI-Women begins with recruiting people who are incarcerated in solitary confinement for interviews. We enter A Pod, because it makes sense to start with the first letter of the alphabet. The unit manager, Tom, lets us in and tells us to go ahead and make our pitch moving cell to cell. He hangs out on the ground floor near the office talking with the counselor, Mark. Tom and Mark don't pay much attention to us and there are no COs around. Another indicator that safety and security are less of a concern when the people incarcerated here, even in solitary confinement, are women.

It's very dark on A Pod. Not that relaxing kind of dark you have in a spa, but more like the kind of dark that reminds us of sadness.

It's about 8:30 in the morning, and though breakfast was at 6:30, no one is awake. At the first few cells, we knock on the cell door to get the occupant's attention. A few women acknowledge our presence but wave us off, not wanting to come and talk. At one cell a Black woman comes to the door. She seems to be in her twenties or thirties. She's thin and very agitated. Bouncing around, asking why we are here. We tell her about the project, but she's not necessarily interested in an interview; she's interested in getting our attention because she has a black eye. Her face looks mottled. She wants to get medical treatment. Everyone hears her pleading with us for help. Another prisoner on the pod hollers back telling her to "shut up." The unit manager Tom and the counselor Mark ignore her. After we finish recruiting in A Pod, we ask to see the list of everyone currently incarcerated in A-pod. The list includes the ID photos of each prisoner and she looks about the same in her intake photo as she looks when we encounter her at her cell door. The discoloration on her face isn't from being beat up; it's apparently an inconsistency in her complexion. But it's hard to tell when we can only see her by peering through the small window on her cell door.

We move up and down the A Pod tier, making sure we stop at each cell that is occupied, which is about one-third of capacity or eight to ten cells. With the exception of a few prisoners who come to the door, we have very few interactions. A white woman who is at the first cell we approach talks with us and agrees to interview. We see her later, being escorted to the visiting room. She is also young, maybe twenty-five, attentive, eager but not too aggressive. Polite. Interested. We're not surprised when she agrees to the interview.

Over and over again we encounter cells holding women who are in their beds, covered from head to toe with blankets, including over their heads, sleeping. Or appearing to sleep. It's late July. The temperature today will approach ninety-five degrees, yet they are wrapped up like babies, in cocoons. Are they tired? Is this what depression looks like? Other women have pulled their mattresses down on the floor, their cocoons, their nests, built, constructed near the cell door. We ask the COs about it and they tell us that the women aren't supposed to sleep on the floor, but as long as they don't cause trouble, they allow them to. It's cooler, they say. In an interview later that day we learn that the prison doesn't have air conditioning and that some women try to get to solitary confinement during the hot summer months where there is AC. But the week or so before we got there, the AC had gone out in the hole. Though it is comfortable the days we are there, apparently this strategy of sleeping on the floor to stay cool has persisted. What's interesting is the blankets, the cocoon. The claim is that the women are sleeping on the floor to stay cool, but they are covered in blankets. So the question is, do the blankets create comfort? Is it about hiding? Covering? Rendering invisible? Is it like the "weighted" blanket that people in the free world buy to ease anxiety? So they sleep on the floor not so much to stay cool but to keep cool enough that they don't swelter in the blanket? Like people in the free world who turn on the AC extra high at night in the summer so that they can sleep under blankets or light a fire in their gas fire place?

A prisoner we meet from C Pod tells us that they sleep on the floor so that they can hear better, hear the footsteps of the guards approaching their cells. Hear the women below them talking. Or maybe this is the same phenomenon that Vivian Aranda-Hughes and colleagues describe.

Aranda-Hughes and her colleagues conducted observations of a women's solitary confinement unit, interviewed administrators, and conducted focus groups with staff, both officers and mental health professionals, working in the unit. Their research reveals that just as women in general population do, much more so than men, women incarcerated in solitary confinement develop and rely on prison relationships in order to survive. In order to establish and maintain relationships, Aranda-Hughes and colleagues find that women will stay up all night talking. According to the staff whom they interviewed, the women prefer to stay up at night talking because it is quiet, which facilitates communication through cell doors and toilet pipes, and because there are fewer staff working who might overhear their conversations. The staff whom Aranda-Hughes and colleagues interviewed reported that in order to stay up all night the women hoarded their psychotropic medications so that they could take larger doses during the day, the side effect of which was sleepiness. Thus, they slept the day away so that they could stay up all night.[1]

Perhaps this is exactly what was happening in A Pod.

★ ★ ★

Just as in SCI-Wannabee, most cells have a shelf outside of the cell door where, in SCI-Women, we find toiletries. The women are not allowed to have their shampoo, conditioner, hair gel, or deodorant in their cells, so it is stored outside the cell on a shelf for their trips to the shower. Shaniqua, who is clearly the expert on all things solitary confinement, tells us about the shower process:

> We only get ten minutes for a shower, every other day, which is ridiculous, and we have to go to the shower fully dressed and take our clothes off in the shower and hang them up so they don't get wet. We have to shove our clothes into the holes in the cage and hope they don't fall out and get wet. [Our observation of the shower indicates that the only place to hang anything is just as she describes.] When we leave our cells we take our towels and wrap our shampoo and soap in them and carry them to the shower—it's awkward . . . and it takes time; they count that against our ten minutes, you know? The time to take off our clothes, push them through the holes in the cage . . . that counts against our ten minutes . . . and just three showers a week. I mean it's gross.

This is one of the key gender differences we observe. In the men's prisons where we observe showers, the men take off their clothes in their cells—it's part of the strip search—and then they are handcuffed and escorted, wrapped in their towels, to the shower.

Is the practice of escorting the women fully clothed to the shower a strategy for being compliant with the regulations laid out in PREA? So that men COs and staff can't be accused of seeing a naked woman? If they are strip searched before they are escorted, that seems very inefficient, because they would strip and then dress again to be transferred to the shower where they undress. Again. Maybe the COs aren't doing the strips when they move women to the shower. We didn't observe any escorts to the shower so we are unable to say for sure.

On a few shelves we see glasses. We wonder, what good are glasses if you can't have them in your cell? It's a busy day, and we forget to ask why. We will find out the next time.

"Juvenile cuffs only" reads a sign outside a few cells throughout solitary confinement. Marina has a sign like this on her door. We ask Unit Manager Tom about the sign, confirming that all the women are over eighteen because we aren't allowed to interview juveniles, and he tells us no, that means that they are small boned and can only be cuffed with juvenile cuffs.

Ok, what does it mean that we, in the United States, have a separate kind of handcuffs for juveniles?

We leave A Pod and we're very unsatisfied. We have recruited maybe two participants, and everyone else is doing their best to sleep through the day. Again, the question is, are they depressed, or is this the same kind of coping mechanism that we in the free world use to deal with grief? Or is this, as Aranda-Hughes and colleagues describe, a strategy to allow them to stay up all night and communicate with their inside "family?"

We head, with Unit Manager Tom and Counselor Mark, to C Pod, and it's empty. The women are all in the yard. We walk through C Pod to be sure that there isn't anyone in their cells whom we should recruit before we go to the yard. We notice that several of the women have pictures of children taped to the walls of their cells.

What's it like to see only the image of your child and not be able to hold her or talk to her?

Finding no one in C-Pod, we ask if we can recruit in the yard, and Unit Manager Tom and Counselor Mark reply, "Sure!" So they take us out to the yard. They warn us that C Pod is lively. Loud.

The yard, which we have described elsewhere, is the same here. Exiting through the back door of the pod, there is access to the yard, which just as in SCI-Wannabee is a series of dog kennels. They are maybe 5 feet wide, 10 feet long, and 10 feet high. There is a wicket on each cage for cuffing and uncuffing the women. In the cage they are both uncuffed and unshackled. This is distinct from the yard at SCI-Wannabee, where the prisoners are all handcuffed and shackled even in the dog kennel–style cage. We guess the COs at SCI-Women believe that when the women are in a dog kennel it's like being in the shower or their cell: they are in a cage, so there is no need for cuffs and shackles—yet another gender difference and evidence of less concern by the COs at SCI-Women about safety and security.

We learn later that the BMU and DTU have "special" yard cages. What makes them special, we are told, is that they have yoga mats in them. At some point we go out into the BMU yard to take a look. The mats are like the kinder mats we had in kindergarten for nap time.

When we enter the yard we immediately observe two prisoners caged next to each other huddled in the back corner talking and perhaps exchanging a little contraband. This pattern is repeated in every other cage. We approach the first cage and invite a woman who is engaged in a conversation with her neighbor at the back of the cage to talk with us, and suddenly it gets very quiet. Clearly the women are all listening to the pitch we give at the door to the cage. Quickly, word begins to spread. One woman we approach is reluctant to participate, and all of the other women holler at her, encouraging her to tell her story. She agrees. As we move down the line, the recruitment shifts to women wanting to tell their stories right there, in the yard. We have to remind them that this is just the time to recruit. We will hear their stories later, when we interview them in private.

All of the women in the yard from C Pod are Black.

Unit Manager Tom stays with us in the yard while we recruit the C Pod women, and it's clear that he has an easy rapport with many of them. While we are on one end of the yard recruiting, he is on the other end of the yard talking with the caged women. Though we can't hear the conversation, it seems like it is a combination of casual conversation and the prisoners making requests of Unit Manager Tom. One woman asks for her property; another says she needs to see psych. Someone else complains about the soap.

We observe this give-and-take between the prisoners and Unit Manager Tom and Counselor Mark many times over the next few days. Though some of it may be put on for our entertainment, maybe Unit Manager Tom and Counselor Mark are more attentive when we are there than when we aren't, but it can't be entirely artificial. It's much too natural, the conversation flowing too easily, for it to be entirely for show. Much like conducting a peer observation in a colleague's classroom, when the students are inevitably on their best behavior, when the interchange is casual, and personal, referencing previous events or conversations, you know it isn't entirely for show.

CHAPTER 28

Meeting the Mass Killer

SOLITARY CONFINEMENT IS HER "HOME"

ON OUR FIRST TRIP to SCI-Women, we had the opportunity to interview one of the most notorious women incarcerated at SCI-Women: "Ms. Rambo," as news accounts have dubbed her.

Ms. Rambo is a petite white woman in her late fifties, with graying hair. The years of incarceration are worn on her face. At the time of our interview she was incarcerated in a "step-down" unit where she had more privileges and more out of cell time as she prepared to transition from solitary confinement to general population. As part of the protocols of this unit, we interviewed her at a table in a day room without handcuffs, shackles, or a CO present. We assumed she was no different than other women we had interviewed, women who were sent to prison for stealing money or driving the getaway car of their partner, or simply having an untreated drug addiction.

We sat across from each other and just talked.

She was unremarkable as she spoke of climate change and drew on paper with a pencil little figures depicting "people" who were "out there." This activity and her references to Hitler led us to believe that she was "off" a bit but not by much. Several news accounts of her trial note that she suffers from schizophrenia, but according to staff at SCI-Women, it is so well managed that she is not restricted to living in a unit like the DTU, which is reserved for those with severe—and unmanaged—mental illness.

Ms. Rambo is smart. She made sense, and she, at least in our interactions with her, seemed harmless, though we were curious about her history given that she is one of SCI-Women's longest "residents," having been incarcerated there since 1985. Because our general practice was not to inquire about the crimes of which the people we interviewed were convicted, upon returning to our motel after the long day of being inside, we immediately logged on to the computer and looked her up.

Much to our surprise, this petite, middle-aged white woman, Ms. Rambo, the woman we sat across the table from, without handcuffs or shackles, and with whom we talked about climate change, was one of the first women mass shooters in U.S. history.

Around 4 p.m. on [a] Wednesday [in] 1985, [Ms. Rambo,] dressed in Army fatigues and black boots, parked her car at the front of the [local] Mall, stepped out and started shooting. Bullets from her .22 semi-automatic rifle missed her first targets—a woman at an ATM and a man walking in the lot.

A group of children standing outside the [Chinese] restaurant were not so lucky. A bullet tore into the tiny chest of [a boy], 2, hitting him in the heart. His two cousins, [cousin who was 10] and [cousin who was 9] were also shot, but they would recover from their wounds.

From there, [Ms. Rambo] dashed into the mall.

People first thought that the pop, pop, pop of the rifle was part of a marketing or Halloween stunt, since the holiday was just a day away.

But then they saw blood on the floor and heard screams. Shoppers scrambled for cover in jewelry vaults, dressing rooms, back offices, any place that would put them out of the gunwoman's sight.

[Ms. Rambo] continued, swinging the rifle, shooting wildly, randomly, into groups in front of the restaurants and stores. It took all of five minutes for her to get off 15 shots, wounding 10, three fatally. In addition to [the others, another person], age 64, died on the spot, [another shopper, age 67], suffered wounds to his head, abdomen and buttocks. He died a few days later at the hospital.[1]

This mild, meek older white woman had committed a heinous crime, but in 2018 you would not know it.

She was in solitary confinement not because she posed a threat to herself or others, not because she had unmanaged severe mental illness, not because she was a "management problem" in general population. She was incarcerated in solitary confinement because she had been there for so long the "white shirts" and COs agreed that it was her "home."

CHAPTER 29

The BMU

IN THE WAKE of the closing of state psychiatric hospitals, one of the main challenges we heard about from everyone we talked with, including "white shirts," COs, and incarcerated people themselves is the role that prisons are now charged with playing in the management and treatment of people with mental illness. As people with severe mental illness were dumped out of state psychiatric hospitals, those who were convicted of violent crimes and sentenced to a psychiatric hospital or those who assaulted staff while in a psychiatric hospital were sent to prison. When they were designed, prisons were not meant to hold people with severe mental illness and psychiatric hospitals were not meant to be prisons. By 2000, many prisons were now incarcerating people with severe mental illness. Staff had not, and admitted openly to us, been trained to deal with people who suffer from every conceivable psychiatric disorder, including schizophrenia, as Ms. Rambo does, bipolar disorder, and borderline personality disorder.

Mary Buser, who wrote extensively about her time on Rikers Island, recounts a similar statement from the staff there: "When I first started working here, we had a few mentally ill inmates here and there, but now the numbers are huge. They don't belong in here. It's no way for a civilized society to treat its mentally ill. But here they are. Jail's their new home. It's really sad."[1]

Though prisoners whose mental illness is treated and managed can live successfully in general population, those whose mental illness is not well-managed often cannot. Because many incarcerated people with severe and unmanaged mental illness act out as a way of coping, the default management strategy is to sentence them to a stay in solitary confinement. As one can imagine, and others have well documented, people experience a degrading and deterioration of their mental health when they are in insolation, locked in cages for twenty-three hours a day with limited human contact, and this is even more so the case for people with untreated or unmanaged mental illness.[2]

Prison administrators responded to the challenge presented by the closing of state psychiatric units by creating specialized units within solitary confinement specifically designed to house prisoners with severe mental illness. These units are often called DTUs (diversionary treatment units) or BMUs (behavioral management units). Because SCI-Women is one of only two prisons in the state that incarcerates women, and it is the only maximum security facility, it has both a DTU and a BMU. In other words, half of the cells in the SCI-Women's solitary confinement unit are reserved for incarcerated people with personality disorders and severe and unmanaged mental illness.

There are many critical elements to the prison reforms that are implemented in these specialized solitary confinement units, including the murals on the walls of which the staff are so proud. Most of the murals in the BMU feature Looney Tunes characters. We can't remember their names, but we recognize them. Black, blue, red, green, yellow. Life-sized images of cartoon characters. The BMU has cartoon characters from the 1970s, the cartoons we watched as kids and young adults, Road Runner and Yosemite Sam, Popeye. In some ways the cartoons seem old-school, but for the women incarcerated in the BMU, many of whom are in their forties, maybe these characters make sense. Maybe they are reminded of childhood. Maybe that's not such a good thing, because in our interviews with the women incarcerated in the BMU, we learned that all of them have histories of child sexual abuse.

Compared with the monochromatic environment of the other solitary confinement units, the bright colors are cheery. Incarcerated people we interviewed in solitary confinement comment on the murals. Some see what we see, that the colors provide some visual stimulation that contrast with the monochromaticity of solitary confinement. One woman who is incarcerated in the BMU identifies the irony of Looney Tunes characters in a unit for "looney tunes"—crazy women. We wonder, but don't have a chance to ask, if this "coincidence" is also not lost on the staff and other women incarcerated in the BMU.

In addition to the murals, some cells have pictures from coloring books taped on the doors, like you might find in an elementary school classroom. On one cell door someone (maybe the inhabitant of the cell) has taped a picture depicting the symbols of the Fourth of July, a brightly colored flag waving on a flagpole, and fireworks in the background. It seems out of place only because today is the second-to-last day of July. But maybe the person confined in the cell likes the picture, much like we like blinking holiday lights that we put up in our offices several years ago. After we returned from winter break, we thought, these are so awesome; why would we take them down? And so we didn't. Maybe she likes the picture, and so even though the day has long passed, it makes her feel good, so she leaves it up or asks the staff to leave it up for her. Maybe it's there because the staff like it, or someone incarcerated in a cell on the other side of the pod likes to look at it, or maybe it's just that no one bothered to take it down. Maybe no one even asks her.

In addition to the murals, both the DTU and the BMU incorporate targeted programming meant to address the rapid, significant, and well documented declines in mental health among people with mental illness who are incarcerated in solitary confinement.[3] For example, those incarcerated in the

BMU and DTU get additional privileges above and beyond those housed in A and C Pods, including twenty hours a week of "out of cell" time, two hours each morning and two hours each afternoon, Monday through Friday. These hours include showers and yard but also structured and unstructured programming. Programming might be therapeutic, like giving the women a journaling prompt, talking with them about resilience or some other concept, or watching a video.

Though we do not know, nor do we ask, about the specific diagnosis of the women incarcerated in the BMU, what we do know, from both observation and interviews with the women incarcerated there and the staff is that at least part of the reason they are incarcerated in the BMU is because they engage in self-harm that is significant enough that it can't be managed in general population.

As professors of women and gender studies, lifelong feminists, and experts in sexual and intimate partner violence, we are well acquainted with cutting and its relationship to sexual trauma. We have had former students who cut. We have a very close friend who cuts. We love her dearly. We don't stand in judgment of anyone who cuts, and cutting doesn't make us uncomfortable except that we know that it is rooted in deep pain, which also doesn't make us uncomfortable; we're not afraid of pain. It does make us sad. It makes our hearts hurt. It makes us angry at abusers who have so little regard for the lives of the innocent children they sexually abuse. It makes us angry that adults who could have intervened and interrupted the violence didn't. But nothing about the women scares us. We're comfortable with their pain. We've seen a lot.

For the uninitiated, the women in the BMU can be scary. They often behave like children. It's as if the cumulative trauma of child sexual abuse, the years in foster care, and being incarcerated as juveniles, has stunted their development. They speak in simple phrases. They tease each other like girls in elementary school do. They color. Not in adult coloring books, which is the latest well-being, meditative fad, but in children's coloring books.

They behave violently, sometimes at each other, rarely at the staff, mostly toward themselves. They cut. They bang their heads against the wall until they are bloody. One woman, Wendi, has track marks on her arms that look like ropes. In addition to cutting, she shoves things into her arms. Pens. Toothbrushes. The scars that remain are a visible and painful reminder of the pain she lives with daily.

We are not psychologists nor do we have training in the area of mental health. We understand that those who do have this specialized training, like Dr. Emma, distinguish between severe mental illness and behavioral problems. To be honest, we had a difficult time making the distinction, and thus we defer to our colleagues. What we did hear from COs and counselors (who are educational specialists not psychologists) in the BMU is that they believe that the women engage in the behaviors they do in order to get attention, not because they have mental illness or personality disorders.

Everyone we spoke with from Unit Manager Tom to the LT to the COs to the women confined in the BMU all agreed that the most common reason for women to be sentenced to the BMU was that they engaged in self-harm and therefore could not be "managed" in general population.

Where the prisoners and COs disagreed was the cause of the self-harm. The COs for the most part considered self-harm a "behavioral" problem that could be managed and even "fixed" with a punitive approach. If you locked women who self-harm into solitary confinement and created a "step program" modeled on those implemented in gang/threat units, not only could you contain the self-harm, but you could stop women from engaging in it.

We are not so optimistic. And we are not alone. Mason and Finelli studied the behavior of chickens in factory farms.[4] Much like people in solitary confinement, chickens raised in factory farms have their basic needs for food, water, and shelter met. In fact, because the whole point of factory farming is to raise chicks into chickens that have unusually meaty breasts and thighs, food is readily available to them. Movement is also restricted. Though this contributes to the rapid growth of the chicken, it disrupts their chicken-ness. For example, as Mason and Finelli note, chickens confined in the tight quarters of factory farms often continue to peck and scratch for food, instinctual behavior, even when food is readily available. Because of the overcrowded conditions in factory farm chicken houses, this often leads to them pecking and scratching each other.

> This pecking can lead to the death of weaker chickens, and even to the "cannibal" frenzy in which chickens not only kill other chickens but they also eat them. (N. Williams 2008; 375). Similar behavior has been observed in intensively confined turkeys and pigs, and self-injurious behavior is so common among primates in zoos and laboratories that an acronym (SIB) is used as shorthand. . . . Sharon Shalev argues that compulsive self-harm is a desperate attempt to confirm one's own existence in the absence of intersubjective recognition—to feel *something* rather than nothing (2009, 196). . . . Another prisoner says, "I found myself curled up in a fetal position rocking myself back and forth and banging my head against the wall. In the absence of sensation, it's hard sometimes to convince yourself that you're really there" (1971).[5]

Women cut and bang their heads against the wall until they are bloody, and jam pens and toothbrushes up their arms to feel *something*. To assure themselves that they are really there. That they are not invisible despite being locked away in the hole. Many have been there a decade or more. To be sure you see them as no one seemed to when they were the victims of child sexual abuse.

Every single woman we interviewed in the BMU had a trauma history. All of them, each and every one, told us harrowing stories of the sexual abuse they experienced as children. Some were as young as three or four years old when it began. Most had been in foster care, sometimes as a strategy to remove them from the sexual abuse, and sometimes that's where the sexual abuse took place. Many of the women we interviewed in the BMU had first been incarcerated as juveniles. They were children. Locked in a psychiatric hospital or a juvenile jail because they had committed violent crimes or because their families couldn't manage their behavior. All of the women we interviewed were self-harming, and many had multiple suicide attempts. In fact, that's how one of the women we interviewed, Sally, ended up in the psychiatric hospital and ultimately in the BMU, locked in solitary confinement at SCI-Women.

All of the women we interviewed in the BMU had been there for years. Most of them couldn't remember how long, but everyone agreed that most of the women had been there for more than five years. Marina had probably been there for at least ten. We knew that this must be true, because on our second visit to SCI-Women two years after our first, when we arrived in the BMU we were greeted by the same faces.

CHAPTER 30

Sally

SALLY FIRST ATTEMPTED suicide at age thirteen and was first admitted to the psychiatric hospital shortly thereafter. Sally has had only brief periods of freedom, a year or two here and there in her late teens and early twenties. When we met her at age forty-two, she had been confined for most of her life.

When we asked her about being admitted to the state psychiatric hospital, she explained that she was caught self-harming in a foster home where she had been placed while her aunt and father fought over her custody. The foster family took her to the emergency room, and after several short stays in psychiatric beds in regular hospitals, it was determined that she needed long-term care, and she was committed to the state psychiatric hospital.

Sally was transferred to SCI-Women because she assaulted a staff member in the state psychiatric hospital.

Sally's horror story began when she was seven years old. Her father was a terrible alcoholic—"I never saw him sober"—and terribly physically abusive. After taking his beatings for many years, her mother fled the abuse but didn't take Sally with her. She admits that this really hurt. She understands why her mother left—she would have done the same thing, she says—but if it had been her, she would have taken her daughter. She felt abandoned. She hasn't seen her mother since she was seven years old and has no idea if she is dead or alive. She was, and likely still is, a drug addict, Sally says. Though her father had been physically abusive to her for "as long as she could remember," he became sexually abusive when her mother left. "He started treating me like his wife. I was a kid. I didn't do anything wrong. He would crawl into bed and beat me and sexually abused me. I hit myself because my dad's not here to hit me. I need to be punished so I punish myself."

She didn't tell anyone about the abuse until age thirteen; she told her aunt after she took Sally in to live with her. This triggered the custody battle between Sally's aunt and Sally's father, and Sally was put into foster care while her custody was being resolved. She began self-harming in foster care because she missed her aunt. Because of the requirements of the custody hearing she wasn't even allowed to talk to her aunt. She was removed to a new school and didn't have any friends. She was very lonely.

She still self-harms "several times a week." When she gets angry she doesn't want to hurt anyone else, so she hurts herself. "When I hit my head I don't mess around. I hit myself to destroy myself. I don't want to die. I just want to hurt. I'm finally getting my anger out."

In 2017, she hit her head so hard that she sustained a concussion and had to have staples put in her scalp to control the bleeding. Her self-induced injuries were so severe that the COs transported her to the local hospital, something everyone agreed only happens when injuries are severe and beyond the capacity of the infirmary to treat.

Sally admits that she needs help with controlling her self-harming behavior. She doesn't want to self-harm in front of her daughter. She doesn't want to go back to the state psychiatric hospital, but she feels she may not have any other choice if she can't prevent herself from self-harming in front of her daughter. When she was out in the past, she cut herself in the bathroom with her daughter just outside the door. Her daughter came in and saw her and she felt terrible about it.

She also engages in self-harm by refusing to eat. She says: "I don't eat because I need to be punished. . . . I get mad at the officers and I think I'm punishing them but I'm really punishing me. Sometimes I think the officers are doing something to the food."

Lisa Guenther's insights help us to make sense of Sally's self-harm, particularly her belief that COs are poisoning her food, not sure if her refusals to eat punish them or her:

> There are many ways to destroy a person, but one of the simplest and most devastating is through prolonged solitary confinement. Deprived of meaningful human interaction, otherwise healthy prisoners become unhinged. They see things that do not exist, and they fail to see things that do. Their sense of their own bodies—even the fundamental capacity to feel pain and to distinguish their pain from that of others—erodes to the point where they are no longer sure if they are being harmed or harming themselves. Not only psychological or social identity but the most basic sense of identity is threatened by prolonged solitary confinement.[1]

Jennifer is another severe self-harmer. She is a severe cutter. In her words, "I will cut with anything . . . cups, crayons, her blues [uniform], toilet paper, shower shoes, security blankets and paper."

As a result, Jennifer is allowed very few possessions, not even security blankets. And she is on pen restriction and can only write with crayons.

Jennifer's compulsion to self-harm and cut is so severe that she has even cut while being in "intermediate restraints"—wearing a belt around her waist, her wrists handcuffed to the belt—while being transported to the hospital to be sewn up after she severely cut her arms.

Jennifer self-harms almost every day. "Sometimes they stitch me and sometimes they don't. I refuse meds because *I'm trying to self-harm.*"

Jennifer tried to kill herself for the first time when she was twelve because she was being molested. She's been locked in a psychiatric hospital or in SCI-Women since her first suicide attempt at age twelve; she's now thirty-nine. Jennifer said that after her first suicide attempt, her mother told her to go ahead and kill herself.

Which is what she has basically been doing ever since, just in slow motion.

Jennifer and Sally and Wendi are not alone, nor are they particularly unique.

A February 2014 study in the *American Journal of Public Health* found that detainees in solitary confinement in New York City jails were nearly seven times more likely to harm themselves than those in general population, and that the effect was particularly pronounced for youth and people with severe mental illness. In California prisons in 2004, 73% of all suicides occurred in isolation units–though these units accounted for less than 10% of the state's total prison population. In the Indiana Department of Corrections, the rate of suicides in segregation/solitary was almost three times that of other housing units.[2]

The belief that many staff in the BMU expressed that the women incarcerated there are "behavioral problems" not suffering from mental illness may shape the ways they respond to self-harm, but it does not lessen their empathy for the women they are charged with keeping safe. All of the staff we talked to and observed were bothered by the self-harm. They all felt a responsibility not simply to stop the self-harming behavior by punishing it, but to help the women stop-harming through interventions, support, and a series of incentives.

We wanted to do more than just interview people incarcerated in the BMU. We also wanted to interview staff and to observe the BMU. So after lunch one day, we headed to the where we knew we would find Unit Manager Tom and Counselor Mark hanging out in the pod office. This is "their unit." We also hoped to interview COs whom we had been observing for several days

CO Lisa is a regular in the BMU. We observed her all day; she works 6 to 2. She's been busy delivering trays, bringing women out for rec (which is how we learn that the time the women spend at the table coloring is their "rec"). She has an easy rapport with the women. Talking to them, making sure they have the items they are supposed to have, like Wendi, the woman who puts things in her arms, is allowed to have a pen when she is supervised during rec time. She and CO Lisa also talk about the fact that Wendi has earned enough points on her incentive plan that she will get a Pepsi today or tomorrow. Her reward for doing what she's supposed to do. As we leave the office and go back to the therapy room for the interview, the women are at the rec tables coloring. One hollers: "CO Lisa is nuts!"

Chapter 31

CO Lisa

CO LISA IS A WHITE WOMAN. We would put her in her late forties or early fifties. She has a daughter who is a drug addict (meth or opioids; we're not sure), who is in and out of jail. CO Lisa is raising her granddaughter, who in her words is "her life." Her face lights up and she smiles when she talks about her routine. When she leaves work, she picks up her granddaughter from school and brings her home, where they eat dinner, read, do homework, all of the normal things that the women she spends all day guarding will never do.

CO Lisa has worked for twelve years at SCI-Women and two years in the BMU. Unit Manager Tom selected her specifically. (We learn from Unit Manager Tom that he gets 100 percent of say in whom he selects for his team in the BMU.)

We ask CO Lisa, "What's the most frustrating part of the job?"

When they self-harm. They're cutting and you're trying to get them to stop. . . . You find someone . . . they went from here [she gestures up] to downhill. It's also frustrating to the other inmates. They start cutting, group is canceled. It throws their routine off. . . . They need consistency. Sometimes with other staff [nurses who come just to administer medications or COs who are "substituting" in the BMU] they [the inmates] get things they're not supposed to get. They need consistency with staff. Sometimes we get copy-cats and sometimes the other inmates lay low. . . . One time we had four of them cutting at once!

Locked in single cells in a solitary confinement unit we wonder how the women incarcerated in the BMU are able to cut. We ask CO Lisa how they cut, what they use to cut, and she responds: "Anything and everything, they can cut with the stem of an apple." We ask, "How do you know when they're going to self-harm?" CO Lisa replies:

Take B: she covers her cell window, just to get attention . . . then she splatters the paper with blood. We contact the bubble and they send a sergeant to talk them down, they don't enter the cell, and see if we can get them to stop. Then we call medical to assess. If they won't stop we have to enter their cell, cuff them and put them in a restraint chair. [CO Lisa points to a restraint chair that they keep stored in the same room where we are doing the interview.] We put them in for a minimum of four hours and a max of eight hours.

"Do you think it works?" we ask, knowing that there is a lot of literature about the restraint chair and how dangerous it is for people experiencing a mental health crisis. CO Lisa says, "We think it helps them recenter."

CO Lisa tells us that the women incarcerated in the BMU do more of the self-harming at night, and we ask why, uncertain of what her answer will be.

They are bored at night, they're up all day and they get tired at night, they start to decompensate and they can't cope as well, and 95 percent of the night shift is new officers. New officers want to do everything by the book, they say "We can't do that." For example, after they cut they go in the strip cell and they are on restriction, they get a security blanket, a security smock, that's it. After two days of good behavior I give them a cup even though they are supposed to be on restriction for three days. *When they are good we need to show them that they are doing good.*

In contrast, she says, the new COs won't give them anything on day two and make them spend the entire three days on restriction.

A security smock is like a hospital gown made out of the kind of blankets that movers use to cover furniture before they put it in the moving truck. It's dark gray quilted material with a royal blue strap that allows it to be closed. It's humiliating to wear, but you can't get any strings out of it to cut with or hang yourself.

It's clear to us that CO Lisa cares about the women she is charged with guarding all day, and so we ask her how she would design the BMU if it were up to her, with her vast experience. No one, of course but us, has ever asked her this question.

In the real world it would be its own unit, not in solitary confinement. It would be a separate building, it would be secure, with doors, a wicket or food pass, handcuffs, shackles and restraint chair, but the staff would be its own dedicated staff, not mixing staff with other solitary confinement units. . . . We talk to intervene, when I tell you to turn around and cuff you need to do that . . . but the women here are impulsive. . . . I don't pull out my spray like the substitute COs; I don't think spray is appropriate in the BMU. Authority is important. The uniform is important. CIT [crisis intervention] training is good training.

CO Lisa's final comment is perhaps the most profound, and honest, of the day. At the end of the day, she says: "*I can't make you stop harming; all I can do is prevent it until the end of the shift.*"

CHAPTER 32

Wendi

FIVE OF THE SEVEN WOMEN incarcerated in the BMU were seated at or near a table in the middle of the room. The table was sort of u-shaped, like a contemporary picnic bench, and had seats that were attached to it. It also had metal clamps near each seat for handcuffing. Near the edge of the table were several desks, the kind you might find in a public middle or high school, with one modification: the same clamp for handcuffing. Three women were handcuffed (they were also shackled) to the table, with a staff member we had never seen observing them while they colored and talked. Marina was handcuffed (and shackled) to the desk nearby.

Each of the women had a journal or some pages from a coloring book. They were joking and laughing and teasing each other like you might see elementary girls doing. A white woman, "B," who is in her forties but who looks like she is in her late fifties and is missing a considerable number of teeth, has been walking around all morning, joking with the staff. When Counselor Mark comes in, she hollers his name; they have an easy rapport. When we go to interview CO Lisa, "B" hollers, "She's nuts! She's going to tell you that we're nuts, but she's the one who's nuts!"

While she's sitting at the table, she reaches over and picks up a notebook that Wendi is writing in. She turns to the back page of Wendi's journal (the black-and-white kind that you might see in the arms of a middle or high school student) and starts to yell: "You're writing about Trump, I knew you were writing about him! He's going to find out!" Wendi pulls the journal away and we see, of course, that she's been looking at empty pages. We wonder if "B" can read.

Wendi is a dark-skinned Black woman in her forties. She wears her hair natural. To be honest, it's a bit wild looking, and Wendi seems to want it that way. The other incarcerated women and staff, are a bit afraid of her. CO Lisa says that Wendi is the only woman in the BMU whom she would fear on the outside. Wendi is short and robust. When she earns an extra food bag, she always chooses Wednesdays, because Wednesday is chicken patty day. Wendi is serving a forty-years-to-life sentence for murder. According to Wendi, she stabbed a woman and threw her out a third-story window because the woman wanted to have sex with her, and Wendi did not want to. According to newspaper accounts of the case, there may also have been some other motives involved in the murder, including a dispute over drugs and money. Wendi was found guilty at trial but also deemed to be suffering from mental illness. When she arrived at SCI-Women, she was initially housed in in general population in a specialized unit for women with mental illness, but she attacked her cellie, according to Wendi, because her cellie refused to have a relationship with her. Angered by her rejection, Wendi raped her and beat her until she was in a coma. The woman Wendi beat up recovered and was released from prison shortly after, and sometime later she died of an overdose. As a result of the brutal attack, Wendi was sent to the BMU.

Wendi takes responsibility for the attack: "I killed my cellie . . . but I shouldn't have had a cellie so early because I was unstable. . . . I wasn't dealing with my life sentence very well."

Because of her violent behavior, Wendi is on restricted release, which means that she will only leave the BMU if and when she is released from prison, which few, including her, believe will ever happen.

Smith walks over to Wendi, who had refused him an interview the day before, and he gives her a hard time.

Wendi says: "I want an interview!"

Smith responds: "Nope. You had your chance yesterday; you can't come back today and say you want the interview."

They both laugh.

Because it is just after lunch, Hattery has a Diet Coke she has purchased from the vending machine in the visitor room. Lunch was awful. We both settle for a very sad salad and some peanut butter on a tortilla. The Diet Coke is like a reward for surviving lunch. As Hattery stands there sipping from the bottle, Wendi says, "I get a soda tomorrow!" We ask CO Lisa about this, and she tells us that because Wendi has earned enough incentive points, she can get a soda once a week.

["What kind of soda will you get, Wendi?"]
"A regular Pepsi!" she remarks.

A toothy grin spreads ear to ear. Wendi keeps eyeing the Diet Coke. Hattery suddenly feels very self-conscious. In the last few years, she has cut back considerably on her consumption of Diet Coke. It is more of an indulgence, when we have lunch out. We don't buy it and keep it at home anymore. Hattery doesn't take cases with her to work anymore. But she can still have a Diet Coke whenever she wants to. Wendi can't. None of the women down here can. It's a hardship for those in solitary confinement; it's a lifetime for those living in the BMU. Hattery's privilege is written by her actions.

We find out later from CO Lisa that when the women are on Level 3, they can have their soda incentive in their cells, but if they are on restrictions, Levels 4 and 5, because they will use the bottles, which are plastic, to cut, they can only have them at the table, where they are supervised, or the soda has to be poured into a cup. Balancing the rights of an adult woman to drink in the privacy of her own cell versus protecting her from further harm—it's a tricky balance.

Wendi shows us her journal. The title, "HOPE," is written in black crayon. Wendi is not allowed pens in her cell because of her proclivity to jam them up her arm. At the table, where she is supervised, she is allowed to use a pen. She has written a paragraph to her daughter about hope. She writes that the light came on in the world the day her daughter was born, that her daughter is her hope. We ask about her daughter. Wendi tells us that she lives with Wendi's sister. We ask if she ever gets to talk to her daughter or see her. We regret the question as soon as it is out of our mouths. Of course she doesn't. We're sure her family thinks she is crazy, especially if they have seen the rope-like track marks on her arms, the scars from jamming pens and toothbrushes in them. She tells us that she gets updates about her daughter from her sister. We have no idea if she has any contact with her daughter, and we're not 100 percent sure she's competent to tell us, but it seems to make her happy to talk about her daughter. So we keep the conversation going as long as we can. It makes us sad to know that this woman will likely never see her child. It makes us sad that this girl will grow up without knowing her mother. We wonder if she shoves pens and toothbrushes up her arm as a way of dealing with all of the pain. Or maybe she harms herself as a way of proving to herself and others that she is not worth it after all, that she is not lovable. Maybe she shoves items up her arm just to feel anything at all.

Obviously it gets tense in the BMU when someone is engaging in self-harm. It can be loud if the one self-harming is banging her head against the door or wall. It can be messy if the one self-harming is bleeding all over her cell. But when it's not tense, only the bars and the handcuffs are there to remind you that this isn't a hospital setting. The interchanges come easily. Staff joke with the women incarcerated in the BMU in a way that communicates intimacy. To be honest, this is the most comfortable, least tense, most relaxed we have ever seen staff across the many prisons we have been to. We have observed some staff in men's prisons give the prisoners a hard time and vice versa: "You back here again? What did I tell you? Come on, you gotta get that right or you'll keep coming back here." But we have never seen this kind of intimacy in the men's prisons. It makes us think about the recommendation that many staff, including CO Lisa, make that the BMU should be its own stand-alone unit, and not part of the solitary confinement unit. Or maybe there are lessons to learn from the BMU that could be implemented in SCI-Wannabee. Lessons that could restore humanity to both the prisoners and the staff. We certainly didn't expect to find so much optimism in a place that is otherwise very depressing.

CHAPTER 33

"Do You Think I'll Die
Here?"—Marina

AFTER OUR FIRST DAY at SCI-Women, we are debriefing our day over beer and fried food: cheese curds, fried peppers, french fries.

SMITH: "I interviewed a woman today. I can't get over her. She went to prison when she was eleven."
HATTERY: "Did she stab a lady with a steak knife on the corner?"
SMITH: "Yes."
HATTERY: "I remember her. It's so tragic."

Marina's story is so tragic that she is impossible to forget. Just a few details were enough for Hattery to immediately recall her.

After we returned home, we reread Hattery's notes on Marina and are reminded of the tragedy of her life.

Marina is a Black woman. She wears her hair cropped short, very close to her skull. She is medium height, though it's often hard to tell because the only time we see her, she is handcuffed, either to a belly chain or to the loop on the table or desk. She sits hunched over. She is thin. As the sign on her cell door indicates, "Juvenile cuffs only," she is so small that COs are only allowed to use handcuffs designed for juveniles on her thin wrists. Though she is in her thirties, she seems very young. Despite the setting in which we are interviewing her and talking with her and observing her, her eyes seem hopeful, as if there could be something good right around the corner—a can of Pepsi, a crayon to color with, news that she is going to be released.

During our first interview with Marina, in the summer of 2017, she was not so hopeful or optimistic. In her first interview she was full of rage, which she expressed openly. Our first interview took place in a strip cage in the CO's office in the BMU. Marina had recently thrown urine and feces on a CO when they had her wicket open to transfer her food. As a result, not only was Marina handcuffed, to a belly chain, and shackled in the strip cage, but for the duration of the interview the COs slid a piece of plexiglass into the top half of the strip cage so that if Marina spit or attempted to throw urine or feces, we wouldn't be hit by it.

Marina was very agitated during the interview. We're sure she was probably very uncomfortable, handcuffed and shackled and stuffed into a plastic chair. Even though she is quite small, it's like her body is folded into the chair. She's loud. We capitalize some of the language from her interview in places where she emphasized her points by yelling. We are quite sure that despite all of our best efforts to keep her interview confidential, she could be heard outside the room.

To be honest, we were a bit afraid of her. Until we heard her story. And then we realized that all of the bluster and antagonism were the rage of a young child being expressed through the body of a grown woman.

Marina has had a journey through various types of facilities, each of which has taken away her freedom, beginning with juvenile detention and then state psychiatric hospitals, prison, and now the BMU.

According to Marina, she was first sentenced to prison in 1998 when she was eleven years old for the stabbing death of a woman she described as "a stranger lady." The woman she stabbed was just that, a stranger, not someone she knew. She stabbed the woman through her heart. When we asked Marina why she stabbed her, she said, "I've wanted to kill people since I was eleven."

Sentenced as a juvenile to eighteen to forty years, she was incarcerated early on in an adult prison and cordoned off from the adults because she was a juvenile. On her behalf, her public defender appealed to the court to transfer Marina to the state psychiatric hospital, where she had been receiving treatment prior to her conviction. Later in the interview, she claimed that she was kicked out of the state psychiatric hospital because "I refused treatment; I said I didn't want help anymore, not because of my behavior. They just said it was my behavior because I was angry with them."

She says she has twice petitioned to be sent back to the state psychiatric hospital but "I was denied because of the attacks."

Marina did a horrible thing. She killed someone. Someone who was innocent, who had done nothing to hurt her or anyone else we are aware of. But we argue that the criminal legal system also did a horrible thing. Actors in the criminal legal system sentenced a *child* to prison for nearly her entire life, far longer than many people who plead or are found guilty of murder. Do we treat Marina like a monster because that's the only way we can conceive of an eleven-year-old who murders someone? Should we instead consider the role that we, as a society, played in creating her? She's not evil, as people perceive her to be. She's broken, perhaps beyond repair, but maybe she could have been repaired when she was a young child. We lock her up, out of sight, out of mind, rather than examine our own role in creating Marina.

Marina was first put into foster care when she was three years old. Her mother put her and her sister, who had just been born, into foster care because "she didn't make enough money to take care of us."

In foster care, she was mad at her mom; she missed her mom.

Beginning at age seven, in foster care, she was physically abused by her foster mom and started running away from home and school. She says she's had mental health problems since she was seven years old.

According to news accounts from her trial, Marina suffers from mental illness. She has attention deficit disorder (ADD), and she has developmental delays; her IQ is under seventy. Many consider her IQ too low to render her legally competent. Nevertheless, she has been incarcerated for more than twenty years.

We asked her if anything makes her feel good, feel happy. She said, "I want to make minimum [her minimum sentence] and go home. But they want to keep me in this hell hole."

She was "kicked out" of the state psychiatric hospital for "being bad," attacking staff and patients, but more so patients. She wanted to kill people.

She described significant mistreatment by the COs:

> They treat me like an animal, harassing me, spitting in my food, messing up my property. I don't have pictures, books, magazines. The staff are all on the same side, they all pick on me, no one more than any others. *I'm the victim here.* They close the wicket on me [this may have been in reference to the fact that she had recently thrown urine and fecal material]. They mess with me because they are jealous of me. They refuse my yard. They starve me. They refuse me food, they refuse me groups, they refuse me clinics, they refuse me medication, they turn off my water. The toilet flooded and they left me in the dirty cell all day long. They are supposed to clean the cells but they don't. They harass me 24/7. They don't care if I die in here. They even talk shit about me to other inmates. . . . I'm tired of all of it . . . *even if I die in here.*

She says, "Solitary is hard on my mind. It's best to be alone against them all. . . . If they keep me any longer I'm going to lose my mind. It's getting worse over time." She says that she has been misdiagnosed, that they claim to know what is wrong with her but they won't admit it. She says that she has ADD, bipolar disorder, anxiety, and speaking problems. "*I wish I knew what was wrong with me.*"

Marina may have a low IQ and mental illness, and she may be a convicted felon, and she may be incarcerated, but she is a human being, and she has a right to know, in her words, *what is wrong with her.*

Marina is very clear that she believes she belongs in a state psychiatric hospital and not in prison: "The best place for me is a hospital where I can get help with my medications and get therapy."

She described solitary confinement using these phrases:

"It's like being in a trance."

"I'm stuck in a hell hole."

She feels "like a slave."

"I'm treated like I'm in a zoo."

"It [solitary confinement] feels like a holocaust prison."

"I'm being treated like an animal. I've needed help for years."

She screams: *"I feel lost and forgotten. I'm somebody. I'm somebody's family member, too."*

Spoken by a grown woman, these are the words of a child. A child we forgot so many years ago. A child we locked in a solitary confinement cage when she should have been learning to read, playing on the playground, dreaming only of what she wanted to become when she grew up, not learning how to survive in a women's prison. We are reminded of the words of a survivor of intimate partner violence whom we interviewed who said of being prostituted as a ten-year-old by her stepfather, "I hadn't even learned to ride a bike yet."

Had Marina ever even learned to ride a bike?

On our second visit to SCI-Women, we encounter Marina in the common area of the pod. We remember her vividly from the first visit we made two years ago, and we tell her so!

["Hey Marina, we remember you, we met you two years ago when we were here!"]

Marina, grinning, responds: "You do?"

["Yep! We interviewed you right in that room over there" [pointing to the office with a cage near the door of the unit.]

Her demeanor this summer, in 2019, is calm, childlike.

Marina grins more.

We ask Marina about the paper she is coloring.

She is using secondary colors that are muted, not bright, purple and pink. We tell her how much we like her picture and that our favorite color is purple. She grins. We leave her table and go conduct our interview with CO Lisa. After we return, about forty-five minutes later, Marina is still sitting at her desk. Her hands still handcuffed to the table and her legs still shackled to the chair. We ask to see her picture and she slides it toward us. We tell her how much we like it and ask if she will share it with us.

"You really want it?" she asks.

["Yes! we do! Then we can remember you!"]

She asks to write our name on the picture, and, remembering that we're not supposed to give our whole names, we say, "Make it to Ms. A."

She looks, nods, and writes: "To: Ms. A."

We ask her to sign the paper, and the other women in the room start yelling: "They call us by our last names, they call you Ms [W], sign it Ms [W]." She does.

We tell her thank you, and then we're off to conduct another interview.

We carefully place Marina's picture in our red research folder. We have decided to hang it on our office wall, unframed, as a reminder, not just of

Figure 7. Art created by "Marina." (Photo by Angie Hattery.)

Marina but of all the women who are in shackles when what they need is an intervention. A reminder of all of the women struggling with self-harm. Managing their demons as best they can. A reminder that every person is a human being and that we as a society must continue to find the most humane ways to take care of them, especially the most vulnerable, no matter what they have done. Maybe Dr. Emma is right about the people locked in solitary confinement. They are our most vulnerable, and they need our highest level of care.

We include an image of Marina's picture here (Figure 7) so that you can remember her and so many others like her. Locked away in the hole. Out of sight out of mind.

The BMU is based on a step program, with 5 being the most restrictive and 1 being the transition phase. When prisoners in the BMU reach level 1, they are moved out into a transition unit for thirty days, and if they are successful there, they transition back into general population. The transition unit is where we interviewed Ms. Rambo. Each level involves a series of carrots and sticks: restrictions that are meant to disincentivize certain behavior, like self-harm, not taking care of hygiene (showering), not being social (staying in one's cell), and incentivize other behavior, like not engaging in self-harm, showering regularly, and coming out and participating in programs. As one moves from level to level, restrictions are lifted and the prisoner gets more privileges, like getting a soda or watching a few hours of TV. The day we chatted with Marina she told us that she had earned two hours of TV.

Between the first and second visits to SCI-Women, the staff modified the rewards associated with good behavior by incorporating a point-based incentive system. Under this revised system, prisoners could earn points to "spend" on things like a soda or an extra meal packet. The point system, rather than dictating rewards, allows the prisoner to choose the rewards they prefer. According to staff, when Wendi earns points, she always selects a food bag. "They get an extra bag on Saturday, right?" we ask.

Unit Manager Mark responds: "No, they can pick any day they want. Wendi always chooses Wednesday because it's chicken patty day and she loves chicken patties!"

If prisoners are not compliant by engaging in behaviors consistent with their behavior plan, like coming out for groups or showering, they can be moved back a level. Some prisoners, like Marina, cycle back and forth between levels 3 and 5. When she is doing well, she gets to watch TV or have a soda. When she is not doing well, she is on restriction and has her privileges revoked.

Though the current policy in most states is that solitary confinement should be limited to fifteen days or maxed at thirty days, all of the women in the BMU have been there for many consecutive years. Perhaps the saddest thing for us was returning two years after our initial visit and recognizing at least three people whom we had interviewed in 2017. Marina has lived in the BMU for perhaps a decade. Her first question to Smith when he interviewed her was "Do you think I'll die in here?"

Sadly, the answer is likely yes.

Marina is serving forty years. By the time she maxes out, she will be in her early sixties. Where would she go? And unless SCI-Women decides to completely restructure the BMU and move it out of the solitary confinement unit, *Marina will die having lived her entire adult life in a cell by herself.*

Marina was sent to prison before she got her first period, and she will still be there after she enters menopause. Her menstrual cycle a marker of her time. Of her life.

Marina is one of the truly invisible. She was invisible when she was a child being sexually abused. Marina was rendered invisible by a mother who didn't want her or couldn't take care of her.

Marina has experienced what philosophers call social death. "Social death is the effects of a (social) practice in which a person or group of people is excluded, dominated, or humiliated to the point of becoming dead to the rest of society. Although such people are physically alive, their lives no longer bear a social meaning; they no longer count as lives that matter."[1]

Former President Jimmy Carter once said: "The measure of a society is found in how they treat their weakest and most helpless citizens."

President Carter's words raise the question, would we have locked Marina away for life if she had been a young, white woman, if she hadn't been diagnosed with both mental illness and developmental delay?

We would never defend the fact that Marina took a life, but it seems clear that Marina's tool kit for responding to her experiences was extremely limited. She was deeply hurt. She was angry. Unique among the women we interviewed in the BMU, she took her anger out on someone else rather than herself. She harmed another rather than self-harmed. But her actions seem rooted in the same need to be visible, to be seen, to manage her deep pain.

We tolerate children who throw tantrums because they don't have the words to express their frustrations, but when a Black, impaired, young woman acts out, when her disturbing behavior is not understood for what it is, a cry for help, we lock her in solitary confinement, *not for the rest of her life, but for her entire life*.

PART SIX

CO Travis

You don't realize how stressful it is inside the walls. You're in jail too. You feel like an inmate. Inmates are running institutions and you have to do things to take care of them and no one is taking care of us. . . . We are Trump's Forgotten.

—CO Travis

CHAPTER 34

We Are the Essential Workers

Most of the COs we met and spent time with are not inherently bad people. They are, like many Germans during World War II, as Daniel Goldhagen describes them, complicit if not "willing executioners."[1] Yes, some were "rah rah huh-ha" hypermasculine men who choose to work in a prison for the same reasons they pursued a career in the military. They loved the adrenaline rush that came from a cell extraction. They were attracted to the disciplined, rule-oriented nature of the work. They believed in a just world in which they played an important role in maintaining law and order.

But as our interviews with CO Porter and others revealed, the majority of COs hated their jobs and worked in the jail because it was the only job in town. They worked in the jail because they believed it offered them the best opportunity to take care of their families, buy a home, provide health insurance, and maybe one day send a child to college, where they had not been able to go themselves. They didn't like the work, they felt alienated from it, and they did their best not to take it home. But the structures of solitary confinement, the requirements of their jobs, demanded that they enforce policies and practices they may not have believed in or fully endorsed but participated in because they felt they had no other choice. Furthermore, like those people incarcerated there, the conditions of solitary confinement wore them down and made them more susceptible to engaging in dehumanizing language and behavior because they too were themselves dehumanized in the hole.

The somewhat controversial contention that COs also lose their humanity as a result of the working conditions in solitary confinement is important for our discussion. We would never suggest that the COs lose their humanity to the same degree as the people incarcerated there do, as they have some control, they have power, and they get to leave the institution every day and go home. But to suggest that they do not pay a consequence for working in the prison is also not true. The COs we interviewed paid serious consequences in terms of their physical and mental health and in their relationships. In the vernacular of Jonathan Metzl, they were literally dying by whiteness. Not so much, as Metzl discusses, by embracing liberal gun laws or policies that defund public education, which they may or may not do, but in this case, by buying into the idea that building jails in rural, white communities, will bring positive economic development. Though we don't disagree that it is by far the best job in town, the question is, at what cost?

The COs we interviewed and observed see themselves, in the vernacular of the COVID-19 global pandemic, as "essential workers." They are responsible for ensuring the safety and security of the prison and for avenging the pain and suffering caused to victims and victims' families. They understand the conditions of solitary confinement not as dehumanizing but strictly as punishment. Many COs told us that they believe that the conditions in solitary confinement are too easy and that as a result, the threat of solitary confinement no longer serves as a deterrent. From their perspective, people incarcerated in general population have no incentive to follow the rules because they no longer fear having to do time in the hole.

We spent significant time with a CO named Travis. CO Travis was the most eager of any CO we met to be interviewed. He sought us out. CO Travis has worked in the Department of Corrections for twenty-four years. He's worked in solitary confinement for the last twelve years. Without a break. He has worked in the hole for longer than anyone else we interviewed, and perhaps it's his experience, or his personality, or a combination of both, but his perspective on solitary confinement was the most distilled of anyone we interviewed. That does not mean he is an outlier. We heard the same perspective from nearly every CO we interviewed. We center CO Travis's articulation of the work of the CO in solitary confinement because of its richness and clarity.

On our second day at SCI-Wannabee, while the students on our research team conducted interviews with the people incarcerated there, we decided to hang out with the officers and other staff to learn more about the work of solitary confinement. We learn over the days and weeks that we spend in solitary confinement units that conducting interviews with the COs and white shirts is more challenging. Unlike the prisoners, who are eager to get out of their cells, whose interviews are bounded by the confines of the visiting room, building rapport with the COs requires a significant investment. We follow them around while they work, we hang out in the offices, we chat them up in the chow hall. Eventually, after earning their trust, some of them agree to speak candidly with us.

Beginning with our interview with CO Travis, and continuing across the day, a window opened up in our project. That's the day we realized that the story the COs have to tell is as important as the story the prisoners have to tell. And CO Travis is the gateway to the story. Not only did we interview and hang out with many COs that day, but our interview with CO Travis led us to place a much greater emphasis on the experiences of the COs, in every prison and on every visit. Were it not for CO Travis, this story would be incomplete; it would not be as full and rich; it would be only one side of the story.

CHAPTER 35

Solitary Confinement Isn't a Daycare!

As soon as we are passed through to the solitary confinement unit that second day at SCI-Wannabee, LT tells us that a CO wants to talk. We say, great. Not sure of what to expect, we prepare to meet CO Travis. Though he's not the first CO we have interviewed, he's physically intimidating, and we were a bit nervous about the interview.

CO Travis is a white man in his mid-fifties. He's tall, well over 6 feet, and burly. He has short hair that is graying but probably used to be blonde. He has a scruffy beard. If you saw him on the street, you might assume he's a lumberjack.

We follow CO Travis down the hallway to the property room that holds prisoners' property and a strip cage. He wants a private space. There is already one plastic chair in the room, so we pull in two more from another office, open up our interview protocol and notebooks, and before we can ask more than a few basic demographic questions, CO Travis launches in:

"Trump won because of forgotten people. In the jail, the *forgotten is the guards.*"

As a veteran of work in the solitary confinement unit, as well as general population at SCI-Wannabee, CO Travis has seen everything, including many of the changes that have taken place in prisons in the state system.

When CO Travis came to work in the jail, SCI-Wannabee had just been built. CO Travis was finishing up his tour in the military and the jail was for him, as it had been for so many others, the best job in town and an easy transition.

SCI-Wannabee was built at the height of prison expansion, and the jail reflected the changes that were happening nationwide, including a steep rise in incarceration, mostly driven by the war on drugs, a "darkening" of the incarcerated population, and a shift in incarcerating rather than hospitalizing those with mental illness. Each of these factors impacts the working conditions CO Travis experiences.

In the "old" days, for the most part, the people sentenced to prison had committed serious, violent crime and as a result they were long-timers. With many years to serve, long-timers have an incentive to maintain "order" in the jail. CO Travis spoke with nostalgia about the days when the jail was filled with long-timers: "There's no more respect or rapport between inmates and guards anymore. We used to rely on the old guys to keep guys in line. If we were having trouble we'd have an old guy go up and talk to the person we were having trouble with. And, it would all get straightened out."

From his perspective, as a result of incarcerating more and more low-level drug offenders, the majority of whom receive relatively short sentences, there is no incentive anymore for prisoners and COs to have a relationship, to work together to maintain a sense of both order and safety in the prison. As a result, more and more fights break out in general population and more and more short-timers who are more likely than not to have been convicted of low-level crimes—they are not the "worst of the worst"—are sentenced to solitary confinement, where they present problems for CO Travis. With no prisoners he can trust, the job of "talking some sense" into a prisoner who continues to present behavioral management issues falls to CO Travis.

> I've been here twenty-five years and the street, young kids have no respect—what do we call them, "millennials?" The old guys used to teach them the ways, now young guys don't want to do that, they want things handed to them, they ask questions for everything, they want an explanation for everything. . . . "You burned me for the shower." "No, you burned yourself!" Rules are part of reform. . . . Old guys accepted what they've done; they treat you with respect; they know you're here to do a job. . . . When you have a conflict between an inmate and a CO, I put him [the inmate] in his cell and I walk away and come back later. . . . Young guys [millennials] don't want to be chumps. Young COs also have some of the same qualities. [He picks up a tube of toothpaste.] They want to know, "Where's my toothpaste?" . . . I say, hold on, let me finish what I'm doing and I'll bring it to you. They want it now.

These experiences shape CO Travis' perspective on solitary confinement, its purpose, its function, and the tools he and the other COs need to manage the people incarcerated there.

First and foremost, CO Travis sees his job as care, custody, and control. But with so many people now locked in solitary confinement, including those with mental illness, his job has changed in two distinct ways. First, because the prison population is primarily composed of people who will ultimately be released back into the free world, CO Travis says that his job has become about ensuring that people incarcerated in solitary confinement leave the unit and ultimately the jail and prison prepared to behave appropriately in the free world. He feels an obligation, much like a parent, to ensure that prisoners have been appropriately punished in order to have confidence that they will reenter society and not cause harm to themselves or others. If you think about it, this is a huge responsibility. Regardless of whether this responsibility is bestowed from the administration or is self-imposed, it weighs heavily on CO Travis.

With long-timers it's much easier, because the long sentences themselves serve as a deterrent to future crime, but also people tend to "age out" of participating in illegal activities while they are incarcerated, reentering a free world in which men their ages are focused on stability and settling down. With short timers, it's much more difficult.

In the hierarchy of punishment, some COs see themselves as the enforcers. If they don't do their jobs, if incarcerated people don't feel adequately punished, and the COs do not establish a deterrent effect, then they have failed in their jobs.

Recidivism, or the cycling in and out of solitary confinement (or jail), contributes to a sense of alienation from work, as Marx so aptly described, for many COs: "I used to work in a machine shop. . . . There was an end product. Here there's no end product. . . . I don't feel like we succeed. . . . Recidivism is failure. . . . One guy dies or leaves and there's another guy back in the same place."

CO Travis referred to recidivism, be it in and out of jail or in and out of solitary confinement, as "doing life on the installment plan."

Punishment then becomes a primary tool for CO Travis to do his job.

CO Travis articulated a perspective that was echoed, though seldom so clearly, by nearly every CO and "white shirt" we talked with or interviewed. From the perspective of the CO, people on the outside have no idea what the work of a CO is like. People in the general public see COs as the "bad guys," the violators of human rights. What the public doesn't see, but CO Travis does, is that he and the other COs are doing the dirty work that the collective "we" refuse to do. In his mind, the people we send to prison are the people that we can't deal with, and we expect him to do the often brutal and dehumanizing work of punishing those people whom "we" deem not fit for society. "Inmates are people who can't make it in the free world. The public doesn't understand. . . . They [inmates] are in here because they did something wrong—I don't mean selling dope—and now they aren't taking responsibility for their own actions. Jail isn't supposed to be *fun!*"

One supermax correctional officer who is cited in Lisa Guenther's book *Solitary Confinement: Social Death and Its Afterlives* remarks:

> Do we have an obligation to take care of them? Yes. But do I have an obligation to provide him touching, feeling, contact with another human being? I would say no. He has earned his way to this unit and he's earned just the opposite. He's earned the need for me to keep him from other people.[1]

COs like Travis resent the fact that they have to do society's dirty work and then, when they do exactly what we ask them to do, they are blamed for violating human rights. For CO Travis it's a no-win proposition.

On top of that, CO Travis feels "sold out" by the fact that when he uses what he sees as forms of punishment—burning a prisoner on a meal because he refused to come to his cell door, didn't put his oranges on, or didn't remove the paper blocking his window—the prisoner files a complaint and CO Travis gets a reprimand.

To add insult to injury, when a team of COs enforces the rules and prisoners make enough complaints, lawsuits get filed. According to CO Travis, "Guys [inmates] are told just act up and you'll get stuff. . . . To me, it's all about them [inmates] and not about us."

Guenther explicates the ways in which prisoner movements and legal challenges around human rights have failed to result in the abolition of solitary confinement and have served rather to establish the minimum standards under which solitary confinement can be implemented. For example, Guenther cites the case of *Gates v. Collier* (1974), in which prisoners brought a human rights case against the Mississippi State Penitentiary (Parchman):

> A federal district court considered the constitutionality of punitive isolation. . . . "The inmates are placed in the dark hole, naked, without any hygiene material, without any bedding, and often without adequate food. It is customary to cut the hair of the inmate confined in the dark hole by means of heavy-duty clippers. Inmates frequently remained in the dark hole for forty-eight hours and may be confined there for up to seventy-two hours. While an inmate occupies the dark hole, the cell is not cleaned, nor is the inmate permitted to wash himself" (Gates, 501F.2d at 1305, quoted in Reiter 2012 95–96). . . . They [the courts] limited its use to one twenty-four-hour period and ordered that "adequate food, clothing, hygiene items, and temperature control" be provided. . . . In each case, egregious violations of prisoners' rights were acknowledged and linked to punitive isolation, but rather than condemning such punishment itself, judges ordered specific changes to ensure that the conditions of punitive isolation met basic standards. These standards were determined by a certain conception of what is necessary for human life, where life and necessity are understood in terms of mere survival rather than relational well-being. By focusing on the provision of basic needs such as food, water, and shelter, judges in these cases were able to evade the question of whether "needs" are sufficient to define (human) life and whether intensive confinement itself might be torture.[2]

In other words, lawsuits amount to a series of *revisions* to the protocols and policies used in solitary confinement rather than addressing solitary confinement *itself* as a violation of human rights.

These lawsuits affirm for COs, on the one hand, that solitary confinement is, in and of itself, OK. It is not judged to be illegal; therefore, the COs are not doing anything illegal when they confine people in solitary confinement. Furthermore, as long as they abide by the letter of the law, for example, by providing hygiene products, then they are in compliance with the law. What they are doing, they tell themselves, is OK. In other words, doling out three rolls of toilet paper each week on a regular schedule and requiring the cardboard tubes to be returned before a prisoner gets a new roll is a practice that meets the minimum hygiene product requirement, as laid out in a court ruling, and thus it is not inhumane or dehumanizing. How could it be? A court, often the *Supreme Court*, said it was "OK."

For the typical CO, lawsuits are a nuisance, in part because they require them to constantly modify their protocols so as to be in compliance. Not surprisingly, many of the people incarcerated in solitary confinement are experts on the latest ruling, and they are not shy about demanding even the smallest modification to their rights. An extra calorie or an extra minute in the shower makes their time in the hole just a little bit easier to endure.

From the COs' perspective, though incremental, lawsuits reduce the number and kinds of tools in their tool kit, making it harder for CO Travis to do the job we have asked him to do.

> The jail responsibility is supposed to be *care, custody and control.* Now the jail has become a daycare. . . . A lot of what happens here I can relate to home. . . . The guys act like my kids. . . . I'm like a giant babysitter of adults. . . . They whine when they don't get their way. At home I can ground my kids; here I can burn a shower. . . . Only difference is, when I ground my kids, I ground them from the Xbox.

CHAPTER 36

Correctional PTSD

UNDOUBTEDLY, AND FOR GOOD REASON, the majority of research and journalist accounts of solitary confinement have focused on the impact of isolation on mental health. Research by psychologists reveals that mental health begins to decline as soon as the first twenty-four hours in isolation. "After six days of social and sensory isolation, the subjects' experience of the world had been altered dramatically."[1]

Yet very, very few people have studied the impact of solitary confinement on the people who work there.

What we know, because we observed it, is that COs are also locked in solitary confinement for eight to sixteen hours a day. Their thirty-minute lunch break, not much longer than the time a person incarcerated in solitary confinement gets in the shower, and shorter than they get in the yard, is their only reprieve, spent eating food that is no more satisfying than what they feed the prisoners, other than the fact that they are allowed a seemingly unlimited supply. They can eat until their bellies are full of chicken patties and the carrot, pea, corn veggie combination. And they have unlimited access to the offerings in the vending machines.

We would never argue that the experiences of the COs who work in solitary confinement compare to the torture that is experienced by the people incarcerated there. The COs are not locked in a cage. The COs are not strip searched, nor are they handcuffed and shackled. The COs get to go home at night and be with their families. Yet the COs do experience the same sensory deprivation that the prisoners do: the monochromatic walls; the stale, uncirculated air; the lack of natural light. They are forced to smell the same smells and eat the same food. And their jobs are extremely dangerous and stressful. They know that at any moment, especially when they are transferring trays or medication through the wicket or escorting an incarcerated person to shower or yard, they may have urine or feces thrown in their faces, they may be spit on or bit or stabbed with a shiv or shank.

Though we suspect that many, if not most of the COs working in solitary confinement experience mental health issues as a direct consequence of their work, few wanted to talk about it. Many denied it or brushed it off, except for

CO Travis. Much of our interview with CO Travis amounted to a discussion of his mental health.

Remember, CO Travis has been working in solitary confinement at SCI-Wannabee for twelve years. If CO Travis averages sixty hours of work a week, and he works fifty weeks a year, he has spent 36,000 hours in solitary confinement. Even if our estimate is high, CO Travis has likely spent at least 30,000 hours in solitary confinement. Thirty thousand hours. Only lifers have spent more hours in the hole than CO Travis.

The impact on his physical and mental health has been significant.

Whereas most of the COs we talked with denied that working in solitary confinement impacted their mental health, CO Travis led with this, and it consumed the majority of our conversation. CO Travis is angry. When he talked about his mental health struggles, his face got red and he raised his voice, not enough to be overheard by people who might be walking by the property room where we interviewed him but loud enough for emphasis. CO Travis is angry because working in solitary confinement is impacting his mental health, and he's angry because he feels like the institution doesn't care. He feels forgotten.

Though he is not trained as a mental health specialist, and this is the second major change in the work of a CO that CO Travis identifies, his job now requires that he deal with incarcerated people who are suffering from serious mental illness. He was adamant that people with mental illness should not be in prison; they should be in a psychiatric hospital. CO Travis blamed the closing of mental health units in hospitals for much of his job stress: "I didn't sign up to have a cup of shit thrown in my face."

Yet his exposure to incarcerated people with mental illness also contributes to his ability to understand and name his own struggles. CO Travis suggested that a new term be coined, "correctional PTSD," to refer to the mental health strain associated with working in solitary confinement. CO Travis is on to something. A study by the Centers for Disease Control revealed that COs have rates of Post-Traumatic Stress Disorder or PTSD that are ten times higher (35 percent) than the general population (3.5 percent).[2]

Christian Curtis synthesizes the literature on trauma and empathy, and he notes: "Dehumanizing activities will indeed dehumanize you, and your brain will reflect that process in the form of damage."[3]

In other words, it's not simply that COs become dehumanized; it's that they, as well as the people they lock up, experience changes in their brain that are similar to the effects of trauma that produce PTSD. PTSD has many significant impacts, including living in a state of hypervigilance, having a short temper, and having a limited capacity for empathy, all of which contribute to the cycle of dehumanization and further the violence inside solitary confinement units.

Curtis continues:

A brain under traumatic stress looks very different from one that is not. In the immediate precipitating moment of trauma, as well as trauma that is later revisited, the brain's deliberative centers—the frontal lobes on both sides—and indeed almost all of the outer cortex, go dark on brain scans. The lower parts of the brain, the source of emotions—the seat of fear, in particular—are fired up. A person in this state is concerned about one thing only, and that is to avoid perceived danger. Absent from this brain at this time is any notion of discretion, judgement, or empathy.

CO Travis describes it this way:

> You get harder. You see a lot of stuff in here no one else sees. Your demons come out. Working 2 to 10 ruins your life. People don't understand us. . . . They don't understand our dark sense of humor. . . . We see stuff and we are involved in stuff. . . . We have no control. No one cares about our mental stability. People call in 'cause they burn out. We have problems outside the job too. . . . Then an inmate acts up and we take it out on them. . . . You don't realize how stressful it is inside the walls. You're in jail too. You feel like an inmate. Inmates are running institutions and you have to do things to take care of them and no one is taking care of us.

What kind of job is this? Is the stress of working in solitary confinement worth the price you pay? As CO Travis so aptly describes his job: *"You're in jail too. You feel like an inmate. . . . No one is taking care of us."*

Further, from CO Travis's perspective, he is invisible. The institution cares about the prisoners, but the institution doesn't care about the impact of working in solitary confinement on him.

> The prison is worried about the mental state of the inmates, *not* the mental state of the COs. We don't get *free* psych. No one asks us if we need support. CEAP [the employee support program] is a joke; you have to use sick time to use it.

Like CO Travis, CO Porter also talked about the ways in which working in solitary confinement is impacting his mental health.

> "My wife and I are divorced. She left me for another man. . . . My callousness goes home. I don't show emotion here; I don't show emotion at home. . . . I go in the extra room and shut down."

["What's the stress?"]

> "Upper management. . . . Honestly, I've been deployed twice and this is worse than combat. . . . At least in combat you know what you're up against every day. . . . [In the jail] You're not just fighting inmates, you're also fighting upper management."

["What are you fighting with upper management about?"]

"Policy. They don't give you enough staff to do what they want. It's nonstop, and it comes into your home. . . . You see things other people don't see. . . . It's just like combat. . . . Its morbid. . . . Am I even right anymore?"
["How do you manage it?"]
"Hunt, fish—everyone has to do something. [He just got back from thirty days of vacation, and he went off the grid hunting and fishing.] "I didn't think about this place once until they called me back. . . . I had no idea how many guys were drinking a fifth every night."

Much like many women who are sent to prison for drug offenses that are a direct result of attempts to self-medicate the pain associated with trauma and abuse, some COs, according to CO Porter, are self-medicating the trauma of working in solitary confinement, by consuming copious amounts of alcohol each night.

Many of the COs and white shirts we interviewed and spent time with talked about the fact that they couldn't take their work home with them. Though they didn't necessarily want to nor did they often socialize with other prison staff, as a result they felt as if no one else understood them. They described feeling like outsiders at family gatherings. In particular, they talked about other people not understanding their sense of humor. Divorce rates are high among correctional officers. In fact, COs are 20 percent more likely to get divorced than the general population.[4] Many of the staff we spent time with told us they had divorced, and many had remarried. When we asked about their divorces and remarriages, a common theme emerged. They had married out of high school or college. When they exited the military or lost their jobs in factories when manufacturing moved "off shore" and they started working in the prison, they started having trouble in their marriages. To a one, all of the staff who remarried found their new spouses at work, in the jails where they worked. They described their new relationships as more successful because their spouses "understood" them. They were no longer on the outside looking in at family gatherings, at least not with their spouses.

CHAPTER 37

"Therapy" with Dr. Emma

THE DAY WE SPENT shadowing Dr. Emma, we asked if we could sit in on her treatment or therapy sessions, and she agreed.

There are two small "treatment" rooms outside of the DTU pod. They look like small offices, except instead of desks the rooms are outfitted with cages, the same kinds of cages where we interviewed Scholar. The first room holds three cages; the second holds five, two cages on one side of the room and three on the other. Dr. Emma holds treatment at the scheduled time, 10 to 11 A.M. on Mondays, Wednesdays, and Fridays, five men (each in a cage) in one room and three in the other, also in cages. Dr. Emma moves in between the two rooms, offering ten minutes of treatment to the first group, then switching rooms and back and forth, alternating for the hour.

Dr. Emma told us during our interview that she gets to select the topics that she wants to cover in their treatment. For this particular day she has chosen resilience. In the first room there was one white man, one Black man, and one Hispanic man, who we're not sure actually spoke that much English. We interacted with this him on several more occasions, and his English was definitely limited. We're not sure how the therapy worked out for him, since Dr. Emma conducted it all in English, but he smiled a lot and seemed happy to be in the cage in the therapy room. The white man, who was closest to us, was older, with long, gray hair and a long, gray beard. He had a lot of tattoos on his arms, neck, and face. He sat on the back of the chair so that even while sitting he was able to look Dr. Emma in the eyes. The Black man, in the middle cage, sat slumped, head and arms tucked into his shirt. He seemed totally disengaged, until the very end of the session.

In the second room there were two white men, caged next to each other, and three Black men in cages on the other side of the room. The white man we could see (we weren't able to walk all the way into the room to observe the other) was young. He alternated between sitting and standing. He nodded his head which seemed to us to indicate his engagement, but didn't say anything. The white man we couldn't see didn't speak except when he received his candy and he asked for a different kind than was offered. The three Black men were all middle aged. Two were very engaged, the two closest to Dr. Emma.

As educators, we were curious about the placement of the prisoners and their relative interaction. Did the COs put the most talkative people in particular cages, or did it just seem that way to us on this one day that we observed? If the COs pulled the prisoners in order by cell, perhaps some of the guys were next to the same people on the tier and in the cages in the therapy room, which could increase or decrease participation and disclosure. It's interesting that on the day we observed, there was some serious, private disclosure. We wonder how that impacts the person who discloses once they are back on the tier, now that other prisoners know their business.

Dr. Emma began the sessions by reading a definition of resilience, and then she asked the people locked in the cages to think about their own resiliency. After giving the assignment, she left and went to the second room and repeated the exercise. We went with her to the second room, so we don't know what happened in the first room after she left. Based on the interactions when we return, we assume not much.

After this exercise, we went back to the first room and Dr. Emma asked the men in the cages what they thought about while she was in the other room and if they had anything to share. No one offered any comment. She then read aloud from a handout she had downloaded from the internet, titled "The Seven Habits of Resilient People." After reading through the entire list, she returned to the top of the list and stopped on each habit. She asked each caged person to mentally rate themselves on a scale from 1to 10. The items were things like having social support, having someone to talk to, recognizing your successes, and not blaming yourself for your failures. She told them that she would be worried if anyone scored lower than a 5 on any item and asked them to share their scores and their personal examples. The white man offered a response to pretty much every prompt and indicated that he thinks his resiliency is pretty high because he has support on the inside. The Hispanic man mostly smiled and nodded. The Black man suddenly found his voice. He sat up and said that he didn't have any support, no one on the outside or the inside, but he rated himself average (a 5) on support. His response didn't make sense to us, but we watched as Dr. Emma navigated the conversation. As she talked to him, he not only perked up but actually moved to the edge of the seat and looked her in the eye and engaged with her. She talked to them all, but especially to the Black man. She talked to him about not blaming himself for his failures and encouraged him to focus on his successes. When they were done talking, the men each stood at the door to their cage and Dr. Emma passed them each two pieces of candy. The men complained that there weren't any chocolates left; there were only Tootsie Rolls and Starburst. When she didn't have the kind of candy the men preferred, they were polite and took what they were offered. She slid the candy, because the pieces were small, between the links in the cage.

In the second treatment room, in addition to the five incarcerated people and Dr. Emma (and us), there was a peer "mentor." The peer mentor program is the highest paid, and one of the most sought-after jobs in the prison. Prisoners are selected for this program based on both their interest in serving as peer mentors and their success in jail, which is measured by completing programs and staying out of trouble. Most have struggled with mental illness, addiction, or both. They receive training, and according to some "white shirts" and unit managers we talked to, incarcerated people who serve as peer mentors are often able to apply the credentials they get in prison to jobs when they are released. Counselor Mark at SCI-Women extolled the peer mentor program. He said that in the beginning many of the COs working in solitary confinement were reluctant to engage the peer mentors and allow them onto the tiers and into the pods because they perceived that the peer mentors would coddle the people incarcerated there or possibly pass contraband. But over time, Counselor Mark was pleased to report, even the most resistant COs saw the benefit of the peer mentors, and peer mentors have become an important asset in the tool kit to manage the people with mental illness who are incarcerated in solitary confinement.

Peer mentors wear white jumpsuits, which are a stark contrast to the brown, blue, and orange jumpsuits the other prisoners wear, and they have a great deal of freedom to move about the prison. They come, unescorted, to the solitary confinement unit to meet with men in the DTU. They are allowed to walk cell to cell to check in with guys, and they also attend, and support, therapy sessions like the one we observe with Dr. Emma. Despite this freedom and the trust it implies, like every prisoner who comes and goes from the solitary confinement unit, they are strip-searched on both their way in and their way out.

As Dr. Emma was asking the incarcerated people about resiliency and how they coach themselves and try to tell themselves good things about themselves, the Black man closest to us asked the others if they ever heard voices. The peer mentor, who is also Black, offered that he has diagnosed schizophrenia. The two men talked at length about the voices they hear, the therapy, and their medications. The Black man in the cage commented that he thinks that people need to talk more openly about hearing voices. The peer mentor agreed and talked about the fact that he knows schizophrenia is something he will live with forever. The best he can do is manage it.

We had several thoughts during this exchange. One, that we are worried about a man in a cage saying that he is hearing voices, and two, that this type of peer mentoring seems really appropriate and potentially really, really helpful.

Dr. Emma let the two men talk for quite some time, not entirely abandoning her agenda, but like any good classroom teacher, letting it go where it needed to go. She was careful to ask the Black man in the cage questions to ensure that he was OK and safe.

As in the first room, Dr. Emma closed out the session by offering the men in the cages a piece of candy.

Because she let the session run so long, she didn't close quite the same way. There wasn't time for each incarcerated person to go around and rate himself on each of the seven habits of resilient people. But in both rooms, she offered each person a copy of the paper with the definitions and habits. Each prisoner took one—perhaps because they wanted to know more about resilience or perhaps because they wanted a piece of paper.

In both treatment rooms but especially in the second, perhaps because of the extended conversation about schizophrenia, Dr. Emma made sure to talk to each person in the cages individually, moving around the room to make eye contact, about their circumstances. She told them over and over again that she knows that they deal with very difficult things but that they are still here and that means they are resilient and if they can learn to draw on their resiliency, the time they have to serve in solitary confinement and in prison will move faster.

In the second treatment room, she also shared about having gone through some difficult times herself. She didn't disclose the details, which is consistent with prison protocol, but she wanted the incarcerated people to know that she knows what it means to be dealing with loss and pain. She is making a human connection. And, for those locked in solitary confinement, her words are one of the few things punctuating the isolation.

After lunch Dr. Emma agreed to let us accompany her on her psych rounds. By law, she's required to have contact with each person incarcerated in the DTU every day, and she meets this requirement of her job by doing rounds. In addition, each person incarcerated there is required to be offered out-of-cell time with her every single day, and they are entitled to out-of-cell time with her at least once a week. Between running two treatment sessions per day, prepping for treatment sessions, documenting the compliance of the people incarcerated in the DTU (they earn points for coming out of their cells, going to programming, and so on), her daily contact with each person confined there is limited to just a couple of minutes per day. Literally.

We begin on the lower tier at one end and work our way to the end, then climb the stairs and work our way back, moving cell to cell.

Dr. Emma looks at the name tag on the door. Then she knocks on the cell door and calls the inhabitant's name. "Jones? It's Dr. Emma. How are you doing today? Good? Anything I can do for you today?"

In conversation, Dr. Emma tells us that when she asks "Anything I can do for you today?" the person incarcerated in the cell understand this as her prompt to them to ask for out-of-cell time if they want it. She asks this way, rather than "Do you want out of cell time," because she knows that if she asks them directly they will all say "yes" and there's no way she can accommodate them all if they each ask for out-of-cell time each week. It's just not possible.

Mostly the incarcerated people we observe while shadowing Dr. Emma on her rounds in the DTU are polite and the exchange is short.

The majority of the people incarcerated there did not, in fact, interact with Dr. Emma other than to acknowledge that they are OK. Mostly they came to the door of their cell to say hello. Sometimes the people incarcerated in the cells did not come to the cell door, in which case Dr. Emma continued to knock and shout their names through the slit in the cell door until she got a verbal response from them, indicating that at a bare minimum they were alive.

Sometimes the incarcerated person needs something, and he views Dr. Emma as the person he can make the request to. Sometimes he just wants someone to talk to. At two cells, we observed Dr. Emma actually "deliver services." In these two cases the people locked in the cells indicated that they were suffering from psychiatric symptoms, and in both cases they indicated that they had not received their appropriate medications. Dr. Emma's role is as a liaison to the psychiatrist. She made notes and insisted that she would pass along their concerns to the supervising psychiatrist. In both cases she seemed very concerned and tried to reassure them that she would get them what they needed, and she offered them other strategies they could employ while they waited for their meds to be ordered and delivered. Both men were suffering from depression, and Dr. Emma talked to them about resiliency, using the same language and thought exercises she used in the treatment room.

Though Dr. Emma is pretty optimistic about her work, we found the psych services to be underwhelming. Dr. Emma was doing rounds in *the DTU*. The men have clear mental health issues; they are suffering from either severe or unmanaged mental illness. They are locked in cages, their only meaningful interaction is with Dr. Emma, the psychologist, who walks by their cell once a day, five days a week, and asks if they are OK. Other than perhaps intercepting a suicide, we can't imagine that much mental health service is being delivered in this setting. This does not mean that Dr. Emma is not working hard or that she is not committed. By our observation, she works hard and cares deeply. Her work, like that of Mary Buser, who wrote about her time delivering mental health services on Rikers Island, is constrained by forces outside of herself, by the administration of the prison and the beliefs about what people who are locked in solitary confinement deserve. Observing Dr. Emma on her rounds reinforces the disconnect between CO Travis' assessment of the treatment he believes the prisoners locked in solitary confinement are receiving and his own lack of access to mental health services. Does CO Travis really believe that these men, locked in cages twenty-three hours a day, seven days a week, who have a one-minute interaction with Dr. Emma have better access to mental health services than he does? If so, what does this say about the working conditions for COs like Travis?

CHAPTER 38

The Grift

FAKING MENTAL ILLNESS TO GET
A CANDY BAR

AT FIRST GLANCE it may seem odd that COs who get to leave prison each day when their shift is over develop deep resentment of the prisoners they keep locked in cages twenty-four hours a day, 365 days a year. When we first heard COs in SCI-Wannabee expressing resentment towards the people incarcerated in solitary confinement, we were taken aback. Yet in interview after interview after interview, COs expressed disdain for the prisoners whom they perceived as scamming the system and getting a better deal than hard-working men like them.

One of the biggest issues of contention between the COs and the people incarcerated in solitary confinement was the D-Code. A D-Code is a diagnosis of severe mental illness. According to the COs, prisoners with a D-Code get all kinds of privileges in the jail, in solitary confinement, and even in the free world.

Prisoners who receive a formal diagnosis and are assigned a D-Code suffer from severe mental illness that is not well managed. In order to address the needs of those with severe and unmanaged mental illness, when prisoners with a D-Code are sent to solitary confinement, they are housed in a separate pod, known as the Diversionary Treatment Unit (DTU). One of the members of our research team, Shannon Magnuson, has focused her analysis on the DTU. We encourage the interested reader to see her work. [1]

In SCI-Wannabee, the DTU is D Pod, which makes it easy to identify. People incarcerated in the DTU wear blue rather than orange jumpsuits so they are easily distinguishable. The DTU is designed as a separate pod in the solitary confinement unit in part because of the special needs of the people incarcerated there and in part because they are entitled to a host of additional privileges. Many COs believe incarcerated people fake mental illness in order to access these privileges, including significantly more time "out of cell" each day. At SCI-Wannabee people incarcerated in the DTU were offered showers and yard every day, and in addition, ten to fifteen hours of "out of cell" programming each week.

Programming, we observed, consisted of offering the people incarcerated there a chance to color sheets designed for preschoolers, play bingo, or watch a G-rated movie that was shown, no kidding, on a VCR.

While prisoners were engaged in programming, the "instructors" mostly sat at a desk, watching them or doing paperwork or dozing off while COs moved among the prisoners desks to ensure that no one was fighting, or stabbing another prisoner with a shank or shiv, or passing contraband.

No wonder the COs believed programming was a waste of time. It was much more work for them (strip searching, handcuffing and shackling the prisoners to desks), and they didn't see any benefit to it. But programming was more than a waste of time from the vantage point of the COs.

Programming is a sea of Black and brown faces, all handcuffed and shackled to desks. It reminds us of a waiting room in an emergency room or at the social security administration or the DMV or the visiting room at a jail or prison. Spaces where people wait, often for what seems like an endless amount of time. Punctuated only by the calling of a number which wakes the unconscious, papers gathered up, scurrying to a window to plead their case, to be seen by medical personnel or renew a driver's license or file for social security benefits, or see a loved one locked up behind a wall. In our visits to these spaces it seems that more often than not, the service people are seeking is denied. The resemblance of programming spaces to welfare offices cannot be lost on the COs. Stereotypes of the "welfare queen" activated, as they watch Black men clamor for a candy bar or to be certified for SSI, short term and long-term grifting. They resent Black people who they perceive as getting something for nothing while hard working men like them get up and come to work every day risking their lives to keep the rest of us safe.[2]

CO Travis offers this analysis:

> It bothers me. . . . Legit people [like vets] don't get what they need. . . . The same guy [who is acting up] is recruiting other inmates in the DTU to act crazy to get money. . . . Guys think SSI is a lot of money—in here it is, but in the streets it's not much. . . . They got nothing on the outside; they gotta get some game. . . . Look, we [COs] know these guys better than our own families. . . . I know their game. In here they're like "I'm entitled, society let me down."

From the perspective of those incarcerated in the DTU, programming brought tremendous benefit. They were out of their cells. They could see each other, talk, probably pass all kinds of contraband, from a piece of food to a scrap of paper, to a small amount of a drug like suboxone, a heroine derivative that was rampant at SCI-Wannabee because it could be smuggled in under something as small as a postage stamp.

People incarcerated in the DTU and who participated in programming also received a much-coveted, regular-sized candy bar for every day that they participated in programming. In a setting in which food is one of the most highly contested items, a candy bar provided not only much-needed calories but taste that contrasted significantly with the bland food that dominated the diet in solitary confinement.

Before we observed the DTU, it was hard to believe the claim of the COs that incarcerated people faked mental illness to get a candy bar. But in this context of solitary confinement, where everything but time is a carefully managed, scarce resource, it became easier to understand the perspective of the COs.

Mary Buser describes a similar tension in the Bing, the solitary confinement unit at Rikers Island that houses more than five hundred men. She articulates the tension between psyche staff and COs:

> I extended my hand to a squat officer with a whiskered chin. But Putney simply glared at me. "There's a lot of knuckleheads in here, nothing wrong with 'em!" "Oh come on, Putney," George chided, "A lot of these guys are very sick, and you know it." "Yeah—and alot of 'em ain't." George didn't have to explain this scenario to me. It was an all-too-familiar example of the tension between the Mental Health staff and the Department of Corrections when it came to the mentally ill. For the most part, the DOC was of the view that the mentally ill were faking it. . . . *To us, the mentally ill are patients; to them they are inmates. To us they are sick and often misunderstood; to DOC they are manipulators who are always trying to "get one over."*[3] [emphasis ours]

Although it was commonly believed among COs that incarcerated people faked mental illness in order to get extra privileges, the research suggests otherwise. National studies suggest that as many as 40 percent of men and upward of 80 percent of women who are incarcerated suffer from some mental health challenges. This is not surprising, given that 20 percent of our incarcerated population is serving time for drug possession. Among the most common mental health issues is addiction, but there are also high rates of anxiety and depression. Bruce Western and his colleagues who conducted research in solitary confinement units in a similar state system found that people incarcerated in solitary confinement were twice as likely as people incarcerated in general population to have ever received a mental health diagnosis (51 percent compared with 24 percent).[4] Additionally, people incarcerated in solitary confinement had relatively high rates of severe mental illness: 21.2 percent had received a formal diagnosis, which was also twice the rate of people incarcerated in general population.

Furthermore, research on solitary confinement reveals, after just twenty-four hours in solitary, the average, mentally healthy person begins to exhibit signs of mental illness. So perhaps the mental illness we observed in the DTU is in some part simply a manifestation of the conditions of solitary confinement itself, a feedback loop if you will, or a chicken-and-egg puzzle to which there is no answer, no matter how much time you spend pondering it.

From our perspective, psychological treatment in prisons is extremely limited. Many incarcerated people are managing serious mental health issues, which all experts agree decompensate or malinger while they are in solitary confinement, even in the DTU where they get some programming. Though they may get programming and group therapy like that which we observe with Dr. Emma, they get very little in terms of mental health *treatment*, and certainly not the kind of care that people in the free world who have insurance are able to receive. We wonder what chance these folks have to successfully reenter general population, let alone the free world if their mental health does nothing but decompensate while they are locked up twenty-four hours a day in cages.

Yet from the perspective of CO Travis, people incarcerated in the DTU are getting something he needs and doesn't have access to: mental health care. Another CO at SCI-Wannabee complained that incarcerated people think they are the only ones who have a hard time, who are struggling with a life that is unfair: "COs have problems, too. . . . My wife is ill." . . . ["I'm sorry."] "It's life . . . but I want to go back to the inmates and say it's all life. Deal with it. We've all dealt with stuff. . . . I'm tired of hearing the inmates complain."

It's not so much a matter of CO Travis and his colleagues making an accurate assessment of the therapy and programming that incarcerated people are receiving; rather, it's his perception that counts, and his perception is that the institution and the world care more about people who have done terrible things, committed horrible crimes, or even just refused to follow the rules than they do about him, a man who does the dirty work that the rest of us don't want to do in a place that impacts his physical and mental health. Out of sight, out of mind. Just like the incarcerated persons. Trump's invisible people.

CO Travis argued that these privileges also extended into the free world in ways that disadvantaged people like him, white people who had worked hard, served their country, and were falling behind while people like the men he took care of for a dozen years while they served time in solitary confinement zoomed ahead, as if they were on an escalator that was moving faster.

Many COs believed the incarcerated people pursued the assignment of a D-Code so that when they were released from prison they would qualify for Supplemental Security Income (SSI), which are government payments to those with disabilities who can document an inability to be employed. In other words, COs like Travis believed that incarcerated people scammed the system on the inside so that once they were released from prison, they could collect a government check rather than work a low-skill, low-wage job. Like CO Travis does. At a job he hates.

CHAPTER 39

The Flipped Script

TVS, TRAYS, AND [FLUSH] TOILETS

MANY OF THE COs we interviewed and spent time with talked about the fact that they felt like glorified babysitters. For those who have not been in a solitary confinement unit, this might seem like an odd analogy, but in fact, many of the fundamental features of solitary confinement require COs to do the same kind of work we associate with daycare.

One of the intended or unintended consequences of the twenty-three-hour lockdown in solitary confinement units is the requirement that all meals be eaten in the prisoner's cell. In practice this means that correctional officers must hand-deliver trays to the people who are incarcerated there three times a day, and pick them up after each meal. Each tray must be passed through a wicket in order to safeguard the CO from the possibility that the inhabitant may "hold their tray hostage" or throw urine or feces at the CO, putting the CO in danger during this exchange. As a result, "passing trays" is a labor-intensive, time-consuming task that some people we interviewed who were incarcerated in solitary confinement ranked as a "benefit" because they didn't have to walk in the rain or cold weather to the chow hall. This otherwise simple and straightforward task was one many correctional officers, on the other hand, came to resent. Trays, for example, are contested terrain not only because their passing is considered a dangerous or high-risk activity but also because they are an instance of "flipping the script" of racialized roles in the United States. In the free world, Black people serve white people. But in the hidden world of solitary confinement the script is often flipped: COs, who are almost always white, serve prisoners, who are disproportionately Black.

Through the lens of men who already feel like they are "forgotten" and "left behind," solitary confinement comes to be viewed not as a place of punishment but rather as a place of service. Service by the COs to the people incarcerated there. Not only must trays be delivered, but mail must be delivered. Shampoo and toilet paper must be dispensed. Razors must be handed out, a tedious process because all razors must also be collected or there is the risk someone will get cut or cut themselves. When the book cart comes, COs must supervise the distribution of reading material. TV channels must be changed in response to the collective wishes of the prisoners locked in the cages in the pod. In the DTU, COs must escort "students" to therapy sessions and classes, which from the perspective of the COs are disguised as "programming." Every thirty minutes, a CO must walk the entire pod to ensure everyone there is still alive.

These duties often take up nearly an entire eight-hour shift and must be repeated day after day after day, for years. A CO working in solitary confinement in SCI-Wannabee will deliver thousands and thousands of meals, pick up thousands and thousands of trays—all while at risk for having urine or feces thrown at them, all while insults are hurled by the people incarcerated there, who are often relentless in their requests: "Where's my property?" "Change the channel!" "Flush my toilet!"

COs' only mechanism for retaining power and control in this social structure is to arbitrarily enforce rules that deny people who are incarcerated access to the things they desire or believe they are entitled to. COs burn prisoners on showers and meals when they are not standing at their cell doors, paper off their windows, light on in their cell at the precise moment the CO walks on to the pod. People who are incarcerated view this as a human rights violation. COs view it as a punishment strategy. We are left pondering the importance of such arbitrary rules. Why do cardboard toilet paper rolls have to be turned in before an incarcerated person can get a new roll of toilet paper? Not because toilet paper or ChapStick is a matter of national security, but because COs view burning people who are incarcerated as one of their only strategies for leveling the playing field, for holding on to their place in the hierarchy. A place they feel they are slowly losing.

Despite the fact that prisoners are locked in their cells twenty-three hours a day and the COs get to go home at night, COs see the hole as a place that rewards the worst of the worst, while the COs and their families and neighbors struggle, where the victims get nothing.

Sometimes COs witness situations in which they truly believe that people incarcerated in solitary confinement get more than they and their families do. For example, as CO Travis emphasized over and over again, he feels that he needs mental health treatment, but he can't get it; he can't afford to pay for it; he would have to take time off from work to utilize it; but every day he is required to escort prisoners, the worst of the worst, to therapy sessions with Dr. Emma, a therapy session he would like to have, albeit minus the strip search and the cage.

CO Porter adds: "I have an elderly family member who had to give up their house to get a medical procedure and the inmates get the best medical care for $5. . . . I knew a guy on death row that got chemo. Imagine that . . . paying to keep a guy alive just to kill him!"

Between 2017 and 2019, when we were conducting research in Larrabee County, though the unemployment rate was relatively low, the median household income is \$10,000 lower than the national median (\$51,000 compared with \$61,000 nationwide).[1] Larrabee County is a county of the working poor. People in Larrabee County struggle to pay their bills and send their kids to college. The COs at SCI-Wannabee are stuck working in a job they hate, and every day they see prisoners who are not working hard, some of whom have committed horrible crimes, get access to things they don't have access to or can't provide. Quite literally, CO Porter sleeps in his car. In the winter. Sure, maybe it's only two nights a week, but he spends all day serving men who sleep in a cell that has heat in the winter.

CO Bunker, who served several tours in Iraq, returned to a place where he feels, to use Arlie Hochschild's phrase, like "a stranger in his own land." Despite the fact that he personally locks people in cages twenty-four hours a day and enforces a set of policies and practices that denies them their basic human rights, he believes that incarcerated people are more privileged than the people they victimized and even himself. "The biggest downfall of the DOC is *there are no victim's rights anymore*. Inmates get TVs, tablets, kiosks, email, *victims get nothing they don't get their family member back*. I lived in a bunker in Iraq for a year and these guys have a better shitter . . . not made of wood that they don't have to burn."

As CO Tom said: "Most of us are here because of choices we made in the past, both the guards and the inmates." And through the lens of the COs, their bad choices, which they define as not going to college when they should have, result in worse outcomes, from their perspective, than those facing the people who are incarcerated.

As Arlie Hochschild argues in her book *Strangers in Their Own Land*, published in 2018, the COs perceive a world in which they have been standing in line, doing the right thing, working hard, waiting patiently, and they look up and other people are jumping the line. At work, mostly Black and brown men, although they are locked in cages, get medical care for \$5 and mental health sessions three times a week with Dr. Emma. Black and brown people are moving into their communities, like Larrabee County, from the urban areas to take advantage of newly constructed public housing, and they are bringing drugs and crime with them, as LT House told us. A Black man was elected president not once but twice. Though few and far between, women now work in the prison, even in solitary confinement. Gay people can get married. Trans people can use any bathroom they want, and now they are transitioning in prison, which presents an entirely other set of circumstances.[2] The world is changing in ways that continue to reinforce a narrative that while they work hard, in a job they hate, other people, including men locked in cages twenty-four hours a day, are getting something for nothing.

To add insult to injury, though not all of the people incarcerated in solitary confinement are Black, in their daily lives, white men, the COs are required to "serve" Black men. They serve them their meals, they bring them their toilet paper, and they change their TV channels. In their worldview, Black people serve white people, not the reverse. Though they may not have regular contact with Black people in Larrabee County, they know from traveling to urban areas in the state or even just from watching TV that Black people clean houses and cook the food in restaurants, even when the owner is white, and as far as they are concerned, it's always been this way. Now, they look up and Black people are lying back, relaxing, not working at all while they bust their butts hauling food up and down the stairs, risking their lives every time they open the wicket. It is precisely this "flipping" of the traditional racial script that forms the basis of the racial resentment experienced and expressed by many of the officers we interviewed.

CHAPTER 40

Not Always in Sync

THE JOB OF THE CO AND THE WORK OF THE CO

FOR MANY COs WORKING in solitary confinement, the job of the CO—care, custody, and control—has become disconnected from the actual work of the CO, which CO Travis refers to as glorified babysitting. In her decisive investigation of organizations and professions that deal with rape, Pat Martin, author of *Rape Work*, details the processes most organizations employ to handle cases of rape, which more often than not result in individual and collective resentment of this aspect of the job. Martin's research focuses on the five institutions in most communities charged with handling some aspect of a rape incident: law enforcement (police and sheriff), the judicial system (prosecutors and judges), hospital emergency rooms, and rape crisis centers.

With the exception of rape crisis centers, the organizations responding to rape allegations maintain larger missions and see rape, at best, as tangential and, at worst, as a distraction from the "real work" of the organization. Law enforcement agents poignantly note, "We're responsible for all crime and rape is only one crime."[1] At least law enforcement agencies include rape as a part of their missions. Hospitals, whom Martin terms "the reluctant partner," in contrast, view the requirement to perform a forensic rape exam as competing directly with their real mission: to heal the sick and wounded. From the perspective of hospitals and their staff, a rape kit is a legal exam, not a medical exam, and they will, in many cases, do anything they can to avoid performing it: "We have one doctor. . . . He will see a child with a cold before a rape victim."[2]

As Martin's research reveals, when organizations and their staff do not view handling rape allegations as central to their mission and/or their jobs, staff are more reluctant to do the work associated with a report of rape, and institutions do not invest in and may even sabotage individual efforts to address rape in their organizations.

The same can be said for the job of the CO. As CO Travis and CO Bunker articulated, many COs view their job as the care, custody, and control of people who have violated the rules of society and been sent to prison as punishment. This sense of urgency in their jobs is exacerbated in solitary confinement,

where they believe they are guarding the worst of the worst. Though CO
Travis and CO Bunker know this is not entirely true—in fact, they are well
aware that many of the incarcerated people they are charged with guarding
each day were sent to prison on low-level drug violations, and they were sent
to the hole for violating minor rules—they construct their job as one in which
their role is first and foremost to punish bad people and second to uphold the
memories of the victims of their crimes. In their minds, they are the only
people in the world who bear this great responsibility, and as much as they
hate their work, they love this aspect of their jobs. This disconnect is precisely
what makes them hate their jobs: they believe they are no longer doing this
important work; instead, they are babysitting.

Rather than punishing bad people, they are serving them! CO Travis
remarks: "Guys don't want to leave solitary. Especially guys who owe debts.
They want to stay. Why wouldn't they? They watch TV all day. Big TV. I change
the channel for him. I take him to the shower. I feed him three hots a day.
One guy's been here two years. We can't kick him."

COs are bringing food to people incarcerated in cells and clearing their
dirty dishes, much like they see waitresses doing in the local diners they frequent. They are escorting them to shower and yard, and bringing them shampoo and soap and razors and toilet paper, much like a housekeeper restocking
motel rooms or providing turn-down service. This is not at all the work COs
want to do, and this is not the work they were trained to do. To add insult to
injury, this work flips the racial hierarchy on its head. From COs' view, Black
men lie back in their cells and watch the Golf Channel while being waited on
by the COs, many of whom, as CO Porter reveals, can't afford the Golf Channel in their own cable package. It is precisely this disconnect between job and
work that Martin points out, that contributes to the white racial resentment
COs experience.

CHAPTER 41

Intimate Interracial Contact
and Intimate Surveillance

ONE OF THE MOST COMMONLY held beliefs in white America is that having a Black friend means you are not racist. This belief is based on the assumption that if we can like someone who is different from us, then we can't or won't discriminate against that person. Though this is a pleasant way to see the world, there is a mountain of scientific and anecdotal evidence that leads us, and many, many, many other scholars, to conclude quite the opposite. Liking, even loving, someone who is different from you does not protect you (or that person) from engaging in discriminatory behavior. In fact, many people not only engage in discrimination against the very people whom they claim to like or love, but more so, they endorse policies that harm the entire group to which their friends or loved ones belong.

Having a Black friend doesn't make one immune to engaging in racism. Contact alone with people who are different from us doesn't reduce our individual level prejudice or our complicity in structural systems of inequality.

In fact, research suggests that contact alone, without meaningful dialogue, can have quite the opposite effect: it can reinforce stereotypes and produce racialized resentment.

THE CONTACT HYPOTHESIS

One might assume that intimate contact could create opportunities for prejudice reduction, and this is just what social psychologist Gordon Allport sought to investigate.[1] Allport developed the contact hypothesis to describe what he and many others believe to be one of the most effective strategies for reducing racial bias. According to Allport, five specific conditions are necessary for prejudice reduction:

> *Equal status.* Both groups must engage equally in the relationship. Members of the group should have similar backgrounds, qualities, and characteristics. Differences in academic backgrounds, wealth, skill, or experiences should be minimized if these qualities will influence perceptions of prestige and rank in the group.

    Common goals. Both groups must work on a problem or task and share
        this as a common goal, sometimes called a superordinate goal, a
        goal that can be attained only if the members of two or more
        groups work together by pooling their efforts and resources.
    Intergroup cooperation. Both groups must work together for their com-
        mon goals without competition. Groups need to work together
        in the pursuit of common goals.
    Support of authorities, law, or customs. Both groups must acknowledge
        some authority that supports the contact and interactions between
        the groups. The contact should encourage friendly, helpful, egal-
        itarian attitudes and condemn ingroup-outgroup comparisons.
    Personal interaction. The contact situation needs to involve informal,
        personal interaction with outgroup members. Members of the
        conflicting groups need to mingle with one another. Without
        this criterion, they learn very little about each other and cross-
        group friendships do not occur.

In contrast to the conditions that Allport identifies for reducing prejudice,
solitary confinement units create a context in which nearly every aspect of the
contact hypothesis is violated, with the exception of personal interaction. As
we have detailed, prisoners and staff in solitary confinement units have significant personal interaction, much of it quite intimate, and yet almost none
of it is cooperative. Rather, much if not most of it is antagonistic. The wicket
is the greatest point of contention, as it allows COs to pass food and allows the
inhabitant to pass the most intimate of bodily fluids. As such, this highly intimate contact in the absence of equality and shared common goals, does the
opposite of what is predicted by the contact hypothesis; rather than easing
racial biases, it intensifies racial prejudice.

    Psychologists refer to this process as "confirmation bias." Confirmation
bias occurs when contact with someone about whom you hold stereotypes
confirms rather than dislodges those stereotypes. So, for example, one of the
most commonly held stereotypes about Black men is that they are criminals.
Evidence of this bias is everywhere. The vast majority of roles played by Black
actors reinforce this stereotype. This is in part why Chadwick Boseman's portrayal of a superhero in the film *Black Panther* was not only noteworthy but
inspirational. There were no Black superheroes, ever, before Boseman. The
news reinforces this stereotype. Images flood the screens of our nightly news,
the front pages of our newspapers, and our social media feeds with images of
Black men committing crimes or being arrested. The more recent phenomenon involves white people calling the police on Black people who are waiting
in Starbucks or having a barbeque in a park, or asking you to leash your dog in
Central Park, which Christian Cooper did when Amy Cooper (no relation)
called the police and claimed she was being attacked by a Black man. Amy

Cooper was invoking one of the oldest tropes available to white women, and one of the most dangerous for Black men: the Black male rapist.

Solitary confinement units around the United States are not any different than SCI-Wannabee: tens of thousands of Black bodies locked in cages. Treated like animals. Sometimes acting like animals. White COs, who absorb directly and indirectly all of the racial stereotypes of Black men have these biases confirmed over and over again, day after day after day, contributing to the furthering rather than the diminishing of white racial resentment. Recall the Black officer who we quoted in chapter 9: "Everything we are taught [stereotypes] is reinforced. White officers don't know the culture of the community they are policing."

As CO Travis points out, compared with the old days, COs and prisoners locked in solitary confinement units together, are structurally positioned as adversaries, and thus they are denied the opportunity to develop even a working relationship, let alone a relationship of mutual respect. Both the incarcerated and CO are in fact more isolated, rather than less isolated, as a result of the intimate nature of solitary confinement.

As Lisa Guenther argues:

> Today's control prisons do not merely leave inmates to their own solitary devices; they force prisoners to interact with guards in specific ways, punishing them with physical force or with further levels of deprivation when they fail or refuse to comply with the rules. The SHU [secure housing unit] is a highly mediated, intensely "social" space insofar as it leaves incarcerated persons no room to withdraw from the forced relationality of constant surveillance and control; and this forced relationality only compounds the social isolation of prisoners, structurally undermining the possibility of an open, reciprocal relationship with others. Here . . . the basic structure of intensive confinement emerges as a forced isolation that excludes the possibility of genuine solitude, and as a forced relationality that excludes the possibility of genuine relationships.[2]

Intimate contact is one of the structural features unique and central to everyone—both COs and prisoners—in solitary confinement. People who are incarcerated there must be strip-searched every time they are moved, which in practice, especially in units like the DTU, can result in COs having to strip-search each and very prisoner multiple times in one shift. Multiplied by thirty or forty prisoners on a pod, an officer might conduct one hundred strip searches a day.

Like the wicket, the strip search is a point of tension as well as control. People who are incarcerated experience the strip search as invasive, and some of them told us that they consider it a violation of PREA. Other prisoners told us it's just something you get used to. We heard the same from COs. Some hated this job duty, and others considered it just routine business. Something that must be done. Regardless of an individual's feelings about the strip search, as Lisa Guenther argues, it is a site both for extreme intimacy and for the expression of power.

> A dialectic of force and resistance sweeps up the bodies of both prisoners and guards. On the one hand, guards are separated from prisoners by highly mediated space where prisoners are sealed within solid walls and monitored from a distance through constantly running surveillance cameras, with doors as the only threshold between inside and outside and cuff-ports [we refer to these as wickets] as the only gaps, the only permeable points in this threshold. On the other hand, guards *come into the most intimate contact possible with prisoners, cuffing and uncuffing their hands through cuffports, restraining their hands and legs, doling out squares of toilet paper or menstrual pads, dispensing food, searching their anal cavities, and sometimes getting feces or urine thrown in their faces.* The separation between prisoners and guards cannot be absolutely enforced, and yet the dialectic of force and resistance that springs up between them remains asymmetrically weighted toward the guards, who have the power of *legitimate* physical violence on their side. . . . The most extreme manifestation of this asymmetry is the strip search, which could be traumatic for anyone but is especially so for the many prisoners who are survivors of sexual and physical abuse.[3] (emphasis ours)

The logic of the COs dictates that in order to maintain security, prisoners must be surveilled at all times. Thus, it's not just the COs who conduct the strip search who have intimate interactions with people incarcerated in solitary confinement; officers in the bubble as well as those on the pod observe prisoners in the most intimate behaviors we on the outside engage in daily and in private, including showering, using the toilet, eating, and sleeping.

Lisa Guenther points out that there is also an impact of this constant surveillance on those doing the surveilling: the COs.

> If I am constantly monitored in my prison cell, without having the chance to return the other's gaze—or if I spend eight hours a day in the surveillance booth, watching prisoners who cannot see me watching them—what effect does this have on my experience of . . . being? On the one hand, the positions of guard and prisoner are tightly bound to one another as subjects and objects of vision; on the other hand the irreversibility of these positions disconnects them from each other, such that the two do not interweave. . . . And yet, the prisoner and the guard are stuck in the same dreary landscape of segmented hallways, razor-wire perimeters, and booming concrete interiors. They are positioned differently within this landscape to be sure, but it is not at all clear that the guards have greater access to the chiasmatic structure of being than do prisoners, as long as they are bound to watch over them.[4]

Solitary confinement is, then, as a result of its very structures, an environment in which there is a tremendous amount of intimate interracial contact. And, yet, because each instance of intimate contact—be it cuffing or uncuffing, passing food or bodily fluids through the wicket, or the strip search—is defined by systemic power the contact functions not to reduce prejudice but to reinforces stereotypes and engender the development of deep racial antagonisms that are the root of white racial resentment.

PART SEVEN

White Supremacy and the Lies White People Tell Themselves

The simple fact was that we still lived in a world in which racism sorts the haves and the have-nots and decides who lives and who dies. Racism, according to Michel Foucault, is the social distribution of death; like an actuarial chart, it predicts who would thrive and who would not.

—Saidiya Hartman, *Lose Your Mother: A Journey along the Atlantic Slave Route*

As Immanuel Kant put it in 1764, the fact that a man "was very black from head to foot," was "clear proof that what he said was stupid." See a Black face, see stupidity, and from this vicious cycle, there was no escape. This is how race ultimately came to function: as a way to divide us. And it has done so with remarkable success—and often brutal results—for hundreds of years.

—Henry Louis Gates Jr. and Andrew S. Curran, "We Need a New Language for Talking About Race"

CHAPTER 42

The "Origin" Lie

THE NEGRO IS THE PROBLEM

THE STORY OF SOLITARY confinement is a story about many things. The story we tell in *Way Down in the Hole* offers a critical analysis of racism in solitary confinement and specifically interrogates the structures and processes of solitary confinement that produce and reproduce white racial resentment. Eddie Glaude Jr.'s argument in *Begin Again* provides the framework for our story.

> In *No Name*, Baldwin recalls his first visit to the South, he says that he "felt as though [he] had wandered into hell." He wasn't talking about the hellish lives led by black southerners, but rather how the racial dynamics of the region had hollowed out white southerners. The lies and violence had so distorted and overtaken the private lives of white people in the region that their lived lives felt empty. . . . What shook Baldwin at his core was a "realization of the nature of the heathen." The white southerner had to lie continuously to himself in order to justify his world. Lie that black people around him were inferior. Lie about what he was doing under the cover of night. Lie that he was a Christian. For Baldwin, the accumulation of lies suffocated the white southerner.[1]

The story of race in solitary confinement is a story about lies. Specifically lies we tell ourselves that allow us to justify locking 80,000–100,000 people a day, who are disproportionately Black, in solitary confinement where they are rendered socially dead, where they lose even the most basic civil and human rights, where, as Scholar says, they are treated like dogs.

In this final part of the book, we consider Eddie Glaude Jr.'s claim that well-meaning white people, white people who believe in the principles of Christianity, even if they do not worship or practice themselves, white people who love democracy and fight to defend the freedoms that we in the United States often taken for granted—as many COs and white shirts in fact did during their time in the military—must do one very painful thing. They must get up every morning and lie to themselves. They must get up every morning and tell themselves that Black people deserve what they get. Because any other explanation for the significant racial disparities in education and wealth and homeownership, and especially in incarceration that exist in the United States would challenge their beliefs in God and democracy.

We opened the book with this question: How can correctional officers, who have all of the power in prisons and especially in solitary confinement, come to believe that the people they lock up in cages twenty-four hours a day, and who they treat like animals, have a better life than they do? How can correctional officers who get to leave every day and go home, come to resent the meals and the TVs and the mental health treatment that prisoners locked in solitary confinement receive? How can correctional officers like CO Travis come to see themselves, and not the prisoners, as the "forgotten?"

And, the answer lies in the lies we tell ourselves. We conclude *Way Down in the Hole* by interrogating the lies that COs working in solitary confinement tell themselves so that they can engage in the dehumanizing work demanded of them, and we ponder the ways in which these lies shape not only the ways the COs treat the prisoners they guard but how they see themselves.

The "Negro" *Is* the Problem

Eddie Glaude Jr. argues that the "founders" of the "American Experiment in Democracy" faced a problem: "the problem of the Negro." He writes, "Jefferson and James Madison worked to reconcile the reality of slavery with their ideas of democracy. Yet what is consistent across these periods is that in terms of 'the Negro problem,' the Negro *is* the problem."[2]

Their solution to the "Negro" problem was the invention of a racialized caste system, built around the principles of white supremacy. This racialized caste system produced a hierarchy of human value on which *literally every point of access to the social, political economy of the contemporary United States has been preordained.* Those who are born white have access to the opportunity to get an education and a good paying job and to buy a house in any neighborhood they can afford. In contrast, those who are born Black face discrimination at every juncture.

Fundamental to white supremacy is the conceptualization of the Black body as less than fully human. As chattel. As a commodity. In her book *Lose Your Mother: A Journey along the Atlantic Slave Route,* Saidiya Hartman describes the commodification of the Black body—commodified even before it arrives in ports like Charleston, New Orleans, or Jamestown:

> Incidental death occurs when life has no normative value, when no humans are involved, when the population is, in effect, seen as already dead. Unlike the concentration camp, the gulag, and the killing field, which had as their intended end the extermination of population, the Atlantic trade created millions of corpses, but as a corollary to the making of commodities. . . . In effect it made it easier for a trader to countenance

yet another dead black body or for a captain to dump a shipload of captives into the sea in order to collect the insurance, *since it wasn't possible to kill cargo or murder a thing already denied life.* Death was simply a part of the workings of the trade.[3]

Black bodies were kidnapped and stolen from Africa, shipped in the bellies of slave ships to the "new" world, and bought and sold on auction blocks alongside horses, hogs, cattle, and any other commodity for which there was a market. Not only were Black bodies defined as less than fully human, as chattel, but that status was politically constructed deliberately so that it passed intergenerationally.

Consider this puzzle: A white woman can have a Black baby, but a Black woman can never have a white baby. Have you ever pondered this and wondered why?

The answer lies in a decision made in the Virginia House of Commons in 1662, less than half a century after the first Africans were kidnapped and brought to the shores of Virginia by slave ships. The ruling, which was adopted across the South, codified into law that the legal status of a person—free or enslaved—*passed only through the mother, and not the father.* The law read: "All children born in this country shall be held bond or free *only according to the condition of the mother.*"[4]

This is the essence of the "one drop rule," one drop of Black blood makes you Black, and just as importantly, not white and the one drop rule not only allowed enslavers like Thomas Jefferson to rape enslaved Black women and enslave the children born from these acts of sexual violence but it defined the category "white."

Sally Hemings bore four children fathered by Thomas Jefferson and as a result of the ruling in the Virginia House of Commons, not a single one of them was white, and none were free.

A second legal move that ensured that people of African descent were not and could never be fully human was the Three-Fifths Compromise. Article 1, section 2 of the Constitution of the United States, penned and signed by founders who include Thomas Jefferson, George Washington, and George Mason, reads as follows:

Representatives and direct Taxes shall be apportioned among the several States which may be included within this Union, according to their respective Numbers, which shall be determined by adding to the whole Number of free Persons, including those bound to Service for a Term of Years, and excluding Indians not taxed, three fifths of all other Persons.

The Three-Fifths Compromise ensured, until the passage of the Thirteenth and Fourteenth Amendments, that people of African descent were defined politically as a *fraction* of a person and thus they could be legally denied the rights that white citizens enjoyed under the constitution, including life, *liberty*, and the pursuit of happiness. Though a series of amendments and Supreme Court decisions have, in theory, restored full citizenship to Black people, nothing can legislate their full humanity.

The power of the racial scheme that Jefferson and his colleagues invented lies in its ability to simultaneously create the category of the chattel slave and construct the political category of white. People of African descent are thus defined both legally and politically as less than fully human, as chattel, who could be bought and sold on the open market, whose labor could be extracted for free, whose offspring, including those fathered by planters who raped enslaved women, would remain in the category of "black" and enslaved thereby limiting and controlling the number of people who could legally claim the status of white. The fact that the racial schema was simultaneously policing both inclusion and exclusion is part of the reason it was able to be so rapidly embedded into the very fabric of the United States, socially, yes, but perhaps most importantly, politically and legally. The literal definition of who is and who is not a citizen and who can lawfully claim all of the rights we associate with citizenship, the rights we are guaranteed in the U.S. Constitution and in the Bill of Rights that many of us memorized in our middle school history classes.

Prisoners, who Lisa Guenther and others argue experience social and legal death, live in a state of *suspended citizenship.*

When taken together, these laws lay the groundwork for rationalizing the dehumanizing practices we witnessed, firsthand, and heard about, in solitary confinement. They create the basis on which we build the lie.

Even the Thirteenth Amendment to the United States Constitution which formally and legally ended slavery includes a provision to retain the social and legal status of "slave." It reads, in part,

> Neither slavery nor involuntary servitude, *except as a punishment for a crime whereof the party shall have been duly convicted*, shall exist within the United States, or any place subject to their jurisdiction.

In other words, people who are incarcerated can legally be considered and treated as slaves. Like the enslaved bodies Saidiya Hartman writes about, the incarcerated are rendered socially dead: "Joy James argues that, by leaving open the loophole for the enslavement of convicted criminals, the Thirteenth Amendment did not abolish slavery, rather, it 'resurrected social death as a *permanent legal category* in U.S. life. (2005, xxviii–xxix).[5] [emphasis ours]

Rendering incarcerated people, most of whom are Black, as socially dead, as less than fully human, with limited citizenship status, allows COs to reconstruct "rights"—like showers, and meals and yard—as "privileges," and rationalize burning prisoners on showers and yard and meals as a form of punishment, as tools to ensure "care, custody, and control" and later to stoke the COs' resentment of these same prisoners when the COs perceive that these bodies locked in cages get more than they do.

Scholar notes: "All human privileges are gone; they treat you like a dog. They bring you food, they throw it to you, you shower in a cage, you exercise in a cage. Just because I'm wearing orange [the color of the jumpsuit for incarcerated people confined in solitary] doesn't mean I'm not human."

Incarceration and Democracy seem to be inherently incompatible. And, yet, the United States, the founder of democracy, leads the world in both the percentage of our citizens who we incarcerate and those we isolate in solitary confinement. The cognitive dissonance created by this incompatibility is resolved by invoking the big lie: "The Negro Is the Problem."

As we argued in our book *Policing Black Bodies*, the rise of the prison system in the United States begins with the emancipation of millions of formerly enslaved bodies. In order to continue to control a group of people, as well as to continue to harness free labor, plantation prisons and the convict leasing system first emerged in the southern regions of the United States, and later expanded across the entire country. In simple terms, the transition from plantation to prison generates and cements a revised racist ideology. Black bodies are transformed from "chattel" to "criminal." Neither status is fully human or fully alive. To be a criminal is to occupy the status of social and legal death. Or, as Joy James argues: "The encoding of slavery or criminality onto blackness reflected a counterpart construction: the inscription of 'whiteness' and nonincarceration as freedom and civility."[6] Frantz Fanon, a psychiatrist and philosopher of French West Indian descent who focused his work on racism and colonization, comes to a similar conclusion: [there were] "distinct problems with the racialization of crime. . . . Colonization marks the colonized as 'born criminal,' always already guilty, and never quite open to rehabilitation."[7]

Carol Anderson sums it up in one simple yet powerful sentence: "The United States did not face a crime problem that was racialized; it faced a race problem that was criminalized."[8]

In other words, Black people are constructed by white supremacist ideology as inherently criminal, as born "criminal." To be born criminal is to have that status conferred intergenerationally, if not legally, then socially. This intergenerational transmission of status is eerily similar to the intergenerational transmission of the political status of "chattel." Marked at birth. With no mechanism to escape the inevitable: first labeled as criminal, then predestined for prison. "Always already guilty and never quite open to rehabilitation."

If there is no hope for rehabilitation, then the most efficient manner in which to address the "Negro" problem is not just to criminalize his behavior but, as Carol Anderson argues, to criminalize his very existence, incarcerate him, if necessary, in solitary confinement, deny his human rights, render him socially dead, effectively removing him from the social political economy. Slavery reconstituted. Democracy seemingly intact.

CHAPTER 43

Emancipated Slaves and
the White Sharecropper

By ASSIGNING BLACK PEOPLE to the status of chattel slaves and white people to the status of citizens, the founding fathers were able to write a Declaration of Independence and a Constitution that was simultaneously consistent with Enlightenment-era ideologies of freedom, democracy, and equality and allowed for the enslavement of Black bodies. In reality, there were many poor whites who also lived in the colonies and early states of the United States, and they too had limited access to citizenship rights. The founders understood that the American Experiment with Democracy hinged on continuing to police and enforce the boundaries between the category of "white" and that of "non-white." In economic terms, many white sharecroppers had much more in common with enslaved people than they did with the landed elite. The founders believed that allowing poor, white sharecroppers access to the status of "whiteness" would prevent them from seeking further citizenship rights, like the right to vote, which at the time was guaranteed only to men who owned land, and, perhaps more importantly, prevent them from aligning themselves with the enslaved and soon-to-be emancipated.

In his book *Dying by Whiteness*, Jonathan Metzl argues that not only was this strategy to incorporate poor whites into the category of the citizen deliberate, but it laid the foundation for the strong commitment to whiteness that we see among working-class white people today: "Reconstruction, historian W.E.B. Du Bois famously argued that whiteness served as a 'public and psychological wage,' delivering poor whites to a valuable social status derived from their classification as 'not-black.' '*Whiteness thereby provided 'compensation for citizens otherwise exploited by the organization of capitalism*—while at the same time preventing working-class white Southerners from forming a common cause with working-class black populations in their shared suffering at the bottom of the social ladder."[1]

In other words, access to "whiteness" was defined as compensation for being poor. Rather than offering poor whites access to economic resources, the elite offered them, instead, access to the heavily guarded status of "white" in a racial hierarchy in which to be white is to be better than everyone else.

A racial hierarchy of human value, in which to be Black or non-white is to be less than fully human. As a result of this "compensation," poor white people aligned their identities along racial, rather than class, lines; they identified with landed elites rather than their class counterparts: recently emancipated Blacks, who were also engaged in sharecropping.

In their book *The Politics of Losing: Trump, The Klan, and the Mainstreaming of Resentment*, Rory McVeigh and Kevin Estep describe the role of the Klan in developing and reinforcing an ideology in which racial identity trumps class identity (no pun intended):

> The Klan, emerging from a long tradition of slave patrols and night-riding vigilantes, acted as terrorists in service of the Southern elite who wanted to preserve their source of cheap labor. *But the group became particularly popular among non-elite whites, because through it they could 'hoard opportunities' preventing black Southerners from sharing in the economic, political and social benefits previously reserved for whites.* Because poor whites and poor blacks together greatly outnumbered the white Southern elite, the Klan cemented an alliance between rich and poor whites, one that would keep blacks subordinate and sustain the dominance of the landed elite.[2]

Poor whites were reminded that no matter how bad things seemed, at least they weren't Black. White supremacist ideologies, as embodied by the Klan and other white nationalist groups, ensured that the limited resources that the elite granted to the middle class and the poor could be and were restricted to white people. The Klan policed the boundaries of Jim Crow.

The campaigns of Donald Trump provide countless illustrations of this strategy. Though his exact "worth" is debatable, he is, by all measures, a member of the 1 percent, the elite. Yet he was able, and continues, to project an image of himself as "just like" working-class white people; he is one of them. Trump is not, of course, the only politician to accomplish this lie; Tea Party conservatives including Rick Santorum and Ted Cruz, millionaires, Ivy League educated, convinced poor and working-class whites that they could be trusted because they were "just like them." To be clear, what they are trading on is the importance of being "white," of "whiteness," in a society built on white supremacy. They are trading, as the elite of the eighteenth century did, on the fact that the privileges of being "white" will compensate the poor and working class, for the exploitation they experience under modern, neoliberal capitalism, a system that enriches men like Donald Trump and Ted Cruz and Rick Santorum.

Trump's strategy was nothing new. As McVeigh and Estep note: "Lyndon B. Johnson understood this strategy well. Driving through Tennessee in his motorcade, he saw racial slurs scrawled on signs. 'If you can convince the lowest white man he's better than the best colored man,' he said, 'he won't notice you're picking his pocket. Hell, give him somebody to look down on, and he'll empty his pockets for you."[3]

At first it seemed counterintuitive to many people watching and analyzing the Tea Party movement of the early 2010s that not only were white people, who by all accounts were benefiting from many Obama-era policies, the most vocal in their opposition to these policies, but they were electing politicians based on their promises to dismantle so-called Obamacare and other social welfare programs that Obama endorsed.

> As much as Trump voters valued finally having access to health care [the uninsured rates of low-income whites fell from 25 percent in 2013 to 15 percent in 2016] to deal with chronic illnesses like diabetes, to get screenings for cancer and to make possible a liver transplant, those benefits came with a bitter and unforgivable downside. The ACA was Obamacare, which was bad enough in itself. But there was also the "anger . . . that other people were getting even better, even cheaper benefits—and those other people did not deserve the help."[4]

The hypocrisy in this statement is obvious, and yet CO Travis expressed an identical sentiment: that the people locked in cage, in solitary confinement, who must be strip searched, shower in a cage, exercise in a dog kennel, *who are not deserving*, get better benefits than he does.

But, it wasn't just CO Travis who expressed these sentiments. CO Bunker's rant provides other illustrations of the white racial resentment that many COs expressed. "I lived in a bunker in Iraq for a year and these guys have a better shitter . . . not made of wood that they don't have to burn."

In order to fully understand the impact and irony of CO Bunker's comment that the prisoners have a better standard of living than he does because at least they have flush toilets one must consider the ways in which toilet paper becomes contested in the confines of solitary. COs police toilet paper in a variety of ways, including controlling how much toilet paper a person incarcerated in solitary confinement can have at any given time and requiring that the cardboard roll be turned back in before a new roll is dispensed. We talked with many prisoners who complained that the COs, who can flush the toilets from the bubble, refused to flush their toilets, often for days, as a form of punishment. How, then can the prisoner's access to a toilet that flushes [and doesn't have to be burned] but over which they may not have the power to flush, or even have enough toilet paper to meet their hygiene needs or fill the toilet bowl, be constructed as a privilege that they have that CO Bunker doesn't? It is precisely these kinds of ironies that illustrate the processes by which white racial resentment is produced and reproduced.

But the development of white racial resentment is about more than the structures of solitary confinement, it is about more than the privileges that CO Travis and CO Bunker feel they are entitled to but don't receive. It is also deeply rooted their morals, in their belief that those who are locked in solitary confinement not only get a better deal than they do, but that they are undeserving *because* they have committed terrible crimes. David Wilson offers this framing of white racial resentment: "[We have come to regard] racialized resentment as a reaction to injustice whereby one racial group is perceived by another as threatening standards of morality, civic virtue, and the principles of justice that frame merit in society."[5]

Applying Wilson's framing we argue that the COs not only perceive that people who are incarcerated in solitary confinement get more than they get—especially access to mental health care—but their resentment is exacerbated by the fact that prisoners have, as Wilson notes, broken the moral, justice contract: they have violated the law, sometimes in very serious ways, and other times, not. But either way, from the perspective of the COs the people incarcerated in solitary confinement are getting something they are not entitled to. They are, as CO Travis put it, Trump's "forgotten," they are "strangers in their own land."

CHAPTER 44

Strangers in Their Own Land

WE SPENT A TOTAL of several weeks in Larrabee County. White people there are struggling. The median household income ($51,000) is 20 percent lower than the national average. The only good jobs are those in the prisons. In many ways, white people in Larrabee County are falling behind. Since the coal mines and factories have closed and jobs have left, white people living in these communities are less likely to have a well-paying job with benefits than their parents did, and the prospect that their children will have a better-paying job, or at least one that isn't so difficult, is bleak. They are also falling behind those living in urban areas and tech bubbles. They won't be any more able to send their kids to college than they were able to go themselves. Their resentment is understandable. To add insult to injury, they see Black people as thriving. A Black man in the White House whose daughters are going to Harvard. LeBron James who is from "their community," the blighted Rust Belt, makes tens of millions of dollars per year, and in the summer of 2020, in the wake of the murder of George Floyd, when James's team played in the COVID "Disney World" bubble, he donned a Black Lives Matter mask. Colin Kaepernick, who couldn't be satisfied with the success he had on the football field, had to kneel, protesting not just police brutality but also, from the COs' perspective, their very way of life.

Other scholars, including Carol Anderson, author of *White Rage*, have articulated the ways in which the campaigns of candidate and later President Donald Trump tapped into and mobilized white racial resentment among rural whites who felt as if they were being left behind.[1] Catherine Woodiwiss, writing in *Sojourns* just months before Trump was elected president captured this sentiment precisely:

> Trump supporters, therefore, saw their candidate as "America's last chance" to recreate a nation that reminded them of the good ole days. The country's growing diversity, Obama's very existence in the White House, and the ever-increasing visibility of African Americans in colleges and corporations had fueled a sense that these gains were "likely to reduce the influence of white Americans in society." Trump's win exposed in frightening ways the "ethnonationalist rage centered around a black president" and

the fear that all of the resources and wealth accumulated through centuries of public policy would be subject to "redistribution from older, white America to its younger, more diverse" population.[2]

Though a sweeping wealth distribution policy passed by Congress seems unlikely, from the view of the COs, these sentiments are not so hard to believe and understand. Isn't that what's happening in solitary confinement? Prisoners in solitary confinement are getting more and more privileges, while COs do more and more work. When Donald Trump referred to the "forgotten," COs like Travis heard him speaking to them.

Much like the world of whiteness in southern Louisiana that Arlie Hochschild details in her 2016 book *Strangers in Their Own Land*, COs also live in a world in which they feel like strangers in Larrabee County. In just a few short years, the world as they know it has been turned upside down. Not only can a Black man become president and live in the White House, the irony of which is not lost on them, but gay people can get married, and women can get a man fired by accusing him of sexual harassment. These same social upheavals, as they experience them, have infiltrated their workplace. Even solitary confinement is not immune. For starters, women are now working in the hole, something the men working there deeply resent. As CO after CO told us, because women can't do strip searches, it's like "being a man down" when you have a woman on your team.

PREA dominates their daily work, a change that cannot be overstated. Many COs believe that prisoners use PREA as one of the only tools they have to exert control. When one is PREA'd (accused of a PREA violation), it triggers an investigation that creates mounds of paperwork not only for the CO but for his supervisor, the white shirt. Officers claim that they are PREA'd for ridiculous reasons, like looking too closely at a prisoner during a strip search or watching them shower, something that COs believe is, in fact, a critical part of their job, necessary to ensure that no contraband is being smuggled or handcrafted, makeshift weapons being hid for later use. One CO we met, who routinely works in the bubble, which means that he is surveilling the intimacies of the lives of hundreds of incarcerated people for forty or more hours a week, told us that he has been PREA'd so many times, he worries that he won't be able to coach his kid's Little League team anymore. He also said it has put a strain on his marriage.

COs, more so than perhaps employees in any other occupation, have to deal, almost every single day, with trans issues. As a result of lawsuits, incarcerated transgender people have rights, which in SCI-Wannabee include the right to safety in the prison, the right to order the undergarments of their choice from the DOC commissary catalog, even the right to transition. As was the case with a transwoman we interviewed and heard about in SCI-Women.[3] Most of the COs we talked to in SCI-Women believed that the transwoman they were charged with protecting was not trans at all, but was in fact a man who faked being trans so that "he" would be incarcerated in a women's prison where it's widely believed that time is easier to do.

COs were no more prepared to work with the high numbers of incarcerated people with severe mental illness than they were to deal with women as colleagues and supervisors, PREA, and incarcerated transgender people. They were strangers in their own land.

COs' only mechanism for retaining power and control in this social structure is to arbitrarily enforce rules that deny the people incarcerated in solitary confinement access to the things they desire or are entitled to. COs burn prisoners on showers and meals because they are not standing at their cell doors, paper off their windows, light on in their cell at the precise moment the CO walks on to the pod. Incarcerated people view this as a human rights violation. COs view it as a punishment strategy. We are left pondering the importance of such arbitrary rules. Why do cardboard toilet paper rolls have to be turned in before a prisoner can get a new roll of toilet paper? Not because toilet paper or ChapStick is a matter of national security, *but because COs view burning prisoners as one of their only strategies for leveling the playing field, for holding on to their place in the hierarchy. A place they feel they are slowly losing.*

It's true, as CO Porter shares, that many of the COs we interviewed live in a world in which they are surrounded by people, or may be themselves, unable to pay their bills. They have friends and family members who have lost their homes as a result of medical debt. They struggle with their own physical and mental health. They sleep in their cars because they can't afford a hotel room on the nights they work double shifts. All of this is true.

COs like Travis and Porter are falling behind because the federal government won't invest in economic development for poor white communities. Amazon builds fulfillment centers, which is just a fancy way to say warehouses, in Larrabee County but not tech development labs. The federal government gives states the money to build prisons but not to invest in solar fields or wind turbines. The federal government allows the health insurance lobby to block access to affordable health care and Big Pharma to lobby against free prescription drugs. Tax breaks go to large corporations, many of whom are now moving offshore, rather than to places like Larrabee County. Even the fracking industry brings its own work force from places as far away as Texas and Florida.

But, as we and others argue, their resentment is misplaced. They are not, in fact, falling behind the Black men they lock in cages twenty-three hours a day. No matter how many $5 medical appointments they attend, or sessions they have with Dr. Emma. No matter how many extra food bags or cans of Pepsi they collect over the days and weeks and months and years they are locked in solitary confinement. Yet this is where the COs focus their white racial resentment. All the while they are literally "dying by whiteness."

CHAPTER 45

Dying by Whiteness

IN HIS BOOK *Dying by Whiteness*, Jonathan Metzl explores myriad ways in which white people trade on their own "whiteness" in ways that disadvantage them economically, but like the sharecroppers of the eighteenth, nineteenth, and early twentieth centuries, serve to police the boundaries of "whiteness."

For example, as Metzl documents, suicide by gun is killing more and more white men each year, and yet gun ownership has been embraced as a key marker of whiteness, a phenomenon that is illustrated and re-illustrated every time we experience a mass shooting in the United States. Conservative whites would rather risk safety in schools and shopping malls than pass any meaningful gun reform legislation. Similarly, though the Affordable Care Act, another issue Metzl explores, brought much-needed access to health care to millions of low-income and working-class white people, as both Metzl and Arlie Hochschild's research reveals, they are the group *most likely* to oppose the expansion of Medicare and vote for representatives in Congress who take the most vocal positions in favor of dismantling Obamacare.

In 2020, during the height of the global COVID-19 pandemic, even masks became a battleground for whiteness, all while hundreds of thousands of white people died of COVID-19.

In solitary confinement, Black men and white men in the hole, existing on both sides of the bars, share a common view: they both see the opportunity structure as blocked for them.

For the prisoners, mostly Black, mostly from urban ghettos, their lives are defined by gang activity (even if they don't personally participate), drug dealing, and violence. For the correctional officers, almost all white, from rural, economically disadvantaged communities, the opportunities that their fathers had in mining or the steel industry or manufacturing have disappeared, and they find that the only job that will keep them solidly in the middle class is working in the local jail. The work is physically and mentally demanding, most of them hate it, and just like for the men they are paid to guard, their lives are cut short as a result of disease and violence; the occupational hazards of their work.

Both groups of men pay with their lives, and yet the white men, newer to this landscape of limited opportunity, cling to the one thing they have that makes them better than the men in cages: their whiteness.

As we learned from CO Travis and countless other COs, in solitary confinement, it's not just the incarcerated people who pay a price as a result of the time they spend down in the hole; the lack of natural light and fresh air, the unhealthy food, and the dehumanizing conditions all impact the physical and mental health of the COs too.

Deliberately designing the structures of solitary confinement for maximum dehumanization means that the staff who work in the hole, particularly the COs, also experience dehumanization.

We reiterate, we do not believe nor would we ever argue that the COs experience greater dehumanization than the people incarcerated in solitary confinement. But, as CO Travis articulated, they are locked up, too. They are forced, whether they want to or not, to participate in dehumanizing practices and processes, including conducting hundreds of strip searches a week and surveilling the most intimate behaviors of the people incarcerated there, cloaked as both punishment and a matter of safety.

Some of the COs we interviewed and many more who the prisoners talked about deliberately engage in further dehumanizing practices, including burning incarcerated people on showers, the yard, and even meals. The act of dehumanizing causes the colonizer, too, to experience dehumanization.

Mary Buser, who worked for many years, first as a counselor and later as an administrator, on Rikers Island recalls the day she knew she had to "get out":

> I reluctantly turned to Fernando Dayrit, our newest staff member. Although he was starting to acclimate to the punitive unit, earlier in the week, the timing in a staged suicide was off; although the inmate survived, he'd broken his neck. When Dayrit learned about it, was understandably skittish about going back into the tower [to the Bing], but I was desperate to have the meds renewed. With clipboard in hand and an attached list of notes, I pleaded with him to go back in. I handed the clipboard to him and said, "Listen, it wasn't that bad." "The guy broke his neck!" Dayrit replied. "Yes—but it was just a little bone—not an important bone." What I remember most in that moment was the sound of the clipboard clattering to the floor. Then Dayrit stepped back and eyed me as if I was a monster. He turned and walked out. I retreated to my office and broke into sobs. I kept seeing his face and the look that mirrored back to me just how desensitized I had become.[1]

Dehumanization, violence, and even suicide are such common occurrences that even staff with the best of intentions, as we believe Mary Buser to be, become desensitized. This is the dialectic to which Frantz Fanon refers: "For colonialism has not simply depersonalized the colonized. The very structure of society has been depersonalized on a collective level. A colonized people is thus reduced to a collection of individuals who owe their very existence to the presence of the colonizer."[2]

It's difficult to argue that Black COs resented incarcerated people the same way that white COs did, because there were too few of them for us to draw any meaningful conclusion. Those we interviewed did not express resentment against incarcerated people, perhaps because they could see themselves in the men locked in cages. Perhaps because they had family and friends in prison. But what they did express was a clear understanding of the impact of pitting COs and incarcerated people against each other. As SGT Josh said, "It's something they hear and repeat [racial stereotypes]. . . . It becomes a mantra. . . . As long as we are divided [COs and incarcerated people] the administration controls everything."

What would it look like if the COs and the prisoners began to see their shared self-interest? How might the structures and policies of solitary confinement be reimagined if the COs understood that they, too, were victims of a system, a system that invests in prisons as economic development, a system that rationalizes dehumanization as a condition of confinement and as a form of punishment but also as a form of racism? As SGT Josh notes, this will never happen because prison administrators understand clearly that in order to keep thousands and thousands of people—both incarcerated people and staff—locked in solitary confinement for days and weeks and months and years requires that they never see their shared humanity.

But what if they could?

CHAPTER 46

Bending the Rules

CREATING HUMANITY IN INHUMANE SPACES

WE WANT TO BE extremely clear that for the most part we believe in the abolition of solitary confinement in the United States. We believe that solitary confinement should be used exceedingly sparingly and only when every other option for keeping the incarcerated people and staff safe has been exhausted. Furthermore, in cases where solitary confinement is absolutely necessary, it should be used for the shortest period of time possible, ideally never more than a day or two, and certainly not longer than the fifteen consecutive days dictated by the United Nations. And never indefinitely. But as the United Nations report reveals, "... various regimes in the United States [including SCI-Wannabee] could and do allow for prisoners to be held in solitary confinement for disciplinary purposes *indefinitely*."[1]

We know that there will be some pushback to this argument. Some will argue that if an incarcerated person commits an act of violence that threatens the safety of another prisoner or an officer, then solitary confinement is the only punishment appropriate and it is the only strategy for maintaining safety. We can be persuaded that there are some very limited circumstances in which this may be the case, especially when incarcerated people severely injure or kill each other or the COs. These situations should be handled on a case-by-case basis.

That being said, as we have demonstrated over and over and over again in this book, the vast majority of the 80,000–100,000 people who are incarcerated in solitary confinement every day in the United States are not those exceptions. The majority of people locked in solitary confinement are there because they are experiencing mental health crises or engaging in behaviors that are a result of undiagnosed, untreated, or improperly managed mental illness, often as a response to histories of severe trauma, or they are simply poor and engaged in "illegal" activity such as running a store in order to meet their basic needs.

The United States incarcerates tens of thousands of people in solitary confinement every single day because we have invested in building not just solitary confinement units but supermax prisons, and those beds must be filled. So we invent a series of rules and regulations that ensure that they will be. We are not safer as a result of our approach to solitary confinement. The vast majority of people locked in these cages will emerge not just from solitary confinement but indeed from prison, and as a result of the decomposition they experienced while in solitary confinement, they are more likely to experience long-term mental health consequences after their release, putting us all at greater risk.

A FORMULA FOR EMPATHY

Intimate contact can produce resentment or empathy. We found many examples of empathy, rather than resentment, at SCI-Women. CO Lisa, for example, deliberately bends the rules sometimes: "Sometimes if it's a really good day I give them extra rec time or time at the table. Or candy . . . to say "thank you for a good day." . . . It works; we all stay safe or they don't kill themselves or end up in the hospital or cut up . . . whatever gets us through the day. . . . Food is safe—who's going to harm themselves with candy?"

Rather than seeing her job as simply meting out punishment, CO Lisa conceptualizes her job as safety: keeping everyone alive.

It wasn't just the women COs who developed empathy. Men who worked in SCI-Women also expressed a connection between the women in solitary and the women in their own lives.

CO Daniel is a white man in his forties. He has dark hair and a long, dark beard, the kind that is popular in contemporary white rural culture. He has been dodging us all day, saying he doesn't want to do an interview . . . hiding in the bubble. Finally, while we're in the BMU pod hanging out with Unit Manager Tom and Counselor Mark, CO Daniel walks by and Unit Manager Tom and Counselor Mark strongly suggest he do the interview. It definitely seems more like an order than a suggestion. CO Daniel works in the DTU, so we follow him back to D Pod to a back office where it appears he has been hanging out, not doing anything, hiding all day. He sits at a desk and pretends to do computer work while we get started.

He is watching the clock because it's 3:30 and he gets off at 4.

Near the very end of the very short interview, CO Daniel reveals that he has a daughter who is thirteen years old and has autism. He talks about learning to parent her and help her deal with her anxiety, which he says helps him manage the women in the DTU and BMU. "She is playing some sports, but she's doing much better since she started playing music . . . She's in the band, playing the clarinet."

Though like many of the other COs he believes that for the most part incarcerated people fake mental illness in order to get better treatment and shorter sentences in the DTU, he also sees the value of programming, which he interprets as similar to the programming his daughter with special needs receives at school.

So what is the difference between SCI-Wannabee and SCI-Women that allows for the development of empathy instead of resentment, even among CO Daniel?

The populations of solitary confinement reflect the overall prison population, and as such, women in solitary confinement, with the exception of the BMU, are more likely than men in solitary confinement to be nonviolent drug offenders who were sentenced to solitary confinement for rule infractions, not violence. From our observations of their files in the LT's offices, they are also more likely to be indigent. Do these qualities make them more likable? More sympathetic? Is it easier for COs to see their daughters and wives and mothers in the faces of those they are locking in cages?

SGT Josh, who is Black, mentioned that he sometimes encounters people he knows from the neighborhood where he grew up who are incarcerated in the solitary confinement unit where he works. This is, of course, not an uncommon experience for Black men who work in any part of the criminal legal system, as police officers, attorneys, judges, or even COs. Does his ability to see himself in the incarcerated person lead him to be more humane?

Unlike CO Daniel's comments, we never heard a single white CO in SCI-Wannabee compare the people incarcerated there to people in their families. Perhaps this is because more of the men in solitary confinement are there for violent offenses, either on the outside or on the inside.

Or perhaps it's because of the lies COs tell themselves so that they can go to work each day, including the lie that all Black men are criminals and thugs. Presuming that incarcerated people are guilty, be it of the crimes of which they are convicted or the misconducts that sent them to the hole, unable to be "rehabilitated," is a lie that allows the COs to believe that the men they guard each day are in fact not only *not* like their family members but *deserving* of the dehumanizing treatment they receive.

Perhaps for the white COs at SCI-Wannabee, their whiteness is the only thing that distinguishes them from the men behind the bars, and in order to protect their whiteness, they engage in dehumanizing behaviors as a tool for reinforcing difference and rendering similarity invisible.

Philip Goodman, a sociologist, studied California's prison fire camps for men which are designed in such a way that incarcerated people and COs work alongside one another fighting the wildfires that are devastating California.

These atypical carceral settings generally have no secure boundaries. Prisoners perform manual labor and fight wildfires in exchange for comparatively less austere conditions than those found in most of California's walled prisons. . . . I posit that prisons can be fertile terrain *for understanding the lived experience of race more generally*. . . . In order to really understand the camps and the experiences of those incarcerated and employed in them, it is imperative that we pay more careful attention to . . . the "*racialization of space and the spatialization of race.*" . . . For instance, unpacking the microdynamics of racial identity construction sheds light on the ways in which prisoners and staff collude to construct the camps as more lenient in terms of racial practices (but "still prisons"). . . . At camps with just a few prisoners categorized as other, those individuals often share a table with people categorized as black.[2]

The men working alongside each other to fight the wildfires have a shared self-interest. When they find this shared self-interest, when they work as near equals to save their communities, they begin to chip away at the racist structures that divide them. This is Gordon Allport's "contact hypothesis" in action. Intimate contact, under specific circumstances, can reduce rather than reproduce white racial resentment.

BENDING THE RULES

Fifty, the reader will recall, had been locked in the hole for a year in order to avoid another prisoner, the man who killed his brother. In his interview, Fifty shared with us that he was going to max out and be released directly from solitary confinement to the streets. We wonder, in what universe does it make sense to release someone directly from solitary confinement, locked down twenty-three hours a day, with extremely limited opportunities for human interaction, directly to the streets? How would that facilitate Fifty's successful reentry, and how would it keep society safer?

Frankly, we didn't believe Fifty. Until Hattery saw him the next day.

Hattery was hanging out in the LT's office when she heard commotion in the hallway.

"I met you yesterday!" a man in an orange jumpsuit hollered.

Hattery turned to look, and it was none other than Fifty standing there in the hallway, uncuffed, unshackled, broom in hand.

Because of protocols to protect incarcerated people, researchers are not supposed to let staff know which incarcerated people have been interviewed or what they talked about. But Fifty wasn't thinking about that.

"I talked to her yesterday!" he hollered, as staff watched him sweeping up the trash that littered the hallway.

"What's your name again?"

Knowing Hattery should not share her real name, her brain fumbled around and landed on "Smith."

"What's your first name? I want to look you up when I get out!"

Yikes!

"Umm . . . Debbie, Debbie Smith."

Hattery was floored. What was going on? When we interviewed him, Fifty had claimed he had extra privileges, but we basically didn't believe him.

Later on that day, while we were interviewing CO Porter in the COs' office in the pod, we looked over and there was Fifty, again, naked except for a towel around his waist, walking, not handcuffed, not shackled, *unaccompanied*, to the shower cell.

We asked CO Porter about it, and he explained that he was bending the rules. He knew that releasing Fifty directly from solitary to the streets wasn't in Fifty's best interest or in the best interest of the community where Fifty would be released, *in 10 days*, so CO Porter designed a step-like program for Fifty. Across his last month in the hole, Fifty was gradually given more and more freedom and more and more responsibility, including chores like sweeping the hallway. He was performing well and hadn't violated any rules, and as a result, CO Porter was rewarding him by giving more and more freedom each week.

If CO Porter could think outside the box in this way, was it possible to reform solitary confinement while we are waiting for it to be abolished?

What other kinds of reforms are possible?

As CO Lisa does her work in the BMU, she rewards good behavior with candy. As she says, "Who can cut with candy?"

As Dr. Emma does her work in the DTU, she shares a few insights about herself, a way of establishing a personal connection with people who others treat as if they are less than or not (even) human.

Would it be too much to ask that Scholar, an avid reader, could have more than one book at a time or that incarcerated people who are hearing impaired or taking medications that make them drowsy have a few extra minutes to get to their cell doors before they are burned on breakfast?

Would it be too much to provide healthy food to everyone in prison, and in solitary confinement, to both those who are incarcerated and those who work there? We all know how we feel when we overload on carbs and greasy food. SGT Josh told us that COs gain the "rookie fifteen," a play on the euphemism of the "freshman fifteen" that many college students experience. If we really wanted to make jails and prisons safer and reduce conflict and violence, offering healthy food could be an important part of that overall strategy. We met white shirts who had worked in solitary confinement for a decade or more who told us that in the old days prisons used to make all of their own food, and it was not only tastier but healthier as well. In order to cut costs, most prisons now contract with large corporations like Aramark to provide their food service, and it's not just the incarcerated people who pay the price.

If we can design mirrors for men to shave safely, can we not design mirrors for women, too, so that they can see themselves and feel more human?

As we design college programs like Inside/Out which bring classes and education and even degree pathways to incarcerated people, could we also design similar programs for COs, many of whom never had the chance to go to college either? What would it look like if COs and incarcerated people could study alongside college students together navigating the liberation of education? Isn't this what Paulo Freire meant when he proposed the "pedagogy of the oppressed"? Isn't this what bell hooks meant when she described a pedagogy of hope? When she suggested that teaching (and learning) is an emancipatory process? What would it be like to invite Scholar and CO Porter to sit next to each other in a classroom and discuss Michelle Alexander's *The New Jim Crow* or our book *Policing Black Bodies*, or even this book?

Would it be too much to ask to dedicate a room in the prison for CO Porter to sleep and shower on the nights he pulls a double shift so that he doesn't have to sleep in his car?

Our colleague Kevin Wright argues that as long as we continue to incarcerate people, he suggests that incarceration could be reimagined in such a way as to leave people better off for their "time well spent," as the title of his article implies:

> People often leave prison worse than when they arrived; sometimes, they leave the same. People could leave prison better than when they arrived through a reimagined response to crime. They could be set up to live sustainable, fulfilling, and meaningful lives after prison. This approach could be informed by research on what makes for a meaningful life— regardless of whether a person has come into contact with the criminal justice system. A reimagined corrections [system] could view time spent in prison as an opportunity rather than solely as a punishment; an opportunity to repair harm, empower people, and promote public safety.[3]

What about training incarcerated people in meaningful work? Lisa Guenther highlights an example:

> As the prison population ages, and as the combination of stress, inadequate food and health care, and sometimes a lifetime of substance abuse intensifies the debilitating effects of aging for many prisoners, more and more required extra care to help them deal with everything from personal hygiene to exploitation by other inmates. While some state prison systems have hired more health professionals to deal with their aging prison population, and some non-violent prisoners have been transferred to public nursing homes, California has invested in training prisoners to become caregivers, or Gold Coats, so named for the yellow jackets they wear to distinguish themselves from other prisoners. Gold Coats help dementia patients with daily routines such as eating, showering, and changing adult diapers; they also conduct exercise classes, accompany patients to their doctors' appointments, and help them navigate the potentially treacherous terrain of the yard and the chow hall. . . . These caregivers were not always so supportive of others; Burdick is serving a life sentence for beating a man to death with a hammer, Baxter shot and killed a

coworker after a heated argument, and Canas killed a hitchhiker who had stolen his car. But their caregiving obligations have allowed them to engage with others as responsible subjects and to explore their own emotional and ethical vulnerability in relation to others. As one Gold Coat wrote in an evaluation of the program, "Thank you for allowing me to feel human."[4]

What if everyone in solitary confinement, those locked up and those locked in while they work, had the opportunity to feel human?

CHAPTER 47

The Lies the COs Tell Themselves

COs LIKE TRAVIS and Porter get up each and every morning and begin their day by telling themselves a series of lies. How do we know this? Because it would be impossible for them to do their jobs and come home at night and hug their kids if they didn't. Just as slave owners had to lie to themselves to justify the fact that they owned people, COs, too, have to lie to themselves to justify the fact that their job is to lock men in cages and treat them in dehumanizing ways. Some of the lying is facilitated by desensitization. Over our many hours in solitary confinement units, even we became less attuned to the filth or the clang of the chains or the sight of the dog-leash tether. We can understand how much of the dehumanization we observed becomes highly routinized for COs who experience it every day, sixty hours a week, fifty weeks a year, for twenty-five years.

In her book *Lose Your Mother*, Saidiya Hartman is relating a story about when she was a child and her mother was pulled over by the police when the car she was driving skidded across some ice and ran a red light. Recalling the encounter with the police, Hartman reveals not only her feelings about the officer and what it was like witnessing her mother being hassled but also how her harsh words impaled the officer. She writes:

> I called the officer every foul name a good twelve-year-old girl who attended Catholic school and who was prohibited from cursing could utter, the first being a racist and the second being a bully; had I known the word "facist" then, I would have called him that too. I asked the officer if he was going to lock us up or shoot us because my mother's brakes failed and she left her license at home. He closed the ticket book with my mother's half-written ticket inside and said "Young lady, I'm sorry you believe all that," and walked back to the patrol car. I'm certain the police officer could not have imagined his daughter saying the awful things I had said to him. A black girl with two ponytails and ashy knees and a plaid school jumper had shared her view of the world and it frightened him or shamed him. He recoiled from the ugliness of it. *To put on that uniform each day, he needed to believe it wasn't true.* As he drove away, I'm sure he was thankful no child of his lived in the same country I did.[1]

Do the COs feel this way? What do they have to tell themselves each day to put on their uniforms and go to work?

We imagine that in order to do this job day in and day out, for decades, COs must tell themselves a series of lies until they begin to believe them:

"Black bodies are less than fully human."

"Black people are criminals."

"It's my responsibility to protect the memory of the victims."

"They've committed terrible crimes and it's my responsibility to punish them."

We didn't make these lies up. COs like Travis and Bunker and Porter and so many others literally told them to us. So we know they must tell them to each other and to themselves.

And we are not alone in hearing these lies. As Carol Anderson writes, a disturbingly high number of Trump supporters actually believe that slavery should still exist in the United States: "*Some 20 percent of Trump supporters believed the Emancipation Proclamation had been bad public policy and that the enslaved should never have been freed.*"[2]

In this way, as Eddie Glaude Jr. argues, Trump is not an aberration. He is typical. He understood this when he stood in places like Larrabee County and rallied his base. Many people, including us, begged that Trump quit lying. Fact checkers were constantly tallying his "lies." But was he really lying when it came to race and white supremacy, or was he simply articulating out loud—or on Twitter—the lies white people tell themselves, so that they can get up in morning and get on with the business of racial discrimination?

CHAPTER 48

"Anything But Race" Theories

WE ANTICIPATE THAT we will be critiqued by some who read this book and suggest that what we observed wasn't really racism, or that the perspectives of correctional officers who believed that the prisoners, locked in cages twenty-three hours a day had a better deal than they did, wasn't really about race. People may be inclined to suggest that what we witnessed among the COs was generalized resentment, not racialized resentment. It's true that many of the prisoners they are charged with guarding all day long are not Black, they are Latinx or white. It's not like we ever heard the COs use the "n" word, right? [Though of course Scholar and many other people incarcerated in solitary confinement reported that they were repeatedly referred to as n★★★★.] The question the critics will ask is how do we know for sure that the resentment that the COs expressed is racial, that is it rooted in racism?

And our response to this question is shaped by the perspectives of other race scholars who have faced similar critiques of their own work.

THE LIE: ITS "ANYTHING BUT RACE"

In her discussion of racism in the child welfare system, Black feminist scholar Dorothy Roberts unpacks the perspective provided by Melvin Thomas, a sociologist at North Carolina State University:

He argues that "anything but race perspectives are refuted by empirical studies that show the continuing impact of racial discrimination: They ignore race when key racist practices such as segregated neighborhoods, culturally destructive educational practices or employer discrimination are forgotten in the rush to focus on something-anything or than race. . . ." But "anything but race" theories are even more pernicious in the way they permit whites to ignore their social advantages based on race . . . Professor Thomas [writes] "Because they see whites as somehow 'better' than blacks in some important way, their superordinate position in society is deserved. . . . If discrimination—the inequitable allocation of resources is based on race—is left out of the analysis, there could be no other conclusion: black disadvantage is a result of deficiencies within blacks themselves."[1]

In other words, the claims by white people that they don't see race, or that the explanation is something other than race, is a version of the "anything but race" theory. White COs who report that there are no issues with race in solitary confinement or that the issues are about "culture" not "race," are engaging this well-worn narrative. Additionally, as Roberts notes, engaging this narrative leads white people to the comfortable conclusion that if anything the treatment Black people receive is treatment they deserve. In solitary confinement, this perspective can be used to justify burning prisoners on showers or meals. But it can also be flipped in order to fuel the production and reproduction of white racial resentment. If COs and other staff hold "anything but race" perspectives, then it becomes increasingly difficult to justify the job they are doing: serving prisoners their meals, delivering toilet paper to their cells, escorting them to shower and yard. In short, they are forced to reconcile their belief that the circumstances of their jobs require them to give Black men who have committed crimes better treatment than they themselves receive.

SEGREGATION PRODUCES RACIAL INEQUALITY

Critical race theory was originally developed by legal scholars including Richard Delgado and Kimberlé Crenshaw as a framework for exposing the role that social structures, and white supremacy in particular, played in shaping the legal foundation on which the United States was built.[2] Critical race theorists argued that every social institution in the United States, from public education, to health care, to the legal system, must be interrogated through a lens rooted in an understanding of the role that white supremacy played not just in creating but also in maintaining each of these structures.

Rather than focusing on individual level behavior, critical race theorists interrogate the systemic, root causes of the racial disparities that exist and persist in the United States. Among the many contributions of critical race theory is the illumination of the role that segregation plays in creating and maintaining racial (and gender) inequality. Critical race scholars note, for example, the impact of racial segregation in producing inequalities in education and housing.

And, courts and legislative bodies have accepted arguments for evidence of racial bias based on these widespread patterns of racial inequalities. For example, in *Brown v. The Board Education of Topeka, Kansas* that rendered racial segregation in public spaces unconstitutional, the court did not require evidence of individual school administrators refusing to enroll a Black child; the presence of racial segregation coupled with disparities in educational outcomes was sufficient to convince the court to find in favor of Brown. Similarly, the Fair Housing Act was a response to widespread evidence of housing segregation and racial disparities in housing; its passage did not necessitate that a Black person demonstrate that a bigoted landlord had denied them the opportunity to lease an apartment or that a racist homeowner refused to sell their house to a Black person.

Once again, Black feminist scholar Dorothy Roberts's description of racism and racialized language is useful here: "Some people will say that the racial disparity in the child welfare systems does not constitute racial discrimination without a showing of racial motivation. The system is racist only if Black children are pulled out of their homes by bigoted case workers or as part of a deliberate government scheme to subjugate Black people. . . . As an initial matter, race need not be the only reason a child is removed from the home for the decision to be racially biased."[3]

In the context of solitary confinement, we revise Roberts's statement: "Some people will say that the racial disparity in solitary confinement does not constitute racial discrimination without a showing of racial motivation. The system is racist only if Black prisoners are sent to solitary confinement by bigoted correctional officers, or as part of a deliberate government scheme to subjugate Black people. . . . As an initial matter, race need not be the only reason a person is sent to solitary confinement for the decision to be racially biased."

CHAPTER 49

January 6, 2021

THE BIG LIE

WE RECEIVED OUR BOOK manuscript back from reviewers just a few days after the events of January 6, 2021. On that day, we sat, like many Americans, transfixed as we watched white nationalists storm the U.S. Capitol, an apparent white supremacist coup in real time. We, like so many, were stunned by the brazen actions of so many white men and a few white women who stormed into the hallowed halls of our democracy wearing MAGA hats and shirts and waving Trump flags. The same kinds of flags we saw flying over storefronts and in front lawns all over Larrabee County. What was perhaps more jarring was the number of Confederate flags and other symbols of white nationalism being carried and on full display by the rioters. These were not flags flown under the cover of darkness or by people whose faces were blotted out in news reports or on video taken by protesters. These white people, mostly men, carried these symbols of the Confederacy and of white nationalism proudly. The message was clear: we, white nationalists and patriots of the Confederacy, are here to take our country back.

The MAGA hats represent more than just an attempt to "make America great again." A sociological analysis reveals that they represent a desire to return to a social order in which white men reclaim total control of the entire social political economy.

Luke Broadwater, a journalist working for the *New York Times*, interviewed Black congressional staffers about their experiences on January 6, 2021. Their statements make clear that they experienced the events of January 6 not only as a demonstration of white supremacy but as an attempt to bring the sentiments of the South to the "North" and to reestablish the presence of the Confederacy. He writes:

"This was the ugliest display of racism that I've seen ever. And I'm from the South," says Remmington Belford, 30, the communications director for Representative Yvette D. Clarke, Democrat of New York. "There's a specific demographic of people that you know conduct themselves that way, and you find your way away from them. Those people came to

Capitol Hill. The people who believe in supremacy due to genetics were on Capitol Hill, and they were armed, and they were incensed.

"I never thought I'd see the Confederate flag walked through the halls of Congress," said Mike McQuerry, 50, the communications director for Delegate Stacey Plaskett, Democrat of the Virgin Islands. . . . "As much as we think we've had progress, we haven't progressed that much."[1]

Black police officers, including Officer Eugene Goodman, who is credited with saving Senator Mitt Romney and others, "described the intense racism they endured from the mob; one told Buzzfeed News he was called a racist slur 15 times, causing him to break down in tears."[2]

As the days and weeks after the insurrection passed and investigators and journalists began to comb through the video footage and posts on social media, reports began to fill in one of the more troubling aspects of the coup: the behavior of some Capitol Police officers. On January 6, 2021, not only was there a minimal police presence which was quickly overwhelmed, but many people also noticed that the police seemed to open the doors of the Capitol for the mobs, almost as if welcoming them in rather than protecting the seat of democracy. One video emerged of a rioter taking a selfie with a police officer while others seen in the background were literally looting and desecrating Statuary Hall. As Natasha Bertrand and others reported a few days later, among the rioters were many off-duty cops and military personnel who flashed their badges at the Capitol Police as if to say, "We got this"; "We are you."[3]

More and more images of police officers and military personnel in uniform performing their duties emerged that also showed them displaying, on their uniforms, symbols of QAnon. Their faces in full view, not hiding behind the white hood of a Klan costume.

Though this might be stunning to many Americans, to think that white nationalists have a visible presence in the police force and the military, it wasn't surprising to us. Not after what we heard from many of the COs whom we interviewed.

CO Porter said: "I don't associate with people from work. I don't want to be around people talking about this place."

["Do you talk to anyone?"]

"Family . . . I talk to them, they're supportive, but I have to watch what I say. . . . It's a strong Republican, Catholic home. . . . I'm not a Republican or a Democrat. I'm not pro-Trump; I get tired of hearing about him. I don't like his manner . . . He's a womanizer and he gets away with stuff. There are a lot of Trump supporters among the staff.

["How do you know? How do they show it? Bumper stickers?"]

"They are vocal about it; they talk about it."

Not after what Claude Marks confirmed in our interview with him. Claude detailed the infiltration of white supremacists in the prison guard union and the process by which white nationalist COs allowed prisoners who were aligned with white nationalist groups like the Aryan nation to "run" the prison yard. At SCI-Wannabee we interviewed white men who proclaimed to be aligned with white nationalist groups and who showed us their tattoos as confirmation. We saw the gang affiliation boards in the COs' office, the column for white supremacist gangs filled with a dozen or more white faces.

We began our research in solitary confinement units in the summer of 2017. Trump had been elected president just six months prior. Like many people living and working in so-called liberal bubbles, we were, admittedly, far more out of touch with the landscape of rural white America than we understood at the time. On our first trip to Larrabee County, we were, frankly, stunned by the Trump yard signs, barns with one entire side painted TRUMP, typically red and blue letters on a white background, chain link fences with red and blue solo cups spelling out TRUMP.

At the time we were living in Fairfax County, Virginia, a suburb of D.C., a space where national politics dominates daily life. But even in this heightened political space, though "election-style" yard signs and billboards for candidates appear early in the election cycle, they are taken down and removed shortly after the election. We don't recall seeing a single "Trump" or for that matter "Clinton" yard sign or billboard that was still up in the summer of 2017. In the world in which we lived, the election, even if we didn't like the outcome, was a fait accompli.

Not so in Trump land. The 2016 election might have been over, but the loyalty to Trump, which rises to the level of a secular religion, was evidenced all across Larrabee County.

Our first trip to Larrabee County coincided with our interview with CO Travis. Though we may have been living in a liberal bubble before we met CO Travis, we knew early in the summer of 2017 that we needed to learn much more about white racial resentment.

We spent the next year consuming all of the academic and scholarly literature we could find. As such, our research and writing were shaped significantly by the work of Jonathan Metzl, Arlie Hochschild, Rory McVeigh, and Kevin Estep. We schooled ourselves on white racial resentment. Across our remaining research trips, we paid careful attention to the presence of symbols of white nationalism, including Confederate flags and "Don't Tread on Me" bumper stickers. We focused our interviews, especially with COs, more intently on their perceptions of racial dynamics in solitary confinement and the prison and community more broadly. We asked COs more questions about their experiences and how they felt about their jobs, their families, and their communities. We never explicitly asked anyone about Trump, but conversations emerged organically, as was the case with CO Porter.

What we did not know about at the time were the white nationalist movements taking place on the dark web. We didn't learn about QAnon until after we completed our research trips. And, therefore, we didn't ask about nor know to look for its symbols. As a result, we do not have the evidence to argue that COs we interviewed are members of white nationalist or conspiracy groups like the Proud Boys or QAnon.

But what we do know is that COs live in communities in which their neighbors and potentially their family members are. Though some may actively resist this ideology, as CO Porter does, others are certainly sympathetic if not actively involved. Their rhetoric of Trumpism and white racial resentment echo those expressed by the protesters on January 6, 2021. Many, including CO Travis, longed for a return to a time in which whiteness ensured the maintenance of laws, policies, and practices that ensured that Blacks and others had limited or no access to the opportunity structure, a time like slavery and Jim Crow.

If, in fact, there are sympathizers if not members of white nationalist groups working as COs in solitary confinement units and prisons more broadly, then this helps to explain what we saw and heard, that the Black people incarcerated there were treated inhumanely because their lives were deemed to have no value. Under these circumstances, some of which they inherited and some of which they created, COs grew to resent the men they locked in cages.

White racial resentment is fueled by the lies that white people, including COs, tell themselves so that they can get up each day and go to work and get on with the practice of enforcing laws, policies, and practices that are built on the foundation of white supremacy.

White racial resentment is produced by the specific structures of solitary confinement, and it reproduces the belief that a Black man locked in a cage twenty-three hours a day, fed through a wicket, who eats next to his toilet, exercises in a dog kennel, showers in a cage, and has extremely limited human interaction, is better off than you are.

That you, and not he, is the one who is forgotten.

Epilogue

FINALLY. DONE. The long drives from Virginia deep into this Mid-Atlantic Rust Belt state are now over. What was accomplished for undertaking such an ordeal?

Get up early. Depending on your gender, pack items that you will need to sustain a full eight hours inside, without a break.

Make sure you are not carrying contraband. But what is contraband? My colored socks? My watch? My underwire bra? Or is it anything and everything, depending on who is on duty when we pass through security to the invisible world of solitary confinement?

What was accomplished was the gathering of enough firsthand data to write this compelling book on race inside solitary confinement. This was done using the methodology of the acclaimed British social anthropologist Clifford Geertz. Geertz, doing fieldwork in Central America, introduces us to the ways in which detailed descriptions are critical to demonstrate to the reader exactly what the researchers both saw and heard. This seeing and hearing must be put in context of the events observed.

This is our concern when researching and studying solitary confinement by relying exclusively on "administrative data" collected mostly by the state where the prisons are located. This is not to say these data and interpretations of them are wrong. It is to suggest that something goes missing when you can't hear, feel, smell, or sense what is going on. Geertz put it thus in his *Thick Description: Toward an Interpretive Theory of Culture*:

> Consider . . . two boys rapidly contracting the eyelids of their right eyes. In one, this is an involuntary twitch; in the other, a conspiratorial signal to a friend. The two movements are, as movements, identical; from an I-am-a-camera, "phenomenalistic" observation of them alone, one could not tell which was twitch and which was wink, or indeed whether both or either was twitch or wink. Yet the difference, however unphotographable, between a twitch and a wink is vast; as anyone unfortunate enough to have had the first taken for the second knows. The winker is communicating, and indeed communicating in a quite precise and special way. . . . Contracting your eyelids on purpose when there exists a public code in which so doing

counts as a conspiratorial signal is winking. That's all there is to it: a speck of behavior, a fleck of culture, and—voila!—a gesture. That, however, is just the beginning. Suppose, he continues, there is a third boy, who, "to give malicious amusement to his cronies," parodies the first boy's wink, as amateurish, clumsy, obvious, and so on. He, of course, does this in the same way the second boy winked and the first twitched: by contracting his right eyelids. Only this boy is neither winking nor twitching, he is parodying someone else's, as he takes it, laughable, attempt at winking. Here, too, a socially established code exists. . . . The point is that between what Ryle calls the "thin description" of what the rehearser (parodist, winker, twitcher . . .) is doing ("rapidly contracting his right eyelids") and the "thick description" of what he is doing ("practicing a burlesque of a friend faking a wink to deceive an innocent into thinking a conspiracy is in motion") lies the object of ethnography: a stratified hierarchy of meaningful structures in terms of which twitches, winks, fake-winks, parodies, rehearsals of parodies are produced, perceived, and interpreted, and without which they would not (not even the zero-form twitches, which, as a cultural category, are as much non-winks as winks are non-twitches) in fact exist, no matter what anyone did or didn't do with his eyelids.[1]

You would have to have been there to see what three boys were doing with "twitches, winks, fake winks and parodies" and their intent. Otherwise, the context is missed.

We also accomplished writing what we believe is one of the first critical accounts of race and racism in solitary confinement. Sure, we know from others that solitary is pretty Black and brown as far as incarcerated people go. Sure, we know that staff and COs and officers are mostly white. What most people don't know and don't even consider are the interactions and processes that exist between these two groups of people who are separated by chasms of both race and power. And, it is in the spaces of these intimate, interracial, inter-status interactions where white racial resentment festers.

The question "What is to be done?" is ever present. We have mulled over this question constantly. In the previous pages, we have provided a set of recommendations that we want to stress again here. We are not abolitionists. We are academic scholars reporting on and analyzing what we observed. We believe that if incarcerated people are choosing to be housed in solitary confinement, we cannot issue a blanket recommendation to shut it down. We can, and do, advocate for a more humane general population unit so that no one would voluntarily choose solitary confinement. When used, we agree with the American Bar Association (2011) that solitary be used for the briefest time and under the least restrictive conditions as is practicable.

Goodbye to the *early* morning stops at the Sheetz gas station/convenience stores. Goodbye to the stale air, to the nasty carpeting in the "hotel" where taking off one's shoes was a potentially dangerous activity. Goodbye to prison food and too much greasy take out. Goodbye to the long, often winding roads in the Mid-Atlantic. Goodbye to Fifty; Scholar; Shaniqua; CO Porter; Dr. Emma; CO Travis; CO Lisa; Ms. Rambo; Unit Manager Steve; Counselor Mark; Unit Manager Tom; CO Bunker; Sergeant Jack; Lieutenant House. So long to the women in the BMU: Wendi and Jennifer and Sally and especially Marina.

Thank you for sharing your stories and the intimate details of your lives. We hope you, the reader, have come to see everyone whose stories we feature in the book as deeply complicated and 100 percent human. If so, then we have done our job. The ultimate mission is accomplished!

ABBREVIATIONS AND TERMS

AC	administrative custody
BMU	behavioral management unit
Burn	when an officer denies a person incarcerated in solitary confinement a right, such as a meal, shower, or time in the yard
CO	corrections officer
DC	disciplinary custody
DOC	Department of Corrections
DTU	diversionary treatment unit
Fishing	a strategy that people incarcerated in solitary confinement use to share small items with each other by using a system of strings, often pulled from their bedsheets and the seams of their clothing, which they attach to the item they want to fish, along with a weight, perhaps a small bar of soap which allows the fisher to have some limited control of the line.
LT	lieutenant
PREA	Prison Rape Elimination Act
SGT	sergeant
SHU	secure housing unit
White shirt	an officer, including lieutenants, sergeants, captains and majors

ACKNOWLEDGMENTS

THIS BOOK would never have reached the shelves if it were not for our editor, Peter Mickulas and the production team—including Sherry Gerstein, Daryl Brower, Ellen Lohman and many others whose names we don't know. We pushed hard and they often pushed hard back. Their insights and expertise contributed significantly to the final product you are reading today. A special shout out to Professor Michael Messner who first introduced us to Peter. We remember our first conversation with you, Peter, in a hotel in Vancouver. You asked if we were interested in writing a book about sports and we said we weren't interested in writing another book at all. We were done. I guess it's not the first time we've been wrong. This may not have been the book you expected. Thanks for trusting us!

One of the biggest challenges we faced in the production of this book was acquiring the art work, specifically the two pieces that were created by incarcerated people. We were deeply committed to including the art of incarcerated people and specifically we wanted a cover that featured the design of someone who is currently or had been incarcerated. We are grateful to the staff at the Prison Creative Arts Project, Director, Nora Krinitsky, PhD and Associate Director, Vanessa Mayesky, MPA who facilitated the acquisition of the two pieces we feature.

We owe a debt of gratitude to two people who we have never met: the incarcerated artists. We were inspired by all of the pieces that are part of the Prison Creative Arts Project collection. The two we selected, "Suffocating" by James D. Fuson, which we feature as the cover art and OBSERVATION—"Red" Cell by D. L. Derell which is featured in Part 1 captured the essence of our observations in solitary confinement in ways our words never could. As they say, "a picture is worth a thousand words." We are inspired by your spirit and your work and we hope that everyone who buys the book and reads it checks out the amazing collection at the Prison Creative Arts Project. We are humbled to feature your work.

A special shout out to our former student and dear friend, Taylor Sprague for creating the illustrations "Diagram of the Hole" and "Solitary Cell." You read an earlier version of our manuscript, you listened, and you transformed our words into these amazing illustrations. We know the reader is better able to "see" solitary confinement through your illustrations. What a pleasure it was to reconnect and work with you on this amazing project. Thank you!

We have benefited tremendously from the work of those who have come before us, especially Dr. Terry Kupers, Professor Keramet Reiter, Mary Buser, Professor Lisa Guenther, Claude Marks, and Professor Danielle Rudes. Their approaches are all different. Some, like Terry Kupers and Mary Buser, worked as mental health providers inside prisons, and as a result they had regular, long-term access not only to prisons but to solitary confinement units as well. As professionals, they focus on the mental health impact of solitary confinement. Others, like Keramet Reiter, conducted most of their research with people who had previously overseen the work of solitary confinement as well as those who had survived. Coupled with administrative data, Reiter's work is critical to understanding the development and implementation of solitary confinement, particularly in one of the most notorious prisons: California's Pelican Bay. Philosopher Lisa Guenther's work is more theoretical and relies on the testimony and writings of people who have been incarcerated in solitary confinement. Guenther's insights, as they pertain to the impact of isolation, including sensory deprivation and "time," were instrumental in our own analysis. Professor Kevin Wright, whom we got to know while writing this book, was instrumental in sharing not only his research but his thoughts about the controversies surrounding the movement to abolish solitary confinement. We are grateful for his perspective, which stretched our own and is reflected in our discussions of abolition and reforms.

One of our earliest interviews with a correctional officer was with CO Travis. After our interview with him, in which he proclaimed that the guards are Trump's forgotten, his left behind, we knew there was much more to the story and we needed to learn more about the process by which COs came to believe that the men they lock in cages have a better deal than they do. We dedicated one summer to reading the literature on white racial resentment. The work of Rory McVeigh, Kevin Estep, and Arlie Hochschild greatly informed our perspective and provided the frame in which to understand CO Travis's prophetic words. We are also grateful to Christian Curtis. In conversations with Christian, we explored the neurobiology of trauma. His new book *Anthropolitics: The Rise of Homo Civilis* informs our thinking about CO Travis's argument that there should be a diagnosis of correctional PTSD and the impact that the trauma of solitary confinement has on the people who work there. Chris's work also helps us think about the ways in which empathy could be built inside the hole.

Professor Leah Adams, a colleague and friend in psychology and women and gender studies at George Mason, is a stats goddess. When we had trouble with some of the analysis of our Qualtrics survey, Leah graciously jumped in to help. Any errors in the Qualtrics analysis remain our responsibility, but we are grateful for her help. Professor Wendi Manuel-Scott is both a dear friend

Acknowledgments

and a conversation partner when it comes to issues of race, anti-Black racism, white supremacy, and intersectionality. Though most people will read this book as a book about solitary confinement, which it is, it is really a book about race. Wendi has always understood that and not only engaged in conversations about white racial resentment but recommended the work of scholars, including Jonathan Metzl, Saidiya Hartman, and Eddie Glaude Jr., whose analysis of race, the transatlantic slave trade, and white racial resentment greatly informed the frame in which the data in this book are analyzed. Claude Marks, a former political prisoner in the federal prison system, generously shared his time with us. We had conversations and conducted informal interviews with Claude over Zoom. He was particularly useful in helping us understand the linkages among the military, white supremacy, and the prison staff. He also directed us to Solitary Watch, an activist organization that provides advocacy and policy recommendations focused on reforming and abolishing the use of solitary confinement. Their book, *Hell Is a Very Small Place*, which features the voices of people who have survived solitary, informed our own work. A deep, special thanks to Shannon Magnuson, who not only was a partner on so many of the research trips but always found the best comfort food, and she pushed us to stand by our race analysis even when it was unpopular.

With deep gratitude we offer thanks to our colleague and friend Danielle Rudes, who spent time, as we did, observing conditions and interviewing staff and people incarcerated in solitary confinement. It is because of her generosity that we were able to join the research team, and her voice is threaded throughout this book. Though each of their approaches is unique, each has informed our own work. We stand, as Robert K. Merton famously said, "on the shoulders of giants."

Finally, we are grateful to the people who allowed us into their lives. We hope we have done you justice. We hope that after reading this book, more people will care about those locked away in solitary confinement, both the people incarcerated there and the staff, and the conditions that contribute to the production and reproduction of racism and white racial resentment that ultimately hurt not only the individuals but all of us as we attempt to navigate our history, as a society, built on the foundation of white supremacy, and imagine a society in which all people are truly equal.

Notes

Introduction

1. Ruth Gilmore, *Golden Gulag: Prisons, Surplus, Crisis, and Opposition in Globalizing California* (Berkeley: University of California Press, 2007).

Chapter 1 A Day in the Hole

1. Radley Balko, *The Rise of the Warrior Cop: The Militarization of America's Police Forces* (New York: PublicAffairs, 2013).
2. Angela Hattery and Earl Smith, *Policing Black Bodies: How Black Lives Are Surveilled and How To Work For Change* (Lanham, MD: Rowman & Littlefield, 2021), 60.
3. Guenther, *Solitary Confinement*, 96.
4. Charles Baxter et al., "Live from the Panopticon: Architecture and Power Revisited," in *The New Abolitionist: (Neo) Slave Narratives and Contemporary Prison Writings*, ed. Joy James, (Albany: SUNY Press, 2005), 208
5. Baxter et al., "Live from the Panopticon," 208.
6. Saidiya Hartman, *Lose Your Mother: A Journey Along the Atlantic Slave Route*, New York: Farrar, Straus and Giroux, 2007), 87–88.
7. Raj Chetty, Nathaniel Hendren, Maggie R. Jones, and Sonya R. Porter, *Race and Economic Opportunity in the United States: An Intergenerational Perspective*, March 2018, http://www.equality-of-opportunity.org/assets/documents/race_paper.pdf.
8. Lorna A. Rhodes, *Total Confinement: Madness and Reason in the Maximum Security Prison* (Berkeley, CA: University of California Press, 2004), 45.
9. Mary Buser, "Let's Help Frank!," Go Fund Me, September 13, 2021, https://www.gofundme.com/f/q3jzy-lets-help-frank?utm_campaign=p_lico+share-sheet+spider1c&utm_medium=copy_link&utm_source=customer
10. United Nations, *Seeing into Solitary: A Review of the Laws and Policies of Certain Nations Regarding Solitary Confinement of Detainees*, United Nations Special Report, 2016, https://www.weil.com/~/media/files/pdfs/2016/un_special_report_solitary_confinement.pdf; Terry Kupers, *Solitary: The Inside Story of Supermax Isolation and How We Can Abolish It* (Oakland: University of California Press, 2017).
11. Ed Pilkington, "Albert Woodfox Released from Prison after 43 Years in Solitary," *Guardian*, February 19, 2016, http://bit.ly/2F8GLy0.
12. National LGBTQ Task Force, "CeCe McDonald Released from Prison," https://www.thetaskforce.org/cece-mcdonald-released-from-prison/.

Chapter 2 Solitary Confinement in Context

1. Michel Foucault, *Discipline & Punish: The Birth of the Prison* (New York: Vintage Books, 1995); Jeremiah Olson, "Race and Punishment in American Prisons," *Journal of Public Administration Research and Theory* 26 (2010): 758–768, http://bit.ly/2LcEqc1.
2. Eileen McHugh, *Auburn Correctional Facility* (New York: Arcadia Publishing, 2010).

3. Ashley T. Rubin and Keramet Reiter, "Continuity in the Face of Penal Innovation: Revisiting the History of American Solitary Confinement," *Law & Social Inquiry*, 43, no. 4 (2018):1604–1632, https://doi.org/10.1111/lsi.12330.

4. "Who We Are," Vera Institute of Justice, accessed April 7, 2022, https://www.vera.org/who-we-are.

5. Gustave de Beaumont and Alexis de Tocqueville, *On the Penitentiary System in the United States and Its Application in France* (Philadelphia: Carey, Lea & Blanchard, 1833), http://www.houseofrussell.com/legalhistory/alh/docs/penitentiary.html.

6. Yale Law School, "Reforming Restrictive Housing: The 2018 ASCA-Liman Nationwide Survey of Time-in-Cell" and the related report, *Working to Limit Restrictive Housing: Efforts in Four Jurisdictions to Make Changes*; United Nations, *Seeing into Solitary: A Review of the Laws and Policies of Certain Nations Regarding Solitary Confinement of Detainees*, United Nations Special Report (2016), 40, https://www.weil.com/~/media/files/pdfs/2016/un_special_report_solitary_confinement.pdf.

7. United Nations, *Seeing into Solitary*,10.

8. Marisa Endicott, "A 2015 Case Was Supposed to Overhaul California's Solitary Confinement. The Reality Is Much More Complicated." "It's clear that monitoring alone is not going to fix the situation." *Mother Jones,* February 13, 2019, https://www.motherjones.com/crime-justice/2019/02/california-ashker-brown-solitary-confinement-status-appeal/.

9. Marisa Endicott, "A 2015 Case Was Supposed to Overhaul California's Solitary Confinement. The Reality Is Much More Complicated." "It's clear that monitoring alone is not going to fix the situation." *Mother Jones,* February 13, 2019, https://www.motherjones.com/crime-justice/2019/02/california-ashker-brown-solitary-confinement-status-appeal/.

10. Freedom Archives, accessed April 8, 2022, https://freedomarchives.org/.

11. Kim Rohrbach, "SHU-shifting: An Update on and Overview of the Ashker v. Brown Class Action," *Bay View*, March 28, 2015, https://sfbayview.com/2015/03/shu-shifting-an-update-on-and-overview-of-the-ashker-v-brown-class-action/.

12. Joshua Cochran, Elisa L. Toman, Daniel P. Mears, and William D. Bales, "Solitary Confinement as Punishment: Examining In-prison Sanctioning Disparities," *Justice Quarterly* 35, no.3 (2018): 381–411.

13. Erik Wright, *Class Counts: Comparative Studies in Class Analysis* (New York: Cambridge University Press, 1997; emphasis ours).

CHAPTER 3 IDEAL TYPES

1. William Wilson and Anmol Chaddha, "The Role of Theory in Ethnographic Research," *Ethnography* 10, no. 4 (2009): 549–564; Steven Lubet, *Interrogating Ethnography: Why Evidence Matters* (New York: Oxford University Press, 2017).

2. Janice Morse, "Cherry Picking: Writing from Thin Data," *Qualitative Health Research* 20, no. 1 (2010): 3–3, https://doi.org/10.1177/1049732309354285; Michael Quinn Patton, *Qualitative Research and Evaluation Methods: Integrating Theory and Practice*, 4th ed. (Thousand Oaks, CA: Sage, 2015), 264.

3. Richard Swedberg, "How to Use Max Weber's Ideal Type in Sociological Analysis," *Journal of Classical Sociology* 18, no. 3 (2018): 181–196, https://doi.org/10.1177/1468795X17743643.

4. Matthew Desmond, "Relational Ethnography," *Theory and Society* 43 (2014): 547, www.jstor.org/stable/43694733.

CHAPTER 6 RACISM IN SOLITARY CONFINEMENT

1. Hannah Pullen-Blasnik, Jessica T. Simes, and Bruce Western, "The Population Prevalence of Solitary Confinement." *Science Advances* 7, no. 48 (26 November, 2021), DOI: 10.1126/sciadv.abj1928.

2. Angela J. Hattery and Earl Smith, *Policing Black Bodies: How Black Lives Are Surveilled and How to Work for Change* (Lanham, MD: Rowman and Littlefield, 2018).
3. Mary E. Buser, *Lockdown on Rikers: Shocking Stories of Abuse and Injustice at New York's Most Notorious Jail* (New York: St. Martin's, 2020), 247.
4. Jason Tripp, "Most Segregated Hour in America—Martin Luther King Jr.," YouTube, April 29, 2014," https://youtu.be/1q881g1L_d8.
5. Terry Kupers, *Solitary: The Inside Story of Supermax Isolation and How We Can Abolish It* (Oakland: University of California Press, 2017).

CHAPTER 7   THE CELL ASSIGNMENT

1. This same observation is confirmed by Vivian Hughes and her colleagues who conducted focus groups with staff in a women's prison. Vivian Aranda-Hughes, Jillian J. Turanovic, Daniel P. Mears, and George B. Pesta, "Women in Solitary Confinement: Relationships, Pseudofamilies, and the Limits of Control," *Feminist Criminology* 16, no. 1 (2020): 47–72, https://doi.org/10.1177/1557085120961441; Joane Martel, "Telling the Story: A Study in the Segregation of Women Prisoners," *Social Justice* 28, no. 1 (2001): 196–215.

CHAPTER 8   IT'S "CULTURE" NOT "RACE"

1. Eduardo Bonilla-Silva, "Rethinking Racism: Toward a Structural Interpretation," *American Sociological Review* 62, no. 3 (1997): 465–480.
2. Adia Harvey Wingfield, *No More Invisible Man: Race and Gender in Men's Work* (Philadelphia, PA: Temple University Press, 2013), 116; Adia Harvey Wingfield, *Flatlining: Race, Work and Health Care in the New Economy* (Berkeley: University of California Press, 2019).

CHAPTER 9   LOCATING PRISONS IN RURAL SETTINGS

1. Pennsylvania Economy League, *The Economic Impact of the Coal Industry in Pennsylvania* prepared for the Pennsylvania Coal Alliance, (March 2014), https://www.ourenergypolicy.org/wp-content/uploads/2014/05/PA-coal.pdf.
2. For a full examination of prison locations and how those who advocate for bringing prisons to their town, see Gregory Hooks, "Prisons, Jobs and Privatization: The Impact of Prisons on Employment Growth in Rural US Counties, 1997–2004," *Social Science Research* 42, no. 3 2013): 596–610, https://doi.org/10.1016/j.ssresearch.2012.12.008.
3. Andy Hoover, "SCI-Retreat Closing: Prisons Should Never Be a Community's Economic Development Strategy | Opinion," *[State] Capital Star*, September 13, 2019, https://www.penncapital-star.com/commentary/sci-retreat-closing-prisons-should-never-be-a-communitys-economic-development-strategy-opinion/.

CHAPTER 15   DEHUMANIZATION

1. Rick Raemisch, "My Night in Solitary," *Opinion* (blog), *New York Times*, February 20, 2014, https://www.nytimes.com/2014/02/21/opinion/my-night-in-solitary.html?_r=0.

CHAPTER 16   LANGUAGE

1. Mary E. Buser, *Lockdown on Rikers: Shocking Stories of Abuse and Injustice at New York's Most Notorious Jail* (New York: St. Martin's, 2015), 243.

CHAPTER 17   STUDIES WITH MONKEYS

1. Harry F. Harlow, Robert O. Dodsworth, and Margaret K. Harlow, "Total Social Isolation in Monkeys," *Proceedings of the National Academy of Sciences*, July 1, vol. 54, no. 1 (1965), pp. 90–97, https://www.ncbi.nlm.nih.gov/pmc/articles/PMC285801/pdf/pnas00159-0105.pdf.

CHAPTER 18   HYGIENE PRODUCTS

1. Joshua Rhett Miller, "Guard Demanded Sex for Toilet Paper at New Jersey Prison, Ex-inmate Claims," *New York Post*, July 3, 2020, https://nypost.com/2020/07/03/guard-demanded-sex-for-toilet-paper-at-nj-prison-ex-inmate/.

CHAPTER 21   TIME

1. Lisa Guenther, *Solitary Confinement: Social Death and Its Afterlives* (Minneapolis: University of Minnesota Press, 2013): 195–196.

CHAPTER 23   CHOOSING THE HOLE

1. This same observation is confirmed by Vivian Hughes and her colleagues who conducted focus groups with staff in a women's prison. Vivian Aranda-Hughes, Jillian J. Turanovic, Daniel P. Mears, and George B. Pesta, "Women in Solitary Confinement: Relationships, Pseudofamilies, and the Limits of Control," *Feminist Criminology* 16, no. 1 (2020): 47–72, https://doi.org/10.1177/1557085120961441; Joane Martel, "Telling the Story: A Study in the Segregation of Women Prisoners," *Social Justice* 28, no. 1 (2001): 196–215.

CHAPTER 24   FREELIMO THE SILENCING OF THE POLITICAL PRISONER

1. *Merriam-Webster*, s.v. (black nationalist" (*n.*), accessed March 13, 2022. https://www.merriam-webster.com/dictionary/black%20nationalism.
2. Chris Hayes, *A Colony in a Nation* (New York: Norton, 2017), 38–39.

CHAPTER 25   EXTREME VIOLENCE

1. Terry Kupers, "How to Create Madness in Prison," in *Hell Is a Very Small Place: Voices from Solitary Confinement*, ed. Jean Casella, James Ridgeway, and Sarah Shourd (New York: New Press, 2017), 164–165.
2. A *New York Times* feature story by Michael Winerip and Michael Schwirtz on the New York State prison system titled "Prison Brutality at Clinton Correctional," *New York Times*, December 22, 2015, can be found here: https://www.nytimes.com/2015/12/22/insider/prison-brutality-at-clinton-correctional-getting-the-story.html?searchResultPosition=6.
3. PAUL HENRY v. MATTHEW L. LIBERTY, et al., 9:15-CV-1108 (MAD/DEP) (2012).
4. Mary E. Buser, *Lockdown on Rikers: Shocking Stories of Abuse and Injustice at New York's Most Notorious Jail* (New York: St. Martin's, 2015), 98.
5. George Floyd was killed on May 25, 2020, in Minneapolis, Minnesota, by police officer Derek Chauvin. On April 20, 2021, Derek Chauvin was found guilty on three counts of murder and at the time of this writing is in custody awaiting sentencing.
6. John Neville died on December 4, 2019, a few days after Forsyth County Detention Center (Winston-Salem, North Carolina) officers placed him in handcuffs and restrained him on the floor following an apparent medical episode.

7. Azi Paybarah, "Sheriff Apologizes to Family of Inmate Who Died after Being Restrained," *New York Times*, August 4, 2020, https://www.nytimes.com/2020/08 /04/us/john-neville-death-winston-salem-nc.html.

CHAPTER 26   WELCOME TO SCI-WOMEN

1. Malika Saada Saar, Rebecca Epstein, Lindsay Rosenthal, and Yasmin Vafa, *The Sexual Abuse to Prison Pipeline: The Girls' Story* (Washington, DC: Center for Poverty and Inequality, Georgetown University Law Center, 2015), 7, http://bit.ly /1DqeScy.
2. Danielle Rudes, Shannon Portillo, Shannon Magnusson, and Angela Hattery, "Sex Logics: Negotiating the Prison Rape Elimination Act (PREA) against Its' Administrative, Safety, and Cultural Burdens," *Punishment & Society* 23, no. 2 (2020), 241–259, https://doi.org/10.1177/1462474520952155.

CHAPTER 27   THE WOMEN'S HOLE

1. This same observation is confirmed by Vivian Hughes and her colleagues who conducted focus groups with staff in a women's prison. Vivian Aranda-Hughes, Jillian J. Turanovic, Daniel P. Mears, and George B. Pesta, "Women in Solitary Confinement: Relationships, Pseudofamilies, and the Limits of Control," *Feminist Criminology* 16, no. 1 (2020): 47–72, https://doi.org/10.1177/1557085120961441.

CHAPTER 28   MEETING THE MASS KILLER

1. Mara Bovsun, "[Ms. Rambo] Went Psycho and Killed Three Innocent People at the [Mal]l," *New York Daily News*, December 2, 2012, https://www.nydailynews .com/news/justice-story/ms-rambo-kill-spree-article-1.1211691.

CHAPTER 29   THE BMU

1. Mary E. Buser, *Lockdown on Rikers: Shocking Stories of Abuse and Injustice at New York's Most Notorious Jail* (New York: St. Martin's, 2015), 20.
2. Craig Haney, "Restricting the Use of Solitary Confinement," *Annual Review of Criminology* 1 (2018): 285–310.
3. Haney, 2018, "Restricting the Use."
4. Jim Mason and Mary Finelli, "Brave New Farm?" in *In Defense of Animals: The Second Wave*, ed. Peter Singer, 104–122 (New York: Wiley-Blackwell, 2006; emphasis ours).
5. Lisa Guenther, *Solitary Confinement: Social Death and Its Afterlives* (Minneapolis: University of Minnesota Press, 2013), 152–153.

CHAPTER 30   SALLY

1. Lisa Guenther, *Solitary Confinement: Social Death and Its Afterlives* (Minneapolis: University of Minnesota Press, 2013), 152–153.
2. United Nations, *Seeing into Solitary: A Review of the Laws and Policies of Certain Nations Regarding Solitary Confinement of Detainees* (United Nations Special Report, 2016), 11, https://www.weil.com/~/media/files/pdfs/2016/un_special_report_solitary _confinement.pdf.

CHAPTER 33   DO YOU THINK I'LL DIE HERE?

1. Lisa Guenther, *Solitary Confinement: Social Death and Its Afterlives* (Minneapolis: University of Minnesota, 2013), xx.

CHAPTER 34   WE ARE THE ESSENTIAL WORKERS

1. Daniel Jonah Goldhagen, *Hitler's Willing Executioners: Ordinary Germans and the Holocaust* (New York: Vintage, 1997).

CHAPTER 35   SOLITARY CONFINEMENT ISN'T A DAYCARE!

1. Sharon Shalev, *Supermax: Controlling Risk Through Solitary Confinement* (Portland, OR: Willan, 2009), 142.
2. Lisa Guenther, *Solitary Confinement: Social Death and Its Afterlives* (Minneapolis: University of Minnesota Press, 2013), 132.

CHAPTER 36   CORRECTIONAL PTSD

1. W. Heron, B. K. Doane, and T. H. Scott, "Visual Disturbances after Prolonged Perceptual Isolation," *Canadian Journal of Psychology/Revue canadienne de psychologie* 10, no.1 (1956), 16. https://doi.org/10.1037/h0083650.
2. Michael D. Denhof and Caterina G. Spinaris, *Depression, PTSD and Comorbidity in United States Corrections Professionals: Prevalence and Impact on Health and Functioning* (Desert Waters Correctional Outreach, 2013), https://desertwaters.com/wp-content/uploads/2013/09/Comorbidity_Study_09-03-131.pdf.
3. Curtis Christian, *Anthropolitics: The Rise of Homo Civilis* (November 8, 2021, Independently published).
4. Gary Aumiller, "Divorce in Cops and Corrections," *Police Psychologist* (December 2, 2016). http://policepsychologyblog.com/?p=4245.

CHAPTER 38   THE GRIFT

1. Shannon Magnuson, *Solitary Diversion: Reforming Restricted Housing Units for Individuals with Severe Mental Health Diagnoses* (Unpublished Dissertation, George Mason University, 2022).
2. Dana DeHart, Cheri Shapiro, and Stephanie Clone, "The Pill Line Is Longer Than the Chow Line: The Impact of Incarceration on Prisoners and Their Families," *The Prison Journal* 98, no.2 (2018), 1–25.
3. Mary E. Buser, *Lockdown on Rikers: Shocking Stories of Abuse and Injustice at New York's Most Notorious Jail* (New York: St. Martin's, 2015), 20.
4. Bruce Western, Jessica T. Simes, and Kendra Bradner, "Solitary Confinement and Institutional Harm" (unpublished manuscript, 2019, Department of Sociology and Columbia Justice Lab, Columbia University).

CHAPTER 39   THE FLIPPED SCRIPT

1. At the time of this writing, during the summer of 2020, in the midst of the COVID-19 pandemic, unemployment in Larrabee County skyrocketed to nearly 20 percent.
2. To read more about the challenges of incarcerating transgender people we recommend our chapter, L. Cait Kanewske, Angela J. Hattery, Shannon Magnuson, Danielle Rudes, and Zachary Zaborowski, "Experiences of Transgender and Gender Nonconforming Individuals in Jail/Prison: Navigating Tensions," In *Handbook on Inequalities in Sentencing and Corrections among Marginalized Populations*, ed. Eileen M. Ahlin, Ojmarrh Mitchell, and Cassandra Atkin-Plunk (New York: Routledge, 2022).

CHAPTER 40   NOT ALWAYS IN SYNC

1. Patricia Yancey Martin, *Rape Work: Victims, Gender, and Emotions in Organization and Community Context* (New York: Routledge, 2005), 53.
2. Martin, *Rape Work*, 74.

CHAPTER 41   INTIMATE INTERRACIAL CONTACT AND INTIMATE SURVEILLANCE

1. Gordon Allport, *The Nature of Prejudice* (Cambridge, MA: Perseus Books, 1954).
2. Lisa Guenther, *Solitary Confinement: Social Death and Its Afterlives* (Minneapolis: University of Minnesota Press, 2013), 147.
3. Guenther, *Solitary Confinement*, 189.
4. Guenther, *Solitary Confinement*, 170.

CHAPTER 42   THE "ORIGIN" LIE

1. Eddie Glaude, Jr., *Begin Again: James Baldwin's America and Its Urgent Lessons for Our Own,* (New York: Penguin Press, 2020), 49–50.
2. Glaude, *Begin Again*, 104.
3. Saidiya Hartman, *Lose Your Mother: A Journey along the Atlantic Slave Route* (New York: Farrar, Straus and Giroux, 2007), 31 (emphasis ours).
4. Virginia Statutes can be found in the collection by William Waller Hening: *The Statutes at Large; Being a Collection of All the Laws of Virginia, from the First Session of the Legislature, in the Year 1619; Published Pursuant to an Act of the General Assembly of Virginia: by William W. Hening, Vol. 1, 1619–1660* (New York, 1819), 252, http://llmc.com/titledescfull.aspx?type=6&coll=50&div=201&set=99863 (emphasis ours).
5. Lisa Guenther, *Solitary Confinement: Social Death and Its Afterlives* (Minneapolis: University of Minnesota Press, 2013), xvii (emphasis ours).
6. Guenther, *Solitary Confinement*, 48 (emphasis ours).
7. Guenther, *Solitary Confinement*, 57.
8. Carol Anderson, *White Rage: The Unspoken Truth of Our Racial Divide* (New York: Bloomsbury, 2016), 137.

CHAPTER 43   EMANCIPATED SLAVE AND THE WHITE SHARECROPPER

1. Jonathan Metzl, *Dying of Whiteness: How the Politics of Racial Resentment Is Killing America's Heartland* (New York: Basic Books, 2019), 17 (emphasis ours).
2. Rory McVeigh and Kevin Estep, *The Politics of Losing: Trump, the Klan, and the Mainstreaming of Resentment* (New York: Columbia University Press, 2019), 44–45 (emphasis ours).
3. McVeigh and Estep, *Politics of Losing*, 160; Bill D. Moyers, "What a Real President Was Like," *Washington Post*, November 13, 1988, https://www.washingtonpost.com/archive/opinions/1988/11/13/what-a-real-president-was-like/d483c1be-d0da-43b7-bde6-04e10106ff6c/.
4. M. J., "Why Republicans Hate Obamacare: Why Is the Affordable Care Act So Despised by So Many Conservatives?" *Economist*, December 11, 2016, https://www.economist.com/the-economist-explains/2016/12/11/why-republicans-hate-obamacare; Sarah Kliff, "Why Obamacare Enrolled Voted for Trump: In Whitely County, Kentucky, the Uninsured Rate Declined 60 Percent under Obamacare. So Why did 82 Percent of Voters There Support Donald Trump?" *Vox*, December 13, 2016, https://www.vox.com/science-and-health/2016/12/13/13848794/kentucky-obamacare-trump.
5. David C. Wilson. "Justice: The Racial Motive We All Have and Need." *Journal of Race, Ethnicity, and Politics* 6 (2021), 64. Doi:10.1017/rep.2020.36 2056-6085/21.

CHAPTER 44   STRANGERS IN THEIR OWN LAND

1. Carol Anderson, *White Rage: The Unspoken Truth of Our Racial Divide* (New York: Bloomsbury, 2016); Jonathan Chait, "Donald Trump Has Proven Liberals Right about the Tea Party," *New York*, December 7, 2016, https://nymag.com/intelligencer /2016/12/donald-trump-has-proven-liberals-right-about-the-tea-party.html; Libby Nelson, "Nearly 20 Percent of Trump Supporters Disapprove of Lincoln Freeing the Slaves," *Vox*, February 24, 2016, https://www.vox.com/2016/2/24 /11105552/trump-supporters-slavery.
2. Catherine Woodiwiss, "The Era of White Anxiety Is Just Beginning," *Sojourners* (March 8, 2016), https://sojo.net/articles/era-white-anxiety-just-beginning.
3. We also interviewed transwomen in SCI-Wannabee. There COs also confused gender identity with sexuality, believing that they were just "gay men." In SCI-Wannabee transwomen were also allowed to order the undergarments of their choice, an act we heard many COs deride and complain about.

CHAPTER 45   DYING BY WHITENESS

1. Mary E. Buser, *Lockdown on Rikers: Shocking Stories of Abuse and Injustice at New York's Most Notorious Jail* (New York: St. Martin's, 2015), 253 (emphasis ours).
2. Frantz Fanon, *The Wretched of the Earth*, trans. Richard Philcox (New York: Grove, 1963), 219–220.

CHAPTER 46   BENDING THE RULES

1. United Nations, *Seeing into Solitary: A Review of the Laws and Policies of Certain Nations Regarding Solitary Confinement of Detainees*, United Nations Special Report (2016), 40, https://www.weil.com/~/media/files/pdfs/2016/un_special_report_solitary _confinement.pdf.
2. Phillip Goodman, "Race in California's Prison Fire Camps for Men: Prison Politics, Space, and the Racialization of Everyday Life," *American Journal of Sociology* 120, no. 2 (2014): 352–394 (emphasis ours).
3. Kevin Wright, "Time Well Spent: Misery, Meaning, and the Opportunity of Incarceration," *Howard Journal of Crime and Justice* 59, no. 1 (March 2020): 44–64, https://doi.org/10.1111/hojo.12352.
4. Lisa Guenther, *Solitary Confinement: Social Death and Its Afterlives* (Minneapolis: University of Minnesota Press, 2013), 248–249.

CHAPTER 47   THE LIES THE COs TELL THEMSELVES

1. Saidiya Hartman, *Lose Your Mother: A Journey along the Atlantic Slave Route* (New York: Farrar, Straus and Giroux, 2007), 131 (emphasis ours).
2. Carol Anderson, *White Rage: The Unspoken Truth of Our Racial Divide* (New York: Bloomsbury, 2016), 170–171 (emphasis ours); Libby Nelson, "Nearly 20 Percent of Trump Supporters Disapprove of Lincoln Freeing the Slaves," *Vox*, February 24, 2016, https://www.vox.com/2016/2/24/11105552/trump-supporters-slavery.

CHAPTER 48   "ANYTHING BUT RACE" THEORIES

1. Dorothy Roberts, *Shattered Bonds: The Color of Child Welfare* (New York: Civitas, 2002), 97–98; Melvin Thomas, "Anything But Race: The Social Science Retreat from Racism," *African American Research Perspectives* 6 (Winter 2000), 79, 90.
2. Richard Delgado and Jean Stefanic, *Critical Race Theory: An Introduction* (New York: New York University Press, 2001).
3. Roberts, *Shattered Bonds*, 93.

CHAPTER 49   JANUARY 6, 2021

1. Luke Broadwater, "For Black Aides on Capitol Hill, Jan. 6 Brought Particular Trauma," *New York Times*, February 17, 2021, https://www.nytimes.com/2021/02/17/us/politics/black-staff-capitol-attack.html.
2. Broadwater, "For Black Aides."
3. Natasha Bertrand, "Justice Department Warns of National Security Fallout from Capitol Hill Insurrection," *Politico*, January 7, 2021, https://www.politico.com/news/2021/01/07/capitol-hill-riots-doj-456178.

EPILOGUE

1. Clifford Geertz, *Thick Description: Toward an Interpretive Theory of Culture* (New York: Basic Books, 1973), 6–7.

Bibliography

Abbott, Jack Henry. *In the Belly of the Beast: Letters from Prison*. Introduction by Norman Mailer. New York: Random House, 1981.

Allport, Gordon. *The Nature of Prejudice*. Cambridge, MA: Perseus Books, 1954.

American Bar Association. *Standards for Criminal Justice on the Treatment of Prisoners*. Chicago: American Bar Association, 2011.

Anderson, Carol. *White Rage: The Unspoken Truth of Our Racial Divide*. New York: Bloomsbury, 2016.

Aranda-Hughes, Vivian, Jillian J. Turanovic, Daniel P. Mears, and George B. Pesta. "Women in Solitary Confinement: Relationships, Pseudofamilies, and the Limits of Control." *Feminist Criminology* 16, no. 1 (2020): 47–72. https://doi.org/10.1177/15570 85120961441.

Aumiller, Gary. "Divorce in Cops and Corrections." *Police Psychologist* (December 2, 2016). http://policepsychologyblog.com/?p=4245

Aviram, Hadar. "Are Private Prisons to Blame for Mass Incarceration and Its Evils? Prison Conditions, Neoliberalism, and Public Choice." *Fordham Law Journal* (2015): 39. http://repository.uchastings.edu/faculty_scholarship/994.

Balko, Radley. *The Rise of the Warrior Cop: The Militarization of America's Police Forces*. New York: PublicAffairs, 2013.

Bauer, Shane. "My Four Months as a Private Prison Guard: A Mother Jones Investigation." *Mother Jones*, August 18, 2016. http://bit.ly/28TZwIP.

Baum, Dan. "Legalize It All: How to Win the War on Drugs." *Harper's Bazaar*, April 2016. http://harpers.org/archive/2016/04/legalize-it-all.

Baxter, Charles, Wayne Brown, Tony Chatman-Bey, H. B. Johnson Jr., Mark Medley, Donald Thompson, Selvyn Tillett, and John Woodland Jr., with Drew Leder. "Live from the Panopticon: Architecture and Power Revisited." In *The New Abolitionist: (Neo) Slave Narratives and Contemporary Prison Writings,* edited by Joy James, 205–216. Albany: State University of New York (SUNY) Press, 2005.

Beaumont, Gustave de, and Alexis de Tocqueville. *On the Penitentiary System in the United States and Its Application in France*. Philadelphia: Carey, Lea & Blanchard, 1833. http://www.houseofrussell.com/legalhistory/alh/docs/penitentiary.html.

Bertrand, Natasha. "Justice Department Warns of National Security Fallout from Capitol Hill Insurrection." *Politico*, January 7, 2021. https://www.politico.com/news/2021/01/07/capitol-hill-riots-doj-456178.

Boger, John Charles, and Gary Orfield. *School Resegregation: Must the South Turn Back?* Chapel Hill: University of North Carolina Press, 2005.

Bonilla-Silva, Eduardo. *Racism without Racists: Color-Blind Racism and the Persistence of Racial Inequality in America*. 5th ed. Lanham, MD: Rowman & Littlefield, 2018.

Bonilla-Silva, Eduardo. "Rethinking Racism: Toward a Structural Interpretation." *American Sociological Review* 62, no. 3 (1997): 465–480. http://www.jstor.org/stable/2657316.

Bonilla-Silva, Eduardo. "The Structure of Racism in Color-Blind, 'Post-Racial' America." *American Behavioral Scientist* 59, no. 11 (2015): 1358–1376.

Bovsun, Mara. "Sylvia Seegrist Went Psycho and Killed Three Innocent People at the Springfield, Pa., Mall." *New York Daily News*, December 2, 2012. https://www.nydaily news.com/news/justice-story/ms-rambo-kill-spree-article-1.1211691.

Broadwater, Luke. "For Black Aides on Capitol Hill, Jan. 6 Brought Particular Trauma." *New York Times*, February 17, 2021. https://www.nytimes.com/2021/02/17/us/politics /black-staff-capitol-attack.html.

Bureau of Justice Statistics. *Race and Hispanic Origin of Victims and Offenders, 2012–2015.* Washington, DC: U.S. Department of Justice, Office of Justice Programs, 2017.

Buser, Mary. "Let's Help Frank!" Go Fund Me. September 13, 2021. https://www .gofundme.com/f/q3jzy-lets-help-frank?utm_campaign=p_lico+share-sheet+spider1c &utm_medium=copy_link&utm_source=customer.

Buser, Mary E.. *Lockdown on Rikers: Shocking Stories of Abuse and Injustice at New York's Notorious Jail.* New York: St. Martin's, 2015.

Casella, Jean, James Ridgeway, and Sarah Shourd, eds. *Hell Is a Very Small Place: Voices from Solitary Confinement.* New York: New Press, 2017.

Chait, Jonathan. "Donald Trump Has Proven Liberals Right about the Tea Party." *New York*, December 7, 2016. https://nymag.com/intelligencer/2016/12/donald-trump -has-proven-liberals-right-about-the-tea-party.html.

Chetty, Raj, Nathaniel Hendren, Maggie R. Jones, and Sonya R. Porter. *Race and Economic Opportunity in the United States: An Intergenerational Perspective.* Opportunity Insights. March 2018. http://www.equality-of-opportunity.org/assets/documents/race_paper .pdf.

Cloud, David, Ernest Drucker, Angela Browne, and Jim Parsons. 2015. "Public Health and Solitary Confinement in the United States." *American Journal of Public Health* 105 (2015): 18–26.

Coates, Ta-Nehisi. *We Were Eight Years in Power: An American Tragedy.* New York: One World, 2017.

Cochran, Joshua, Elisa L. Toman, Daniel P. Mears, and William D. Bales. 2018. "Solitary Confinement as Punishment: Examining In-prison Sanctioning Disparities." *Justice Quarterly* 35, no. 3 (2018): 381–411.

Comfort, Megan. *Doing Time Together: Love and Family in the Shadow of the Prison.* Chicago: University of Chicago Press, 2008.

Conover, Ted. *Newjack: Guarding Sing.* New York: Vintage Books, 2001.

Corbin, Juliet, and Anselm Strauss. *Basics of Qualitative Research: Techniques and Procedures for Developing Grounded Theory.* Thousand Oaks, CA: Sage, 2014.

Davis, Angela. "Rape, Racism and the Myth of the Black Rapist." In *Women, Race, & Class,* 172–201. New York: Vintage, 1983.

Davis, Angela Y. *Women, Race, and Class.* New York: Vintage Books, 1983.

Davis, James. "Who Is Black: One Nation's Definition." *Frontline*. PBS Online. http:// www.pbs.org/wgbh/pages/frontline/shows/jefferson/mixed/onedrop.html.

DeHart, Dana, Cheri Shapiro, and Stephanie Clone. "'The Pill Line Is Longer than the Chow Line': The Impact of Incarceration on Prisoners and Their Families." *Prison Journal* 98, no. 2 (March 2018): 188–212. https://doi.org/10.1177/0032885517753159.

Delgado, Richard, and Jean Stefanic. *Critical Race Theory: An Introduction.* New York: New York University Press, 2001.

Denhof, Michael, and Caterina G. Spinaris. *Depression, PTSD and Comorbidity in United States Corrections Professionals: Prevalence and Impact on Health and Functioning.* Desert Waters Correctional Outreach, 2013. https://desertwaters.com/wp-content/uploads /2013/09/Comorbidity_Study_09-03-131.pdf.

Desmond, Matthew. *Evicted: Poverty and Profit in the American City.* New York: Broadway Books, 2017.

Desmond, Matthew. "Relational Ethnography." *Theory and Society* 43, no. 5 (2014): 547–579. www.jstor.org/stable/43694733.

Dickens, Charles. *American Notes for General Circulation and Pictures from Italy.* London: Chapman & Hall, 1913.

Drogin, Eric Y., and Carol S. Williams. "Solitary Confinement: Isolate the Problem or Leave Well Enough Alone?" *Criminal Justice* (Fall 2016): 31+. http://link.galegroup .com/apps/doc/A487433798/AONE?u=upenn_main&sid=AONE&xid=74b3d46e.

Du Bois, W. E. B. (William Edward Burghardt). *The Souls of Black Folk.* New introduction by Herbert Aptheker. Millwood, NY: Kraus-Thomson, 1973.

DuVernay, Ava. "When They See Us." TV miniseries, aired on NETFLIX, 2019.

Dyson, Michael. *I May Not Get There with You: The True Martin Luther King, Jr.* New York: Free Press, 2001.

Edwards, Frank, Hedwig Leeb, and Michael Espositoc. 2019. "Risk of Being Killed by Police Use-of-Force in the U.S. by Age, Race/Ethnicity, and Sex." *Proceedings of the National Academy of Sciences,* 2019. https://www.pnas.org/cgi/doi/10.1073/pnas .1821204116.

Endicott, Marisa. "A 2015 Case Was Supposed to Overhaul California's Solitary Confinement. The Reality Is Much More Complicated." *Mother Jones,* February 13, 2019. https://www.motherjones.com/crime-justice/2019/02/california-ashker-brown -solitary-confinement-status-appeal/.

Epstein, Cynthia Fuchs. "Great Divides: The Cultural, Cognitive, and Social Bases of the Global Subordination of Women." *American Sociological Review* 72 (2007): 1–22.

Fanon, Frantz. *The Wretched of the Earth.* Translated by Richard Philcox. New York: Grove, 1963.

Fitzhugh, George. *Sociology for the South, or, the Failure of Free Society.* Richmond, VA: A. Morris, 1854.

Flitter, Emily, and Chris Kahn. "Trump Supporters More Likely to View Blacks Negatively." Reuters/Ipsos poll, 2016. http://reut.rs/2CSTx5G.

Forman, James. *Locking Up Our Own: Crime and Punishment in Black America.* New York: Farrar, Straus and Giroux, 2017.

Foucault, Michel. *Discipline & Punish: The Birth of the Prison.* New York: Vintage Books, 1995.

Frost, N. A., and C. E. Monteiro. "Administrative Segregation in U.S. Prisons." NCJ 250316. In *Restrictive Housing in the U.S.: Issues, Challenges, and Future Directions.* Washington, DC: U.S. Department of Justice, National Institute of Justice, 2016.

Garland, David. *The Culture of Control: Crime and Social Order in Contemporary Society.* Chicago: University of Chicago Press, 2001.

Gates, Henry Louis Jr., and Andrew S. Curran. "We Need a New Language for Talking About Race." *New York Times Sunday Review.* (March 3, 2020). https://www.nytimes .com/2022/03/03/opinion/sunday/talking-about-race.html?campaign_id=37&emc=edit _rr_20220305&instance_id=54940&nl=race%2Frelated&regi_id=87693497&segment _id=84748&te=1&user_id=8a0f9071445587e7ce5a22b6b8677b36. Accessed March 14, 2022.

Gawande, Atul. "Hellhole." *New Yorker,* March 23, 2009.

Geertz, Clifford. *Thick Description: Toward an Interpretive Theory of Culture.* New York: Basic Books, 1973.

Georgetown University Law Center. *The Sexual Abuse to Prison Pipeline: The Girls' Story.* Washington, DC: Center for Poverty and Inequality, 2020. povertycenter@law .georgetown.edu.

Gest, Justin. *The New Minority: White Working Class Politics in an Age of Immigration and Inequality.* New York: Oxford University Press, 2016.

Ghandnoosh, Nazgol. *Race and Punishment: Racial Perceptions of Crime and Support for Punitive Policies.* Washington, DC: Sentencing Project, 2016.

Gilmore, Ruth. *Golden Gulag: Prisons, Surplus, Crisis, and Opposition in Globalizing California.* Berkeley: University of California Press, 2007.

Giridharadas, Anand. *Winners Take All: The Elite Charade of Changing the World.* New York: Knopf, 2019.

Glaude, Eddie, Jr. *Begin Again: James Baldwin's America and Its Urgent Lessons for Our Own.* New York: Crown, 2020.

Goldhagen, Daniel. *Hitler's Willing Executioners: Ordinary Germans and the Holocaust.* New York: Vintage, 1997.

Goodman, Phillip. "Race in California's Prison Fire Camps for Men: Prison Politics, Space, and the Racialization of Everyday Life." *American Journal of Sociology* 120, no. 2 (2014): 352–394.

Griffin, Eddie. "Breaking Men's Minds: Behavior Control and Human Experimentation at the Federal Prison in Marion, Illinois." *Journal of Prisoners on Prisons* 4, no. 2 (1993): 17–28.

Guenther, Lisa. *Solitary Confinement: Social Death and Its Afterlives.* Minneapolis: University of Minnesota Press, 2014.

Haney, Craig. "Psychology and the Limits to Prison Pain: Confronting the Coming Crisis in Eighth Amendment Law." *Psychology, Public Policy, and Law* 3 (1997): 499–552.

Haney, Craig. "Restricting the Use of Solitary Confinement." *Annual Review of Criminology* 1 (2018): 285–310. https://doi.org/10.1146/annurev-criminol-032317-092326.

Haney, Craig. "The Science of Solitary: Expanding the Harmfulness Narrative." *Northwestern University Law Review* 115, no. 1 (2020): 211–256.

Haney, Craig. "The Wages of Prison Overcrowding: Harmful Psychological Consequences and Dysfunctional Correctional Reactions." *Washington University Journal of Law & Policy* 22 (2006): 265. http://openscholarship.wustl.edu/law_journal_law_policy/vol22/iss1/22.

Harlow, Harry, Robert O. Dodsworth, and Margaret K. Harlow. "Total Social Isolation in Monkeys." *Proceedings of the National Academy of Sciences,* July 1, Vol. 54, no. 1, pp. 90–97, 1965. https://www.ncbi.nlm.nih.gov/pmc/articles/PMC285801/pdf/pnas00159-0105.pdf.

Hartman, Saidiya. *Lose Your Mother: A Journey along the Atlantic Slave Route.* New York: Farrar, Straus and Giroux, 2007.

Hattery, Angela, and Earl Smith. *African American Families: Myths and Realities.* Lanham, MD: Rowman & Littlefield, 2014.

Hattery, Angela, and Earl Smith. *Gender, Power and Violence.* Lanham, MD: Rowman & Littlefield, 2019.

Hattery, Angela, and Earl Smith. *Policing Black Bodies: How Black Lives Are Surveilled and How to Work for Change.* Lanham, MD: Rowman & Littlefield, 2021.

Hayes, Chris. *A Colony in a Nation.* New York: Norton, 2017.

Hening, William Waller. "*The Statutes at Large; Being a Collection of All the Laws of Virginia, from the First Session of the Legislature, in the Year 1619; Published Pursuant to an Act of the General Assembly of Virginia: by William W. Hening.*" Vol. 1, *1619–1660.* New York, 1819. http://llmc.com/titledescfull.aspx?type=6&coll=50&div=201&set=99863.

Heron, W., B. K. Doane, and T. H. Scott. "Visual Disturbances after Prolonged Perceptual Isolation." *Canadian Journal of Psychology/Revue canadienne de psychologie* 10, no.1 (1956): 13–18. https://doi.org/10.1037/h0083650.

Hochschild, Arlie. *Strangers in Their Own Land: Anger and Mourning on the American Right.* New York: New Press, 2016.

Hooks, Gregory. "Prisons, Jobs and Privatization: The Impact of Prisons on Employment Growth in Rural US Counties, 1997–2004." *Social Science Research* 42, no. 3 (2013): 596–610.

Hoover, Andy. "SCI-Retreat Closing: Prisons Should Never Be a Community's Economic Development Strategy | Opinion." *[State] Capital Star.* September 13, 2019. https://www.penncapital-star.com/commentary/sci-retreat-closing-prisons-should -never-be-a-communitys-economic-development-strategy-opinion/.

Hughes, Vivian Aranda, Jillian J. Turanovic, Daniel P. Mears, and George B. Pesta. "Women in Solitary Confinement: Relationships, Pseudofamilies, and the Limits of Control." *Feminist Criminology* 16, no. 1 (2020): 47–72. https://doi.org/10.1177/15570 85120961441.

Jacobs, James. *Statesville: The Penitentiary in Mass Society.* Chicago: University of Chicago Press, 1978.

Jacobs, James, and Lawrence Kraft. "Integrating the Keepers: A Comparison of Black and White Prison Guards in Illinois." *Social Problems* 25 (1978): 304–318.

James, Lois, and Natalie Todak. "Prison Employment and Post-traumatic Stress Disorder: Risk and Protective Factors." *American Journal of Industrial Medicine* 61, no. 9 (2010). https://onlinelibrary-wiley-com.mutex.gmu.edu/doi/10.1002/ajim.22869.

"Jefferson's Attitudes toward Slavery." Monticello.org. Accessed July 1, 2020. https://www .monticello.org/thomas-jefferson/jefferson-slavery/jefferson-s-attitudes-toward -slavery/.

Jenness, Valerie. "From Policy to Prisoners to People: A 'Soft Mixed Methods' Approach to Studying Transgender Prisoners." *Journal of Contemporary Ethnography* 39 (2010): 517–553.

Jenness, Valerie, Lori Sexton, and Jennifer Sumner. "Sexual Victimization against Transgender Women in Prison." *Criminology* 57 (2019): 603–631. https://doi.org/10 .1111/1745-9125.12221.

Jurik, Nancy. "Individual and Organizational Determinants of Correctional Office Attitudes Toward Inmates." *Criminology* 23 (1985): 523–539. http://www.jtbf.org.

Karakatsanis, Alec. "The Punishment Bureaucracy: How to Think About Criminal Justice Reform." *Yale Law Journal Forum*, March 28, 2019.

Kerber, Linda. "The Meaning of Citizenship." *Journal of American History* 84, no. 3 (December 1997): 833–854. http://www.jstor.org/stable/2953082.

Kliff, Sarah. "Why Obamacare Enrolled Voted for Trump: In Whitely County, Kentucky, the Uninsured Rate Declined 60 Percent under Obamacare. So Why did 82 Percent of Voters There Support Donald Trump?" *Vox*, December 13, 2016. https://www.vox.com/science-and-health/2016/12/13/13848794/kentucky-obama care-trump.

Kupers, Terry. "How to Create Madness in Prison." In *Hell Is a Very Small Place: Voices from Solitary Confinement*, edited by Jean Casella, James Ridgeway, and Sarah Shourd, 163–178. New York: New Press, 2017.

Kupers, Terry. *Solitary: The Inside Story of Supermax Isolation and How We Can Abolish It.* Oakland: University of California Press, 2017.

Laws, Ben. "Segregation Seekers: An Alternative Perspective on the Solitary Confinement Debate." *British Journal of Criminology* 61, no. 6 (2021): 1452–1468. https://doi .org/10.1093/bjc/azab032.

Leflouria, Talitha. *Chained in Silence: Black Women and Convict Labor in the New South.* Chapel Hill, NC: University of North Carolina Press, 2016.

Lubet, Steven. *Interrogating Ethnography: Why Evidence Matters.* New York: Oxford University Press, 2017.

Lyon, Edward. "Republican-Appointed Federal Judges Sentence Blacks More Harshly, Women More Leniently." *Prison Legal News*, June 2019. http://bit.ly/2IxkFHV.

Magnuson, Shannon. *Solitary Diversion: Reforming Restricted Housing Units for Individuals with Severe Mental Health Diagnoses*. Unpublished Dissertation, George Mason University, (2022).

Majors, Richard, and Janet Bilson. *Cool Pose: The Dilemmas of African American Manhood in America*. New York: Lexington Books, 1992.

Marquart, James. "Doing Research in Prison: The Strengths and Weaknesses of Full Participation as a Guard." *Justice Quarterly* 3 (1986): 15–32.

Martel, Joane. "Telling the Story: A Study in the Segregation of Women Prisoners." *Social Justice* 28, no. 1 (2001): 196–215.

Martin, Courtney. "The Racial Wealth Gap in Readers' Eyes." *New York Times*, May 15, 2019. https://www.nytimes.com/2019/05/15/opinion/the-racial-wealth-gap-in-readers -eyes.html.

Martin, Patricia Yancey. *Rape Work: Victims, Gender, and Emotions in Organization and Community Context*. New York: Routledge, 2005.

Mason, Jim, and Mary Finelli. "Brave New Farm?" In *Defense of Animals: The Second Wave*, edited by Peter Singer, 104–122. London: Wiley-Blackwell, 2006.

McHugh, Eileen. *Auburn Correctional Facility*. New York: Arcadia, 2010.

McVeigh, Rory, and Kevin Estep. *The Politics of Losing: Trump, the Klan, and the Mainstreaming of Resentment*. New York: Columbia University Press, 2019.

Metzl, Jonathan. *Dying of Whiteness: How the Politics of Racial Resentment Is Killing America's Heartland*. New York: Basic Books, 2019.

Miller, Joshua Rhett. "Guard Demanded Sex for Toilet Paper at New Jersey Prison, Ex-inmate Claims." *New York Post*, July 3, 2020. https://nypost.com/2020/07/03/guard -demanded-sex-for-toilet-paper-at-nj-prison-ex-inmate/.

M. J. 2016. "Why Republicans Hate Obamacare: Why Is the Affordable Care Act So Despised by So Many Conservatives?" *Economist*, December 11, 2016. https://www .economist.com/the-economist-explains/2016/12/11/why-republicans-hate-obama care.

Montagu, Ashley. *Man's Most Dangerous Myth: The Fallacy of Race*. Lanham, MD: Rowman & Littlefield, 1997.

Morse, Janice. "Cherry Picking: Writing from Thin Data." *Qualitative Health Research* 20, no. 1 (2010): 3. https://doi.org/10.1177/1049732309354285.

Moshenberg, Dan. 2015. "Pennsylvania Built a Special Hell for Miriam White." Women in and Beyond the Global, October 13, 2015. http://www.womeninandbeyond.org/?p =19413.

Moyers, Bill. "What a Real President Was Like." *Washington Post*, November 13, 1988. https:// www.washingtonpost.com/archive/opinions/1988/11/13/what-a-real-president-was -like/d483c1be-d0da-43b7-bde6-04e10106ff6c/

Murray, Charles. *Coming Apart: The State of White America, 1960–2010*. New York: Crown, 2013.

National Institute of Justice, "Exploring the Use of Restrictive Housing in the U.S. Issues, Challenges, and Future Directions," November 14, 2016. https://nij.ojp.gov /topics/articles/exploring-use-restrictive-housing-usissues-challenges-and-future -directions.

National LGBTQ Task Force. "CeCe McDonald Released from Prison." Accessed December 30, 2021. https://www.thetaskforce.org/cece-mcdonald-released-from-prison/.

Nelson, Libby. "Nearly 20 Percent of Trump Supporters Disapprove of Lincoln Freeing the Slaves." *Vox*, February 24, 2016. https://www.vox.com/2016/2/24/11105552/trump -supporters-slavery.

Nkomo, Stella. "The Emperor Has No Clothes: Rewriting Race in Organizations." *Academy of Management Review* 17, no. 3 (1992). https://doi.org/10.5465/amr.1992.4281987.

Olson, Jeremiah. "Race and Punishment in American Prisons." *Journal of Public Administration Research and Theory* 26 (2010): 758–768. http://bit.ly/2LcEqc1.

Oshinsky, David M. *Worse than Slavery: Parchman Farm and the Ordeal of Jim Crow Justice.* New York: Free Press, 1997.

Park, Robert. "The Concept of Social Distance." *Journal of Applied Sociology* 8, no. 5 (1924): 339–344.

Park, Robert. "The Nature of Race Relations." In *Race Relations and the Race Problem.* Durham, NC: Duke University Press, 1939: 3–45.

Park, Robert Ezra, and Ernest W. Burgess. *Introduction to the Science of Sociology.* Chicago: University of Chicago Press, 1921.

Patterson, Orlando. *Rituals of Blood: Consequences of Slavery in Two American Centuries.* New York: Civitas, 1999.

Patton, Michael Quinn. *Qualitative Research & Evaluation Methods: Integrating Theory and Practice.* 4th ed. Thousand Oaks, CA: Sage, 2015.

Paybarah, Azi. "Sheriff Apologizes to Family of Inmate Who Died after Being Restrained." *New York Times,* August 4, 2020. https://www.nytimes.com/2020/08/04/us/john-neville-death-winston-salem-nc.html.

Peck, Leonard. 2004. "Hoeing a Long and Hard Row: Long Term Administrative Segregation of a Cohort of Texas Prison Inmates." Unpublished PhD diss., Sam Houston State University. ProQuest Dissertations 3159492.

Pennsylvania Economy League. *The Economic Impact of the Coal Industry in Pennsylvania* Prepared for the Pennsylvania Coal Alliance. March 2014. https://www.ourenergypolicy.org/wp-content/uploads/2014/05/PA-coal.pdf.

Pilkington, Ed. "Albert Woodfox Released from Jail after 43 Years in Solitary Confinement." *Guardian,* February 19, 2016. http://bit.ly/2F8GLy0.

Prewitt, Kenneth. *What Is "Your" Race?: The Census and Our Flawed Efforts to Classify Americans.* Princeton, NJ: Princeton University Press, 2016.

Prison Policy Institute. 2018. "New Report, *Mass Incarceration: The Whole Pie 2018*" (blog), March 14, 2018. https://www.prisonpolicy.org/blog/2018/03/14/wholepie2018press/.

Pullen-Blasnik, Hannah, Jessica T. Simes, and Bruce Western. "The Population Prevalence of Solitary Confinement." *Science Advances* 7, no. 48 (26 November, 2021). DOI: 10.1126/sciadv.abj1928.

Pyrooz, David, and Scott Decker. *Competing for Control: Gangs and the Social Order of Prisons.* Cambridge: Cambridge University Press, 2019.

Raemisch, Rick. "My Night in Solitary." *Opinion* (blog), *New York Times,* February 20, 2014. https://www.nytimes.com/2014/02/21/opinion/my-night-in-solitary.html?_r=0.

Raemisch, Rick. "Why I Ended the Horror of Long-Term Solitary in Colorado's Prisons." ACLU.org (blog), December 5, 2018. https://www.aclu.org/blog/prisoners-rights/solitary-confinement/why-i-ended-horror-long-term-solitary-colorados-prisons.

Ralph, Laurence. "As Soon as I Get Out Ima Cop Dem Jordans: The Afterlife of the Corporate Gang." *Issue 6: The New Frontiers of Race: Culture, Criminalities, and Policing in the Global Era,* 2010. https://doi.org/10.1080/1070289X.2010.533531.

Ray, Victor. "A Theory of Racialized Organizations." *American Sociological Review* 84, no. 1 (2019): 26–53. https://doi.org/10.1177/0003122418822335.

Reiter, Keramet. "Making Windows in Walls: Strategies for Prison Research." *Qualitative Inquiry* 20 (2012): 417–428.

Reiter, Keramet. *23/7: Pelican Bay Prison and the Rise of Long-Term Solitary Confinement.* New Haven, CT: Yale University Press, 2016.

Requarth, Tim. "Why Do So Many Researchers Still Treat Race as a Scientific Concept?" *Slate*, May 30, 2019. http://bit.ly/2IjqIQq.

Resnik, Judith, Hirsa Amin, Sophie Angelis, Megan Hauptman, Laura Kokotailo, Aseem Mehta, Madeline Silva, Tor Tarantola, and Meredith Wheeler. 2020. "Punishment in Prison: Constituting the 'Normal' and the 'Atypical' in Solitary and Other Forms of Confinement." *Northwestern University Law Review* 115, no. 1 (2020). https://scholarly commons.law.northwestern.edu/nulr/vol115/iss1/3/

Rhodes, Lorna. *Total Confinement: Madness and Reason in the Maximum Security Prison.* Berkeley: University of California Press, 2004.

Roberts, Dorothy. *Fatal Invention: How Science, Politics, and Big Business Re-create Race in the Twenty-first Century.* New York: New Press, 2011.

Rodriguez, Nancy. "Director's Message: Restrictive Housing in the U.S." National Institute of Justice (NIJ), November 14, 2016. https://www.nij.gov/about/director/Pages/rodriguez-restrictive-housing-in-the-us.aspx.

Roediger, David. *The Wages of Whiteness: Race and the Making of the American Working Class.* London: Verso, 2007.

Rohrback. Kim. "SHU-shifting: An Update on and Overview of the Ashker v. Brown Class Action." *Bay View*, March 28, 2015. https://sfbayview.com/2015/03/shu-shifting-an-update-on-and-overview-of-the-ashker-v-brown-class-action/.

Rubin, Ashley and Keramet Reiter. "Continuity in the Face of Penal Innovation: Revisiting the History of American Solitary Confinement." *Law & Social Inquiry* 43, no.4 (2018):1604–1632. https://doi.org/10.1111/lsi.12330

Rudes, Danielle, Shannon Portillo, Shannon Magnusson, and Angela Hattery. "Sex Logics: Negotiating the Prison Rape Elimination Act (PREA) against Its' Administrative, Safety, and Cultural Burdens." *Punishment & Society* 23, no. 4 (2020). https://doi.org/10.1177/1462474520952155.

Saar, Malika Saada, Rebecca Epstein, Lindsay Rosenthal, and Yasmin Vafa. *The Sexual Abuse to Prison Pipeline: The Girls' Story.* Washington, DC: Center for Poverty and Inequality, Georgetown University Law Center, 2015. http://bit.ly/1DqeScy.

Saini, Angela. 2019. *Superior: The Return of Race Science.* Boston: Beacon.

Sakoda, Ryan, and Jessica T. Simes. "Solitary Confinement and the U.S. Prison Boom." Paper presented at the American Sociology Association Meeting, Philadelphia, PA. August 2018.

Sakoda, Ryan, and Jessica T. Simes. "Solitary Confinement and the US Prison Boom." *Criminal Justice Policy Review* 66 (2019). https://doi.org/10.1177/0887403419895315.

Sered, Susan, and Maureen Norton-Hawk. 2019. "Triple Jeopardy: Women's Employment Struggles Post Incarceration." *Journal of Offender Rehabilitation* 58, no. 4 (2019): 261–280. https://doi.org/10.1080/10509674.2019.1596191.

Shalev, Sharon. *Supermax: Controlling Risk Through Solitary Confinement.* Portland, OR: Willan, 2009.

Smith, Earl, and Angela J. Hattery. "Cultural Contradictions in the South." *Mississippi Quarterly* 63, no. 2 (2010): 145–166.

Southern Poverty Law Center. "Solitary Confinement: Inhumane, Ineffective, and Wasteful." 2019. https://www.splcenter.org/20190404/solitary-confinement-inhumane-ineffective-and-wasteful.

Stern, Michael. "Like Being 'Buried Alive': Charles Dickens on Solitary Confinement in America's Prisons." *American Prospect*, October 5, 2015. http://bit.ly/2m9vPbM.

Stevenson, Bryan. *Just Mercy: A Story of Justice and Redemption.* New York: One World Press, 2015.

Stuart, Forrest, and Reuben Jonathan Miller. "The Prisonized Old Head: Intergenerational Socialization and the Fusion of Ghetto and Prison Culture." *Journal of Contemporary Ethnography* 46 (2010): 673–698. http://bit.ly/2MVwI2h.

Swedberg, Richard. 2018. "How to Use Max Weber's Ideal Type in Sociological Analysis." *Journal of Classical Sociology* 18, no. 3 (2018): 181–196. https://doi.org/10.1177/1468795X17743643.

Sykes, Gresham. *The Society of Captives: A Study of a Maximum Security Prison*. Princeton, NJ: Princeton University Press, 2007.

Tripp, Jason. "The Most Segregated Hour in America—Martin Luther King Jr." YouTube, April 29, 2014. https://youtu.be/1q881g1L_d8.

United Nations. *Seeing into Solitary: A Review of the Laws and Policies of Certain Nations Regarding Solitary Confinement of Detainees*. United Nations Special Report, 2016. https://www.weil.com/~/media/files/pdfs/2016/un_special_report_solitary_confinement.pdf.

United States Sentencing Commission. *Demographic Differences in Sentencing: An Update to the 2012 Booker Report*. Washington, DC: United States Sentencing Commission, 2017.

Vera Institute of Justice. "Solitary Confinement: Common Misconceptions and Emerging Safe Alternatives." New York: Vera Institute of Justice, 2015. http://bit.ly/2HQu1zz.

Vera Institute of Justice. "Who We Are." Accessed April 7, 2022. https://www.vera.org/who-we-are.

Wacquant, Loïc. "The Curious Eclipse of Prison Ethnography in the Age of Mass Incarceration." *Ethnography* 3, no. 4 (2002): 371–397.

Walker, Michael. "Race Making in a Penal Institution." *American Journal of Sociology* 121, no. 4 (2016): 1051–1078. https://www-journals-uchicago-edu.mutex.gmu.edu/doi/full/10.1086/684033.

Wang, Hansi. "As Legal Battle Persists, Census Citizenship Question Is Put to the Test." NPR, June 13, 2019. https://www.npr.org/2019/06/13/731629018/as-legal-battle-persists-census-citizenship-question-is-put-to-the-test.

Western, Bruce. *Punishment and Inequality in America*. New York: Russell Sage Foundation, 2006.

Western, Bruce, Jessica T. Simes, and Kendra Bradner. 2019. "Solitary Confinement and Institutional Harm." Unpublished manuscript, Department of Sociology and Columbia Justice Lab, Columbia University, 2019.

White, Vernon Franklin. "An Analysis of the Race Relations Theory of Robert E. Park." Master's thesis, Atlanta University, 1948. ETD Collection for AUC Robert W. Woodruff Library. http://digitalcommons.auctr.edu/dissertations.

Williams, Eric. *Capitalism and Slavery*. Chapel Hill, NC: University of North Carolina Press, 1944.

Williams, Gregory. *Life on the Color Line: The True Story of a White Boy Who Discovered He Was Black*. New York: Plume, 1996.

Williams, Jason. "Race as a Carceral Terrain: Black Lives Matter Meets Reentry." *Prison Journal* (2019). https://journals-sagepub-com.mutex.gmu.edu/doi/full/10.1177/0032885519852062.

Wilson, William Julius. *The Truly Disadvantaged: The Inner City, the Underclass, and Public Policy*. Chicago: University of Chicago Press, 1987.

Wilson, William, and Anmol Chaddha. "The Role of Theory in Ethnographic Research." *Ethnography* 10, no. 4 (2009): 549–564.

Winerip, Michael, and Michael Schwirtz. "Prison Brutality at Clinton Correctional." *New York Times*, December 22, 2015. https://www.nytimes.com/2015/12/22/insider/prison-brutality-at-clinton-correctional-getting-the-story.html?searchResultPosition=6.

Wingfield, Adia Harvey. *Flatlining: Race, Work and Health Care in the New Economy.* Berkeley: University of California Press, 2019.

Wingfield, Adia Harvey. *No More Invisible Man: Race and Gender in Men's Work.* Philadelphia: Temple University Press, 2013.

Woodfox, Albert. *Solitary: Unbroken by Four Decades in Solitary Confinement; My Story of Transformation and Hope.* New York: Grove, 2019.

Woodiwiss, Catherine. "The Era of White Anxiety Is Just Beginning." *Sojourners,* March 8, 2016. https://sojo.net/articles/era-white-anxiety-just-beginning.

Wright, Erik. *Class Counts: Comparative Studies in Class Analysis.* New York: Cambridge University Press, 1997.

Wright, Kevin. 2020. "Time Well Spent: Misery, Meaning, and the Opportunity of Incarceration." *Howard Journal of Crime and Justice* 59, no. 1 (March 2020): 44–64. https://doi.org/10.1111/hojo.12352.

Yale Law School. "Reforming Restrictive Housing: The 2018 ASCA-Liman Nationwide Survey of Time-in-Cell." Association of State Correctional Administrators: The Liman Center for Public Interest Law at Yale Law School, 2018. https://law.yale.edu/sites/default/files/documents/pdf/Liman/asca_liman_2018_restrictive_housing_revised_sept_25_2018_-_embargoed_unt.pdf

Yale Law School. *Working to Limit Restrictive Housing: Efforts in Four Jurisdictions to Make Changes.* Association of State Correctional Administrators: The Liman Center for Public Interest Law at Yale Law School, October 2018.

Index

About the Authors

ANGELA HATTERY holds a PhD in sociology from the University of Wisconsin. She has held faculty and administrative positions at Ball State University, Wake Forest University, and George Mason University (where she served as director of women and gender studies). She is currently professor of women and gender studies and codirector of the Center for the Study and Prevention of Gender-Based Violence at the University of Delaware. *Way Down in the Hole* is her twelfth book.

EARL SMITH is a social scientist, having studied social anthropology, sociology, and political economy at the University of Connecticut, where he earned his PhD. He has held faculty and administrative positions at the State University of New York at Brockport; Washington State University (where he held a joint appointment in sociology and comparative American cultures [CAC], also serving as chair of CAC); Pacific Lutheran University (where he served as chair of sociology and dean); Wake Forest University (where he served as chair of sociology); and George Mason University. He is currently professor of women and gender studies and a core faculty member in the Center for the Study and Prevention of Gender-Based Violence at the University of Delaware. *Way Down in the Hole* is his twelfth book.

Available titles in the Critical Issues in Crime and Society series:

Susan L. Miller, *Victims as Offenders: The Paradox of Women's Violence in Relationships*

Torin Monahan, *Surveillance in the Time of Insecurity*

Torin Monahan and Rodolfo D. Torres, eds., *Schools under Surveillance: Cultures of Control in Public Education*

Ana Muñiz, *Police, Power, and the Production of Racial Boundaries*

Marianne O. Nielsen and Linda M. Robyn, *Colonialism Is Crime*

Leslie Paik, *Discretionary Justice: Looking Inside a Juvenile Drug Court*

Anthony M. Platt, *The Child Savers: The Invention of Delinquency*, 40th anniversary edition with an introduction and critical commentaries compiled by Miroslava Chávez-García

Lois Presser, *Why We Harm*

Joshua M. Price, *Prison and Social Death*

Heidi Reynolds-Stenson, *Cultures of Resistance: Collective Action and Rationality in the Anti-Terror Age*

Diana Rickard, *Sex Offenders, Stigma, and Social Control*

Jeffrey Ian Ross, ed., *The Globalization of Supermax Prisons*

Dawn L. Rothe and Christopher W. Mullins, eds., *State Crime, Current Perspectives*

Jodi Schorb, *Reading Prisoners: Literature, Literacy, and the Transformation of American Punishment, 1700–1845*

Susan F. Sharp, *Hidden Victims: The Effects of the Death Penalty on Families of the Accused*

Susan F. Sharp, *Mean Lives, Mean Laws: Oklahoma's Women Prisoners*

Robert H. Tillman and Michael L. Indergaard, *Pump and Dump: The Rancid Rules of the New Economy*

Mariana Valverde, *Law and Order: Images, Meanings, Myths*

Michael Welch, *Crimes of Power and States of Impunity: The U.S. Response to Terror*

Michael Welch, *Scapegoats of September 11th: Hate Crimes and State Crimes in the War on Terror*

Saundra D. Westervelt and Kimberly J. Cook, *Life after Death Row: Exonerees' Search for Community and Identity*